Tradition and Theology
in the
Old Testament

Tradition and Theology
in the
Old Testament

edited by
DOUGLAS A. KNIGHT

with contributions by

Walter Harrelson

Helmer Ringgren

Rudolf Smend

Walther Zimmerli

Arvid S. Kapelrud

Roger Lapointe

Douglas A. Knight

Odil Hannes Steck

Peter R. Ackroyd

James L. Crenshaw

Robert B. Laurin

Michael Fishbane

Hartmut Gese

FORTRESS PRESS Philadelphia

Library of Congress Catalog Card Number 76–007872
ISBN 0–8006–0484–9

5785G76   Printed in U.S.A.   1–484

Contents

Abbreviations

AB	Anchor Bible
AfOB	Archiv für Orientforschung, Beiheft
ANET	J. B. Pritchard (ed.), *Ancient Near Eastern Texts Relating to the Old Testament*
ASNU	Acta seminarii neotestamentici upsaliensis
ATANT	Abhandlungen zur Theologie des Alten und Neuen Testaments
ATD	Das Alte Testament Deutsch
AThD	Acta Theologica Danica
BA	*The Biblical Archaeologist*
BASOR	*Bulletin of the American Schools of Oriental Research*
BEvTh	Beiträge zur Evangelischen Theologie
BK	Biblischer Kommentar: Altes Testament
BSt	Biblische Studien
BTF	*Bangalore Theological Forum*
BWANT	Beiträge zur Wissenschaft vom Alten und Neuen Testament
BZAW	Beihefte zur *Zeitschrift für die alttestamentliche Wissenschaft*
CBQ	*Catholic Biblical Quarterly*
ConOT	Coniectanea biblica: Old Testament Series
CTM	*Concordia Theological Monthly*
DBS	*Dictionnaire de la Bible, Supplément*
EvTh	*Evangelische Theologie*
FRLANT	Forschungen zur Religion und Literatur des Alten und Neuen Testaments
HS	Horae Soederblomianae
HThR	*Harvard Theological Review*
IJT	*Indian Journal of Theology*
Interp	*Interpretation*

JAOS	*Journal of the American Oriental Society*
JBL	*Journal of Biblical Literature*
JQR	*Jewish Quarterly Review*
JR	*Journal of Religion*
JSJ	*Journal for the Study of Judaism*
JSS	*Journal of Semitic Studies*
JTC	*Journal for Theology and the Church*
JTS	*Journal of Theological Studies*
NKZ	*Neue Kirchliche Zeitschrift*
NZSTh	*Neue Zeitschrift für Systematische Theologie und Religionsphilosophie*
OTL	The Old Testament Library
PEQ	*Palestine Exploration Quarterly*
RGG	*Die Religion in Geschichte und Gegenwart*
RoB	*Religion och Bibel*
RSR	*Religious Studies Review*
SBLDS	Society of Biblical Literature Dissertation Series
SBT	Studies in Biblical Theology
SEÅ	*Svensk exegetisk årsbok*
SJLA	Studies in Judaism in Late Antiquity
StTh	*Studia theologica*
STU	*Schweizerische Theologische Umschau*
TDNT	G. Kittel and G. Friedrich (eds.), *Theological Dictionary of the New Testament*
ThB	Theologische Bücherei
ThF	Theologische Forschung
ThSt	Theologische Studien
ThW	Theologische Wissenschaft
ThZ	*Theologische Zeitschrift*
TUMSR	Trinity University Monograph Series in Religion
TWNT	G. Kittel and G. Friedrich (eds.), *Theologisches Wörterbuch zum Neuen Testament*
UT	C. H. Gordon, *Ugaritic Textbook*
VT	*Vetus Testamentum*
VTS	Vetus Testamentum, Supplements
WF	Wege der Forschung
WMANT	Wissenschaftliche Monographien zum Alten und Neuen Testament
WuD	*Wort und Dienst*
ZAW	*Zeitschrift für die alttestamentliche Wissenschaft*
ZDPV	*Zeitschrift des deutschen Palästina-Vereins*

RABBINIC AND QUMRAN ABBREVIATIONS

Av. Zarah	Avodah Zarah
b.	bavli (Babylonian Talmud)
Ber.	Berachot
'Eduy.	'Eduyot
Giṭṭ.	Giṭṭin
Ḥag.	Ḥagigah
Ḥull.	Ḥullin
1J	Targum Jonathan
2J	Pseudo-Jonathan
M.	Mishnah
Onq.	Onqelos
Qid.	Qiddushin
R.	Rabbi
R.H.	Rosh Ha-shanah
Sanh.	Sanhedrin
Shab.	Shabbat
T.	Targum
Tanḥ.	Tanḥuma
Tos.	Tosefta
Yad.	Yadayim

CD	Cairo (Genizah text of the) Damascus (Document)
1QH	Thanksgiving Hymns from Qumran Cave 1
1QM	War Scroll from Qumran Cave 1
1QpHab	Pesher on Habakkuk from Qumran Cave 1
1QS	Manual of Discipline from Qumran Cave 1
4QDibHam	Words of the Luminaries from Qumran Cave 4
4QFlor	Florilegium from Qumran Cave 4
4QpNah	Pesher on Nahum from Qumran Cave 4

Contributors

Peter R. Ackroyd, King's College, University of London, London, England

James L. Crenshaw, Vanderbilt University, Nashville, Tennessee

Michael Fishbane, Brandeis University, Waltham, Massachusetts

Hartmut Gese, Eberhard-Karls-Universität, Tübingen, Germany

Walter Harrelson, Vanderbilt University, Nashville, Tennessee

Arvid S. Kapelrud, Universitetet i Oslo, Oslo, Norway

Douglas A. Knight, Vanderbilt University, Nashville, Tennessee

Roger Lapointe, Ottawa University, Ottawa, Ontario, Canada

Robert B. Laurin, American Baptist Seminary of the West and Graduate Theological Union, Berkeley, California

Helmer Ringgren, Uppsala Universitet, Uppsala, Sweden

Rudolf Smend, Georg-August-Universität, Göttingen, Germany

Odil Hannes Steck, Johannes-Gutenberg-Universität, Mainz, Germany

Walther Zimmerli, Georg-August-Universität, Göttingen, Germany

Preface

Since it is not altogether usual today for several scholars to
join in a collaborative effort to reflect on multiple aspects of a
single problem, it may prove helpful to the reader to learn something about the circumstances leading to this fresh examination
into the theological implications of the tradition process in ancient Israel. Each author was invited to write a new article—
explicitly for this project and not previously in print—on a
topic close to his area of specialization within the Old Testament discipline. Work on these essays had to proceed independently, for there was no opportunity for a common forum or
open discussion in which all could participate. Yet résumés of
each chapter were circulated during the writing stage, and in
certain individual cases where it seemed highly advisable because of overlapping topics a few of the authors read one or
more of the other chapters. Obviously, each contributor was
free to pursue his topic as he found best. Every discussion is
self-contained and can be read separately, without the support
of adjacent chapters. The editor attempted to lend a measure of
cohesion to the book by suggesting certain guidelines for the
whole approach, by making recommendations about problems
to be addressed in each chapter, and by adding occasional foot-
notes throughout to refer to other places within this book where
a given topic is treated in more depth. It is hoped that the result
of this collaboration, with its points of diversity and its areas of
consensus, will stimulate further reflection on these important
issues.

The reader should know that the versification of biblical references in this book follows the Hebrew Bible; where different, verse numbers according to the standard English versions are provided in brackets. Unless otherwise indicated, biblical quotations are the translations of the respective author. If followed by "RSV," the translation is that of the *Revised Standard Version* of the Bible.

With great appreciation I want to acknowledge the interest and support which the twelve other contributors have constantly showed in this undertaking. The interchange of ideas in both correspondence and conversation has made the experience a pleasurable one. I am indebted also to Dr. Werner Klatt and Dr. William Reader for reading parts of the final manuscript, and to Mr. Raymond Newell for assistance in proofreading. And I am certainly speaking for the other authors when I thank my wife Evelyn Knight for preparing the final typescript. For grants to carry out my work on this volume I am grateful to the Vanderbilt University Research Council and the Deutscher Akademischer Austauschdienst.

Göttingen, July 1976   D.A.K.

Tradition and Theology
in the
Old Testament

Introduction:

Tradition and Theology

Douglas A. Knight

Our access to an understanding of tradition is blocked by two
hindrances, quite aside from the many severe methodological
problems. In the first place, tradition appears to have a mysterious power over its recipients, including us today. Each
generation finds tradition already a part of historical reality, of
the situation in which the people must confront life. It is impossible to ignore this wide-ranging body of verbal and practical
materials; whether it is being accepted or rejected it affects all
aspects of life. The power of tradition derives from its very
presence: it represents the truths and experiences of previous
generations and thus holds an implicitly authoritative advantage over the present situation. For this reason it has the potential to be used either constructively or restrictively. On the
one hand, tradition saves each generation from having to start
life entirely afresh, with no accumulation of knowledge, experiences, and institutions on which to draw. As we grow up
within the tradition and become educated in it, we gain the
means for self-realization through critically appropriating and
even transcending this heritage. But beyond this meaning-
content, tradition conveys also meaning-structures. It promotes solidarity with the past and especially with the present,
for through it the clan, the community, and the nation take on
a significance far beyond that of simply meeting the needs for
physical survival. And even more fundamentally, tradition
provides us with the very structures for understanding and
communicating. But, on the other hand, tradition also has a
potential for restraint, and this accounts for the pejorative sense

1

in which the term is often used. Simply because it implies experiential truth, it can become a refuge to which later groups
and individuals flee, rather than a point of departure for their
own struggles with the conditions of life. It can be used as an
excuse for institutional rigidity and personal insensitivity. It
can squelch rather than promote creative living. Both of these
expressions, positive and negative, of the inherent power of tradition have rarely been the object of analytical reflection, and they
continue to affect us as we approach the subject of tradition.

The second hindrance to our understanding tradition is the
very ambiguity, or better, the multiplicity of the phenomenon.
What cannot be considered a matter of tradition? The term is
applied as readily to oral and written literature (of all genres)
as it is to customs, habits, beliefs, moral standards, cultural attitudes and values, social and religious institutions. It is anything in the heritage from the past that is delivered down to the
present and can contribute to the makeup of the new ethos.
Actually, the word tradition can even refer to the process of
transmission (the *traditio*) as well as to the materials themselves that are being handed down (the *traditum*). Quite
obviously, differentiation in method is needed if one hopes to
analyze these diverse types of tradition and to ascertain how
each survives and exerts its influence. It may be noted that in
the essays in this book the term tradition is usually used in the
sense of oral and written literature, although in certain discussions it embraces other aspects as well.

Beginning especially in the middle of the eighteenth century,
diverse types of folk traditions were collected in areas of Europe, and within a century, through the efforts of men like
Jacob and Wilhelm Grimm, such materials gained an ever increasing importance as a subject of scholarly investigation.
Significant studies are presently available, for example, on
African, Balkan, and Nordic traditions. James Frazer has published a massive collection of folklore from cultures in all parts
of the world. Interest has been directed to the traditions in
such ancient societies as Greece, Rome, Arabic cultures, Meso-

potamia, as well as Israel. Prompted by such work on the actual traditions and the historical, sociological, and religious roles which they played, modern philosophy and phenomenology have attended to the structures at work and their obvious implications. Notably Hans-Georg Gadamer has underscored the fundamental importance of tradition in establishing our categories of understanding, in shaping our intellect, our predilections, our perspectives, our communication, our presuppositions. According to him, a person is not determined wholly by tradition but retains the freedom to decide whether or not to accept it and to hand it on further. Yet there is a real sense in which the particular historical situation and the whole historical process contribute to each individual's manner of receiving and interpreting the tradition. (A similar point was made earlier by Rudolf Bultmann about the *Vorverständnis*, the pre-understanding which each interpreter brings to a text or tradition, and it is emphasized below in Chapter 3 with respect to our own perspectives and presuppositions guiding us as we seek to reconstruct the history of Israel.) Gadamer emphasizes, though, that tradition is not therefore something to be overcome or neutralized, for it presents humanity—the ancients as well as us—with the opportunity for affirmative understanding and productive advance.

Such considerations and research in other disciplines lend legitimacy and importance to the modern effort to recover the traditions of Israel. Since Hermann Gunkel at the outset of the twentieth century, it has become entirely common to assume that the Old Testament is not the literary creation of authors working at their desks but is the result of a centuries-long, intricate process of development among the people of Israel. The majority of the literature derives from traditions which circulated relatively freely, underwent changes, and gradually became grouped together into a form which acquired literary stability. These traditions, usually at some point related to the oral sphere, do not represent individuals' private productions. They are the life expressions of various groups, for "traditioning" is the function of the community. The process remains in flux through a steady selection and reinterpretation of the heritage from the past; materials are not preserved merely for their own sake but only insofar as they continue to have—or can be modified in order to have—a significance for new generations. Consequently, the fate of these traditions is quite closely tied to ongoing circumstances in the realms of politics, religion, education, judicial courts, social situations, and intellectual life. This in turn underscores the absolute importance of our understanding the narrower and broader situations in which each tradition is anchored—if we hope to comprehend the depth dimension of meaning which the given text contains.

Interestingly, the Hebrew Bible knows no terms equivalent to tradition or transmission in the sense in which we are applying these concepts to it. Yet we should not necessarily expect to find them there, and the validity of this widely held hypothesis about the Israelite tradition process does not depend on it. The ultimate test of an historical hypothesis is its ability to account for the evidence better than any other explanation. The practitioners of the traditio-historical method, which has been refined considerably since the 1930s, have applied it with greater or lesser intensity to most conceivable parts of the Old Testament, including historical, prophetical, lyrical, legal, sapiential texts. While widespread agreement on many specific points has not been attained, there are few that doubt that we are asking basically the right questions. Internal to the literature, below the surface level, there are indications which point to the formation of that literature, and by retracing its development and determining the forces which affected it we can perceive its intense, vital, dynamic relation to life. Why is a text exactly as it is, and not different in some respect? To answer this is no simple enterprise—yet one of absolute importance and seriousness because it drives us back to the stage in which people are not idly composing traditions but are carving out their very existence in situations of stress, of threat, of routine, of faith, of adjudication, of child-rearing, of social control. The ancient Israelites, not unlike us, had to address their immediate needs, and this was done often by referring to their past and considering their future. The results of this process were as varied as were the situations and the people themselves. This multiplicity, fundamental to the Old Testament, is affirmed, not diminished, by the traditio-historical approach.

All of this has significant implications for theology. How are we to evaluate this process of tradition formation? What theological significance is there in the text's close relation to life, especially at the many points where a kerygmatic intention is not obvious? What does it mean if the theological "message" of the Old Testament was always growing, in flux, adapting to new situations—and not the expression of timeless, absolutistic revelation? Does the involvement of so many people in the formative process affect our understanding of inspiration and revelation? Is it possible to understand the text without knowledge of its prehistory and the situations which produced it? What are the implications if we consider that the tradition was significantly affected by the ancient Near Eastern environment, by the contingencies of history, by social and religious developments, by intellectual streams, by fixed patterns of speech? How could Yahweh, the confessed God of Israel, have been involved in all of this—or despite all of this? Indeed, could not tradition at times have led the people to the abyss rather than to the heights? If we are therefore to be cautioned against an undue idealization of the tradition, what is its actual strength for theology and for anthropology? Might the history of traditions in fact provide us with the key to forming an Old Testament theology or even a biblical theology? Since any given text may conceal a variety of strata, are there any firm rules for how we are to solve the resulting hermeneutical problems? Are we obliged to gain a sensitivity for the whole sweep of the historical formation without arbitrarily preferring one stage or another (whether the original, or the one with the most distinct theological message, or even the final canonical stage)— especially in light of the fact that the meaning at any one such

stage would not necessarily have been amenable or understandable to other persons in the productive process before or after
that point? Is there a relation between the process or the traditions unfolding in Israel's history and the post-biblical Jewish,
Christian, and Islamic traditions? What is our own interest in
the Israelite traditions—only to repristinate ancient ideas and
ways, or to face our own heritage, to examine common concerns
and thereby to strive for self-understanding?

That is an oppressive series of questions. The problems are
neither artificial nor insignificant; they emerge directly from the
postulated tradition process in Israel. Unfortunately, they lead
us into a rather uncharted terrain. Most tradition historians
have not been inclined to examine the general historical and theological implications of their work. Gerhard von Rad's pioneering work in this regard contains significant insights at many of
these points and has prompted some discussion in the discipline,
but several of the questions have as yet received no attention.

The thirteen essays that follow attempt to meet this need for
a systematic reflection on the consequences that traditio-historical research has for theology, especially for Old Testament
theology. A certain selectivity of topics was necessary; the ones
included are essential, while a few other important questions
had to be omitted or simply addressed in the context of some
related discussion. At the same time, certain matters (e.g., the
life relation, revelation, canon, biblical theology) are so basic
that they are mentioned in several essays, although we have
attempted to keep repetitions at a minimum.

A word about the interrelatedness of the chapters may prove
helpful to the reader. The first part does not deal so much with
temporal origins as with the material groundings of the tradition. What are some of the primary impulses and materials
that stimulate tradition development? These two chapters on
life processes, religion, and the wider environment provide an
indication as well as of the fundamental role which tradition
played in Israel.

Part II focuses on problems essential to the development of

much of the Old Testament literature, and on their theological implications. How are we to understand the relationship between history and tradition in view of the community's centuries-long process of reflecting on their past and searching for meaning in it? The prophets' utterances are replete with references to the pre-prophetic traditions about salvation and to earlier prophetic messages as well; are they simply traditionists inclined to adjust the heritage in only minor ways, or is there a more basic theological conviction that is governing their preaching and their use of prior materials? In light of the central role played by the cult in Israel, what theological significance is there in this close relationship between tradition development and Israel's worship, and how does this affect the nature of the Old Testament as well as the task of the exegete? Stimulated by such problems, the final two chapters in this section address more general and fundamental issues: the implications of oral expression for our notion of tradition and for our understanding of the text, and the unavoidable consequences which the traditio-historical hypothesis has for our understanding of biblical revelation.

Part III confronts questions which to the present have scarcely received systematic attention by tradition historians, although these matters are so basic that they are influencing the traditions at most points in their development. Traditionists, those who are producing and preserving traditions, do not exist in a vacuum, unaffected by their surrounding intellectual life, undisturbed by historical and social changes, unconcerned with ideas and positions that differ from their own. Chapter 8 describes the main streams of theological and ideological positions present in Israel throughout its history, and it deals with the impact of such continuous streams on the development of traditions and texts. In light of such lines of continuity, Chapter 9 examines the effects which historical ruptures, political and social changes, had on the traditions and on theology; how could continuity with the past be reestablished after an unexpected disaster? Yet the prevailing doctrines and notions which do

persist and which are propounded with vigor by many traditionists will not necessarily find acceptance by all the people,
and Chapter 10 demonstrates the existence of dissenting opinion in many parts of the Old Testament, especially in the wisdom literature—protest which is not idle talk but which stems
from the experienced dilemmas of life.

The final section considers the effect of the tradition process
on the development of scripture and on the religious life of the
later believing communities, both Christian and Jewish. Was
canonization consistent with the lengthy history of tradition
growth and transformation, and what are the theological and
religious problems of freezing one stage in the developing tradition? Does the Israelite *traditio* help to account for some of the
vitality in early Judaism, especially in terms of the midrashic
process of interpreting earlier traditions? The last chapter
touches on many of the previously mentioned topics and attempts to evaluate their significance for biblical theology.
What difference does it make that the text had a prehistory in
tradition, and how is the biblical theologian to approach these
diverse stages and the developmental process on the whole?

One final word to clarify our intentions: This volume represents a joint effort by a number of scholars to break new ground
in this important field. Decades of intense exegetical and historical work by many tradition historians have provided detailed results that demand reflection on a broader scale. All
contributors are addressing the same general question about the
theological implications of Israel's formation of tradition, and
there is a surprising amount of agreement on the answers which
are found to this question. Yet the attentive reader will discover numerous points where opinions differ. This is all to the
good; the issues are open to numerous approaches, and a monolithic position to which all participants would subscribe—even
if this were possible—would suggest that the problems are less
complicated than they really are. Our primary purpose, consequently, is to carry the discussion further in the hope of
stimulating more engagement with these crucial issues.

Part I

IMPETUS

Chapter 1

Life, Faith, and the
Emergence of Tradition

Walter Harrelson

ORAL COMPOSITION AND TRANSMISSION
IN ANCIENT ISRAEL

It is a commonplace of contemporary biblical scholarship that
behind our several bodies of literature (narrative, legal, prophetic, wisdom, and cultic) there existed early collections that
were transmitted orally and had been composed for oral presentation.[1] Scholars differ as to the extent of such oral composition and transmission, but it is assumed that prior to the literary
production of our present Hebrew Scriptures much of the literature acquired written form after oral composition of some of its
parts and a period of oral transmission.

Such an assumption is entirely reasonable. The issue is not
whether the Israelites were capable of writing down the story of
the patriarchs and lawgivers and judges and prophets, and the
like. It is whether they would have been likely to have done so,
given the place that stories of their beginnings had in their kind
of society. It seems unlikely that early Israel would have
wished first of all to record the stories of its beginning. Cultic
recitation and oral transmission of the narratives within the
family and tribal circles would have been more likely, it is believed.

1. See, e.g., P. Grelot, "Tradition as Source and Environment of Scripture," in
The Dynamism of Biblical Tradition, Concilium, vol. 20 (New York: Paulist
Press, 1967), 7–28.

The existence of such a period of oral composition and oral transmission, therefore, seems not to be in doubt. We may question the extent of oral composition and transmission and the ability of contemporary students of Israelite literature to identify the materials that reflect or belong to this period of oral composition and/or transmission.

The problems are more complex with regard to certain literature than they are with regard to other bodies of material. The wisdom sayings may well have circulated orally in the circle of the wise teacher or in certain strata of Israelite society. Committed to memory, they would have been passed along to the next generation in oral form and would have been written down, perhaps, only at such times as circumstances supported the production of a collection. The book of Proverbs appears to reflect several such collections. With regard to the legal materials the situation is considerably more difficult to reconstruct. It would appear likely that the case law of Exodus (chs. 21–23) arose largely out of decisions rendered by the elders and judges which, in time, were collected and committed to writing, thereafter supplemented by additional decisions of the judges. The Decalogue may originally have been produced and transmitted orally, undergoing supplementation and formal changes in the course of its transmission, later to be written down in connection with political or judicial developments in the North or South. The Deuteronomic laws are thought to be the product of Levitical teaching and proclamation in the North and the South, transmitted orally for a time and then committed to writing.

The prophetic collections of the pre-exilic period seem to have been produced in a similar way. First there were the prophetic utterances, themselves repeated on more than a single occasion by the prophetic composers, and then transmitted orally for some time within the circle of associates of the individual prophets. Particular circumstances led to the collection and recording of such prophetic utterances (see Jer. 36), without thereby cutting off the tradition that could continue to augment and to modify the materials being preserved and passed along, until finally the collection was closed. It was not different with the Psalter and other cultic texts. Priests and other temple officials passed along the cultic directions from generation to generation, while temple poets and singers produced, reused, and modified the hymns, laments, and thanksgivings that we find in the book of Psalms. It may be that well-remembered formulas operated in the development of the Psalter materials, as Culley has maintained.[2] Certainly, there would have been a constant interplay between the forms of psalms in which they were originally composed and the forms of the psalms as they were regularly reused in cultic and other communal settings.

With regard to Israel's early narrative literature the problem is most complex. Here again, it seems highly probable that the early form of narratives concerning the patriarchs, now imbedded in our complex Pentateuchal literature, would have been oral, would have been tied to particular personalities, localities, and cultic sites, and would have developed as materials initially belonging to particular groups or tribes within early Israelite history. Preservation of the oral tradition and its transmission may well have been cultic in large part, although the importance of family and tribal units as bearers of the traditions should not be underestimated.

John Van Seters has maintained recently[3] that the present form of the patriarchal narratives is a product of the exilic and post-exilic periods. In his view, even the so-called Yahwistic portion of the Pentateuch belongs to the exilic period. Van Seters argues, moreover, that the traditio-historical approach to the study of the Pentateuchal narratives has led scholars into numerous byways. He maintains that in our effort to recover

2. R. C. Culley, *Oral Formulaic Language in the Biblical Psalter* (Toronto: University of Toronto Press, 1967).
3. J. Van Seters, *Abraham in History and Tradition* (New Haven: Yale University Press, 1975), pp. 310–12.

the oral traditions it is essential to be guided by careful form-critical and structural studies of the written narrative materials.

There is no need to quarrel with the latter point, whatever one's reluctance to follow Van Seters's arguments for the dating of the literary materials. What we have is literature, written literature, and it is entirely right for him to insist, as many others have before him, that it is not by any means simple to come to conclusive results regarding the preliterary form of the Israelite materials. Even so, it seems plausible to suppose that the material that comprises a large part of the Hebrew Scriptures took shape in part during a period of oral composition and oral transmission.

Such an understanding of the development of Israelite literature carries important consequences for our view of life and faith in Israel. Oral traditions were in large measure the creation of *people*, not only and not primarily of literary or religious geniuses. They incorporated fundamental understandings of groups within Israel, such understandings, however, being open to the critical judgments of other groups. These traditions were susceptible of elaboration, development, and curtailment in the light of changing social and cultural circumstances. Creative individuals surely would have contributed significantly to their shape and character, not only at the inception of a fresh understanding or disclosure but all along the way as the traditions developed. Moreover, since such traditions appear to have contributed to the shaping of all of the distinguishable bodies of Israelite literature, they were influential in the creation of Israelite literature as a whole.

DEFINITIONS

With this sketch before us, we need to underscore certain recent efforts to define what is meant by tradition in relation to Old Testament studies. According to Douglas Knight, a biblical tradition has the following characteristic features:

(1) It is received from others and transmitted further, es-

pecially from one generation to the next.

(2) It has both form and content. The history of a tradition can only be retraced as long as it remains *"formal greifbar"*; beyond this point the elements of content must be examined under the rubric of *Motivgeschichte, Stoffgeschichte, Themengeschichte, Vorstellungsgeschichte, Begriffsgeschichte*, or *Problemgeschichte*.

(3) A tradition is the immediate property of a group or a community, that is, it has a direct function for the people who transmit it.

(4) A tradition is "living," developing, malleable, and only relatively stable; it can become changed and reinterpreted to meet the needs of its transmitters.

(5) A tradition is usually oral but can also be in written form as long as it fulfills the other criteria mentioned here, especially that of being able to develop and adapt.

(6) Tradition tends to be cumulative and agglomerative.[4]

This definition is of course not likely to be satisfactory to all students of biblical traditions. The most narrow of definitions with which I am acquainted is that of the philosopher Josef Pieper.[5] Pieper distinguishes sharply between the passing on and acceptance of tradition, on the one hand, and teaching something to learners, on the other. To pass on a tradition means to receive it from others who themselves have received it from yet others; it means also to pass it on *as received* to those to whom one is responsible to give it. If we move back to the "original" in the line of traditioning, even that original one will understand the tradition to have been given to him, for tradition is itself something given. If we think of the originator of a religious community, the founder of the religion, such a founder will understand the disclosure that he passes on to have come through an act of divine revelation that preserves

4. D. A. Knight, *Rediscovering the Traditions of Israel*, rev. ed., SBLDS 9 (Missoula, Mont.: Society of Biblical Literature, 1975), p. 26.
5. J. Pieper, *Überlieferung, Begriff und Anspruch* (München: Kösel, 1970), pp. 19–29.

the character of tradition as *given*. And all whose task it is to pass along the tradition must take the greatest care to see that they deliver what they have received and nothing else. The handing down of the tradition means handing down *intact* what has been received.

The fact that traditions are changed, are re-formed, take on new shape and character in the course of their transmission should not obscure what the traditionists understand themselves to be doing. If what they are passing down has sufficient significance to be delivered whole to the next generation, then it must be delivered whole. The process of handing it down will be marked by acts of interpretation, of course; even so, the essential elements of the tradition, the *traditum*, must be there and recognizably there.

Pieper's study is devoted not to oral tradition or to early biblical materials so much as to those elements of a people's self-understanding in terms of which they make fundamental sense of life, the world, history, and the destiny of humankind and the world. His examples are drawn largely from the Platonic tradition, the Bible, and the early history of the church. Thus, his definition cannot be used easily for our purposes here.

Nonetheless, it is useful to consider his more restricted definition along with that of Knight. Knight begins as Pieper begins —with emphasis upon the receiving of traditions from others and their being passed along to others to come. If tradition has a function for those who transmit it (Knight, #3), does it not perhaps have a very weighty function, as Pieper maintains? Should we not therefore recognize two aspects of tradition? (1) There are elements in the culture of a people that are passed along by the people primarily because of their interest in such elements, an interest that need not be viewed as weighty or decisive for their self-understanding. These may be distinguished from (2) those that have genuine weight, elements in terms of which the group recognizes something of decisive importance for the maintenance of its life and faith.[6] In this sense, Pieper's view seems to me of great importance: not everything that the ancient Israelites passed along orally or in writing was felt to be of such significance. There was Tradition and there were traditions.[7]

Is such a distinction usable, however, when applied to the biblical materials? Is it possible to determine what traditions may belong in the category of Tradition and which of them simply represent important but not decisive elements of the culture? We might well turn to Gerhard von Rad's little historical credo,[8] or to Martin Noth's Pentateuchal themes.[9] Better examples might be the confessional passages of the New Testament (1 Cor. 15:3–7; Phil. 2:5–11; etc.). One need look only at this question to see how very unsatisfactory such an approach appears to be. The language of the confessional statements treated by von Rad is certainly later language, marked by the passage of time and later interpretation. The passages in the New Testament also have by no means been handed down entirely in the language in which they presumably took shape in the earliest Christian community.

The only alternative way to make the distinction that Pieper wishes to make is to deal with the central *content* of the tradition, not with (or not primarily with) its literary form. Thus, Martin Noth's themes may be more satisfactory points of reference. But themes are not a tradition; themes appear within a

6. This feature of tradition corresponds well to the construction and maintenance of a social world, as dealt with in contemporary sociology of religion. See P. L. Berger, *The Sacred Canopy* (New York: Doubleday, 1969), pp. 3–51.

7. See the World Council of Churches' *Commission on Faith and Order Paper No. 40* (Geneva: World Council of Churches, 1963), which bears the title *Tradition and Traditions*.

8. G. von Rad, *Das formgeschichtliche Problem des Hexateuch*, BWANT 4/26 (Stuttgart: Kohlhammer, 1938) = *Gesammelte Studien zum Alten Testament*, ThB 8 (München: Chr. Kaiser, 1958), 9–86 = "The Form-Critical Problem of the Hexateuch," in his *The Problem of the Hexateuch and Other Essays* (Edinburgh/London: Oliver & Boyd, 1966), 1–78.

9. M. Noth, *Überlieferungsgeschichte des Pentateuch* (Stuttgart: Kohlhammer, 1948) = *A History of Pentateuchal Traditions* (Englewood Cliffs: Prentice-Hall, 1972).

tradition. John Van Seters warns against our constructing hypothetical traditions lying behind the present literary shape of our materials.[10] How, then, might the *Tradition* that is to be received and passed along intact be discoverable at all?

A distinction might be drawn between a central or a core tradition and its later embellishment and modifications. If, however, we mean a tradition and not merely a theme or a set of motifs, then we have to be able to detect a process of traditioning, of handing down, that is concerned with a discernible content that goes beyond a theme or set of themes. Is it possible to reconstruct, even very hypothetically, a core tradition that functioned orally to account for (to use a very complex example) the origins of Israel? If so, it should be possible to identify its basic themes, the motifs that articulate the themes, the plot that emerges, and the tradition as something to be received and handed down intact.

LIFE AND FAITH IN EARLY ISRAEL

The effort to reconstruct such a core tradition should only be undertaken on the basis of some judgment concerning the life and faith of early Israel. Clearly, the differences of judgment on early Israelite life and culture have perhaps never been so wide as they are in contemporary scholarship. The patriarchal traditions, for example, have been identified recently by Thompson as having assumed their present shape during the period of the early monarchy.[11] Van Seters would place the Abraham traditions in the period of the exile.[12] A large number of scholars judge that they took shape in the period shortly before the monarchy, as a connected tradition. Others believe that they go back to the early or middle part of the second

---

10. Van Seters, *Abraham in History and Tradition*, p. 263 and passim.
11. T. L. Thompson, *The Historicity of the Patriarchal Narratives*, BZAW 133 (Berlin: de Gruyter, 1974).
12. Van Seters, *Abraham in History and Tradition*, pp. 310–12, and his argument throughout the book.

millennium. Given such wide variations in judgment, is it not better to leave the entire question open?

We should at least be able to work on the basis of relative dating. I find it convincing that behind our present literary materials in the Pentateuch were oral materials that had assumed some connection with one another to form a central tradition, accounting for the origin of the people of Israel. If there is no way easily to defend an absolute date for the emergence of this core tradition, it certainly can be maintained that it antedated the present layers of literary material that are assigned the designations J, E, D, and P. I believe, with Van Seters and several Scandinavian scholars, that it is better to assume a process of literary development of the Pentateuch in which the antecedent literary tradition was known to the writer whose work came next in chronological line. It has never been convincing to me that E, for example, did his work without knowledge of J. Assuming this literary dependence of the later writers or collectors upon the earlier ones, we may still maintain that there was in the preliterary stage not simply a set of themes, not only a set of confessional passages, but an oral tradition—something akin to Noth's G.

Our initial question about this core tradition must be: what was the setting in life and faith that produced, or contributed to the production of, such a core tradition? It was, at its center, belief in Yahweh. There may have been antecedent belief in a tribal deity identified with particular tribes or groups. There may have been influence from Western Semitic conceptions of the high God El or Ba'al. But belief in Yahweh as Israel's God is certainly what precipitated a core tradition that was to be remembered and handed down intact.

Yahweh will surely have been understood in this core tradition as one who accompanied the worshipers on their movements throughout the land, who took note of the oppression of his people and took steps to ease their lot, who offered promise of a radical change in their circumstances if the worshipers held fast their trust in him. The basic themes of this core tradition are probably rightly identified by Noth: promise to the fore-fathers, exodus from Egypt, guidance in the wilderness, revelation at Sinai, and guidance into the settled land. But reduced further to their essential features, on our hypothesis, they consisted necessarily of only those features noted: Yahweh's accompaniment of his people in their movements, his concern for the plight of the oppressed and his readiness to ease their plight, and his promise of new and decisive things to come.

How this core tradition developed is impossible to say. No religious genius need be presupposed, although the work of the patriarchs and of Moses in the shaping of such a core tradition cannot be excluded. My point is that if we ask what can reason-ably be presupposed as to the contents of this core tradition, the minimal statement above seems to include its essential features.

If we now ask whether this core tradition seems actually to underlie the traditions that we have, the answer seems to be clear. It does indeed represent what can be called the essential tradition that is to be received from others and passed along to the next generation. But is such a core tradition *"formal grief-bar"*? Have we not simply reduced the themes of Martin Noth, taken together, and called this reduced content a tradition? We have indeed; but any statement of the core tradition will perforce be hypothetical. Certainly, Noth's development of the several themes, originally independent of one another, taking shape in premonarchical Israel is equally hypothetical. And I am searching for that irreducible core tradition that was under-stood to be essential to the life and faith of successive genera-tions, which had therefore to be passed along intact.

The plot of such an oral narrative tradition would run some-what as follows:

> Yahweh called our forefathers from their Eastern home-
> land and brought us into a new land. He accompanied us
> in our wanderings throughout this land, providing protec-

tion for us and requiring of us that we place our trust in him. When our forefathers were enslaved and oppressed in Egypt, he delivered us from oppression, guided us back toward the homeland, and continued to assure us of his protection and of great things to come. Despite all trials and difficulties, Yahweh remains faithful to his promise. We are required also to be faithful to him.

Such a core tradition is formally comprehensible. It has both form and content, the form probably consisting of both a narrative to be related in the family and at tribal gatherings and a confessional form for recitation at cultic assemblies. It is the core tradition of the early tribes who associated themselves with God under the designation Yahweh. It was composed orally and was circulated orally for many generations in all probability. It was suitable for elaboration and modification while at the same time it maintained its core content. Thus, this hypothetical early form of the tradition of ancient Israel seems to meet the criteria suggested by Knight.

But how did such a core tradition develop? What were the factors that led to the adoption of just these central understandings? Were the understandings widely shared, or did they belong to some particular group within Israel, only later to become a part of the life and faith of the larger community? Were they shaped and shared primarily through cultic acts at one of the places of worship? Or was the ethos of family and tribe the more important bearer and establisher of such understandings?

We cannot proceed beyond reasonable hypotheses. In my view, the appearance of belief in God under the personal name Yahweh antedated the period of Moses. Even so, it was the set of events that some ancestors of Israel lived through that gave specificity to their belief in Yahweh as the God who noted the oppression of his people and took steps to ease their lot. The belief in God as the accompanying Presence of his people in their journeyings is a firm element of the period prior to Moses in my view. The promise of new and decisive things to come seems to me also to be characteristic of pre-Mosaic religion and to have been given fresh impetus through the experience of the exodus and the wilderness wanderings.

Thus, the three elements may all be claimed to be a part of the understanding of some of Israel's ancestors prior to the settlement in the land of Canaan. The only element that seems traceable no earlier than the time of Moses is the special concern for the oppressed.

How were these elements shaped, brought into close relationship, and solidified? Again, we cannot know. I doubt that the cultus was the decisive reality, although its importance certainly would have been considerable. The elements arise out of the life and experience of the people. They assume the form of a story of the beginnings of the people under divine guidance. As a story, the core tradition need not be assigned exclusively to certain bearers of tradition alone: families will have preserved it, along with the gifted tellers of tales. Guardians and officiants of sanctuaries will have known and recounted it as well. As movements occur leading toward larger associations at central places of worship, the core tradition will have assumed firm and definitive form. Even so, it is a mistake, I believe, to understand early Israelite life and faith as dominated by cultic practices. Nothing in the core tradition as hypothetically reconstructed above calls for cultic celebration and re-presentation as its essential bearer and shaper.[13]

Our conclusion, then, is that the core tradition developed in such a way in early Israel that the religious existence of the people was shaped by events that led to the domination of these core elements in their existence: Yahweh was the God of this people (no matter how small the actual number of persons involved); he accompanied them in their movements; he was particularly concerned with the oppressed and mistreated

13. On the antiquity of certain patriarchal religious themes and motifs see V. Maag, "Malkût JHWH," VTS 7 (1960), 129–53. See also the comprehensive study of H. D. Preuss, *Jahweglaube und Zukunftserwartung*, BWANT 7 (Stuttgart: Kohlhammer, 1968), 9–39, 109–25. James Barr deals illuminatingly with the notion of "story" in ancient Israel in "Story and History in Biblical Theology," *JR* 56 (1976), 1–17.

among them; and was leading them into a future the features of which remained open.

When we examine the present literary shape of the Pentateuch we are able to relate this core tradition to it. One noteworthy difference between the above reconstruction and those of Noth and von Rad is that our reconstruction accounts for the fact that the Pentateuch ends with the death of Moses in Transjordan. Our core tradition closes with the promise of momentous things to come, with an open future for the worshipers of Yahweh. The Pentateuch portrays the death of Moses after his successor has been designated, records his burial, and closes. Yet, it is Torah that thus ends: the most fundamental part of Israel's sacral traditions ends with the people of God on the way to the fulfillment of the divine promise but with that promise not consummated. I maintain that this closing of the Pentateuch must rest on ancient tradition—and not merely on the possible historical fact that Moses died in Transjordan. Entrance into the settled land, the establishment of the tribal groups in their allotted portions, the provisions of tribal leaders in times of crisis—all that must be a later elaboration of the core tradition.

Note also that there is much that need not have belonged to this core tradition: the plague tradition; the deliverance by the Sea of Reeds; the covenant act at Mt. Sinai; the promise of land and progeny, etc. I do not wish to insist that none of those features belonged to the core tradition; it is enough simply to say that the core tradition did not depend upon their presence. Nor have we maintained that Alt's treatment of patriarchal deities[14] need be accepted as sound.

This core tradition will have been elaborated from the time of its inception. Tradition does not remain fixed; it grows. But the process of traditioning depends upon certain features of

---

14. A. Alt, "Der Gott der Väter" (1929), in *Kleine Schriften zur Geschichte des Volkes Israel*, vol. 1 (München: Beck, 1953), 1–78 = "The God of the Fathers," in *Essays on Old Testament History and Religion* (Oxford: Blackwell, 1966), 1–77.

the tradition that do have a solidity and fixity about them, in content if not in form. These, I maintain, consist of more than themes. They have the character of the fundamental revelatory disclosure or discovery. They lie near the beginnings of a community that later appears as bound to a large and complex body of traditions. Such a community knows who it is in virtue of a story of its origins. In ancient Israel, this core tradition functioned very much in the way in which ancient creation myths and other myths of origin functioned in other societies. It provided a common identity, a shared story in terms of which the people's origins, present life, and future possibilities were unveiled.

Such core traditions also, by their existence and their significance for life and faith, encourage the development of other traditions and expand the place of tradition in the life of a people. Not everything by any means depends upon the core tradition; there is Tradition and there are traditions, as we have maintained. The core tradition invites the people's reflection upon it, encourages the bold critic to dissent, opens the way for healthy and often vigorous debate (see Chapter 10 in this book). In particular, such a core tradition confronts the reality of the people's experience of a God who appears to have abandoned them (see Ps. 44).

Does this hypothetical core tradition accord well with what is known of ancient Israelite life and society? In my judgment, it does. I have deliberately sought not to overstate the core tradition and have not speculated on the historicity of many elements in the patriarchal and Mosaic traditions about which there is much doubt today. If we compare the above core tradition with the confessional passages in Deut. 26:5–11; Deut. 6:20–25; and Josh. 24:1–13 we can see that they represent elaborations of the core tradition. And yet, we already have in such confessions more than the themes of Noth; we have a tradition, the plot of which can be traced and one which has a place for the developed themes and their elaboration.

THE REVOLUTIONARY CHARACTER
OF THIS CORE TRADITION

An additional point needs to be made. In Israel, it is precisely this core tradition that seems to incorporate some of the most nonconventional materials. Tradition normally has a leveling effect: early recollections are smoothed out, the tradition is accommodated to the later developments, the more revolutionary understandings are tempered and made to support the successive changes in the social and political life of the community. This is not the case with Israelite traditions. This early core tradition already contains the most striking element of early Israelite religion: Yahweh's concern for the oppressed of the earth and his determination to come to their aid. In addition, it underscores the active presence of God in the guidance of his people in their movements, and it emphasizes the openness of the people's future under the leadership of God. Such elements are unlike the religious developments of Israel's neighbors. There, God and cultic localities are connected; God protects the weak and the fatherless, according to many ancient religious traditions, but God's coming to the aid of a *people* under oppression has no counterpart in the ancient world. And most important of all, the future normally lacks this openness, this prospect of the new, this understanding of a people's waiting for the consummation of the divine purpose.

In all the modifications and elaborations of the core tradition, these elements remain. God gives the land, but not fully. God protects his people, but not when they spurn their responsibilities. God accompanies his people in their movements, but his eye is fixed especially upon those who are defenseless and helpless; these he will not forever allow to suffer mistreatment.

This preservation of ancient Israelite tradition with its remarkable and revolutionary features is one of the most striking elements in Israelite religion. It underscores the connection of tradition with the life and faith of the people. Whether we go back to Moses or behind Moses to the patriarchal period, we do not find social and cultural conditions that "naturally" give rise to such a religious understanding.   The three features of the core tradition, when taken together, mark a break with ancient Near Eastern religions that represents the fundamental mystery of Israelite religious beginnings.   Semi-nomads moving to the fringe of the desert for pasture when the time was right, then back to the settled land when the time for engagement in farming came, may have found the notion of an accompanying God, closely related to them by ties of family, very congenial.   An enslaved group with a sense of identity and strong family and tribal ties might well have come to believe that their God was leading them from oppression to freedom.   A band of wanderers in the wilderness, recently freed from bondage, may have developed some sense of destiny under God.   Even so, these cultural conditions provide no more than a set of social realities that would support the religious understandings found in the core tradition.   Tradition, we see, does arise in faith and aims at the transmission of that faith intact, as Pieper maintains. And nothing in the later elaboration of the tradition undercuts these basic understandings born of faith.   On the contrary, the elaboration offers particularity and subtle transformation of the basic tradition.   Moses becomes the lawgiver, specifying what binds Israel to Yahweh.   The accompanying presence of Yahweh is seen as both judgment and blessing; Yahweh punishes a faithless and oppressive people just as he protects and brings blessing in times of faithfulness.   The entrance into the land of promise is accompanied by great acts of deliverance by Yahweh; his alone is the victory in the acts of holy warfare.   The land belongs to Yahweh who is "giving" it to his people, but never in such a way as to enable the people to understand it as their possession.   The future remains open and full of promise; reverses come, but God is faithful when his people are not; new and fresh starts occur.

The same core tradition may be claimed to underlie the developing narrative traditions of the period of judges and kings.

It also is evident most particularly in the work of Israel's prophets. It finds expression in a variety of ways, and with much elaboration, in the cultic texts of the book of Psalms. Nor is it alien to the wisdom tradition or to that of apocalyptic, even if it finds little direct expression in those bodies of literature. It is challenged, as are all of the more elaborate traditions of Israel, by the authors of Job and Ecclesiastes.

LIFE, FAITH, AND THE CORE TRADITION

With the aid of the notion of a core tradition, it may be possible to trace the development of traditions as they reach the stage of literary fixation and cease to develop. Such an effort would not differ markedly from current traditio-historical investigations, of course. Referring to the work of Martin Noth, one might claim that had Noth given greater attention to the development of such a tradition he would the better have been able to explain the emergence of his G, the basic tradition or writing which he supposes to have come into existence in the period of the judges. His own account is not very convincing.[15] He begins with the identification of themes that develop separately among different groups and in different localities. He allows for much additional material arising out of the curiosity of the ancestors of Israel over the peculiar sexual customs of the Canaanites, the rude kind of life lived by groups on the fringes of the settled land, the fierce application of blood vengeance by peoples of the South, and the like. The themes are connected with the early cultic life and practices and issue in creed-like summaries at a later time, with the basic themes first articulated into some traditional whole in the period of the settlement in the land.

But if a tradition, in order actually to represent that which

---

15. H.–J. Kraus makes a somewhat related criticism, pointing to Noth's disregard for the "intentional continuity" of the traditions; cf. "Zur Geschichte des Überlieferungsbegriffs in der alttestamentlichen Wissenschaft," *EvTh* 16 (1956), 383ff. = *Biblisch-theologische Aufsätze* (Neukirchen-Vluyn: Neukirchener Verlag, 1972), pp. 291ff.

sums up the meaning of a people's life and hopes, must be of a sort that is received and passed along intact, it seems evident that the early Israelite themes, as independent features of Israel's cultic existence, would not have constituted a tradition at all. Yet the life and faith of Israel, we maintain, would in all likelihood have produced such a core tradition. It is difficult to believe, though, that the life and cult of the tribal confederacy would have provided sufficient impetus to bring the consolidation of the separate themes into a basic tradition that was to be passed along. One's doubts are increased by criticism of the notion of the tribal league as a firmly established entity in the land of the settlement.

If we assume, however, that a core tradition existed that enabled the community to understand its life and heritage in the terms contained in that tradition, then we can the better understand both the common features of Israelite life in the settled land and the continued independence of the tribes. The core tradition would have reminded those who had been in Egypt and those who had not that Yahweh guided the forefathers in their movements and acted decisively to free the Israelite slaves. They would have seen the entrance into the land and the spread of Israelite holdings within it as signs of that open future promised in the core tradition. They would have been reminded, at the same time, that settlement in the land did not constitute the consummation of the divine promise; the promise still awaited realization, for new things were characteristic of Yahweh's dealings with his people.

The development, then, begins with mystery: the mystery of how certain peoples in the second millennium came to the understandings found in such a core tradition. The mysterious disclosure is caught up in the tradition and handed along. It guides the development of tradition and the accompanying self-understanding, while also drawing into its orbit other features of ancient culture that do not have the weight of the core tradition. The present themes of the Pentateuch, including the primeval history, represent the further articulation and elaboration of the core tradition. Noth's G, the basic but elaborated story of the beginnings of humankind and of Israel, tracing the story into the settlement of the tribes in Canaan, had at its center this core tradition. The Yahwist and his successors further elaborated and articulated this expanded tradition.

CONCLUSION

This essay has assumed that oral composition and oral transmission were characteristic features of the production of Israelite literature. One area in the production of such oral traditions has received chief attention: the development of what is called a core tradition that goes back to the early beginnings of Israel. Such a core tradition needs to be identified in terms of its content, not its existing shape in the literature. It seems unlikely that any form-critical or structural analyses of the surviving literature will enable the analyst of traditions to recover its form. The form, it is maintained, is more likely to have been narrative than poetic. The setting is likely not to have been cultic alone; such a core tradition would have circulated within the family and the tribe, as story, just as easily as it would have been passed along in cultic acts.

As the core tradition was passed along, continuity and change occurred at one and the same time. What was received was passed along intact. It was preserved intact for purposes of transmission even when the form was expanded to allow for fresh disclosures and fresh understandings and experiences, so long as the content of the core tradition remained. The expansions represented fresh interpretations of the core tradition, whether or not they were so understood. Tradition is a living reality; it is "cumulative and agglomerative." Additions changed the original character of the core tradition to some degree. At the same time, changes in form and style are necessary precisely to maintain the essential content of the tradition.

Nevertheless, the continuity in the life and faith of Israel was provided precisely by such core traditions.[16] What holds Israel together as Israel is a foundational mystery that is caught up in a story that recounts the minimally essential character of the mystery as disclosed: Yahweh appears to a people as one who accompanies them on their pilgrimage; this Yahweh has a special bias in favor of the poor and the oppressed of the earth; he continues his accompanying presence with the people in their movements, requiring of them that they trust his promise of new things to come, a future the lineaments of which have not as yet been fully disclosed.

And Torah (the Pentateuch) clearly maintains that fundamental core tradition in its present shape. Yahweh is the accompanying Presence. He will not forever let oppression go unchecked. He holds before his people a promise that beckons and requires their trust in that promise. Moses may die outside the land of the promise, but Moses' death is no bitter tragedy. God's people prepares for the new event under the leadership of the One who has always been their guide and their deliverer from oppression.

The basic theme of this core tradition, then, is "Yahweh's Promise on the Way to Consummation." It can be maintained that such a basic theme is the theme of the Hebrew Scriptures as a whole and of the Christian Bible as a whole. So pervasive is this core tradition that we have sought to identify.[17]

---

16. It should be noted that I understand this core tradition to be one of several in ancient Israel, not by any means the only one. Analogous traditions of the settlement, the period of the judges, the establishment of the kingship may have existed. More clearly, the theological streams of tradition (see Chapter 8 of this work), which are not to be confused with core traditions, may also have at their base such core traditions. Nevertheless, the core tradition with which I am dealing does seem to me to have a distinctive weight and place within Israel because of its being so fundamental to Israel's self-understanding.

17. I do *not* understand this core tradition to provide anything like a "center" of the Old Testament, theologically viewed. See R. Smend, *Die Mitte des Alten Testaments*, ThSt 101 (Zürich: EVZ Verlag, 1970); and G. Hasel, *Old Testament Theology: Basic Issues in the Current Debate* (Grand Rapids, Mich.: Eerdmans, 1972), pp. 49–63.

Chapter 2

The Impact of the Ancient Near East on Israelite Tradition

Helmer Ringgren

Tradition is an ambiguous word, not the least when it is used in Old Testament exegesis. "Oral tradition" has become a slogan among those scholars who fight literary criticism and consider the oral transmission of texts as the normal procedure of handing down narrative or poetic material in Old Testament times. "History of tradition" (*Überlieferungsgeschichte*) deals with the preliterary stage of the shaping of the Old Testament texts. In this paper, however, "tradition" is taken in a somewhat wider sense as denoting the religious practices and texts that have been handed down from generation to generation and have contributed to shaping the religious and cultural life of ancient Israel. In a way, it includes also the way of life itself that is shaped by this inherited material—it could perhaps also be called the religious heritage of ancient Israel.

Now, it is obvious that Israelite tradition did not develop in an isolated vacuum. Geographically, Israel was part of the ancient Near East, and history and archaeology inform us that its political, commercial, and cultural relations with its neighbors were manifold and varied. Even if the Old Testament itself considers the history of Israelite religion as a constant, and in the end victorious, struggle against the infiltration of Canaanite elements, any objective consideration of the facts shows that the historical truth is much more complicated than this.

The question that we ask, then, is this: To what extent and in

31

what way have factors from outside Israel contributed to the formation of the religious tradition, or heritage, of Israel? Ever since the discovery and decipherment of the hieroglyphic and cuneiform documents, the problem of foreign influence on biblical tradition has been a burning issue.

In his lectures on *Babel und Bibel* (1902–5) Friedrich Delitzsch argued in favor of a strong Babylonian influence on biblical thought. The pan-Babylonian school found traces of Babylonian astral mythology throughout the Old Testament. S. H. Hooke and his followers[1] found it possible to reconstruct a common "myth and ritual pattern" in the ancient Near East, a pattern which was originally developed in Mesopotamia and then spread to other parts of the area, partly in disintegrated form. New material was brought into the discussion by the discovery of the Ugaritic texts, which were especially utilized in the patternist sense by I. Engnell.[2]

The point of departure for this discussion is the simple fact that there are many similarities between biblical ideas, practices, or narratives on the one hand and extra-biblical material on the other. Nobody would deny this. But Old Testament scholars have not reached any consensus on the method for utilizing this material. All too often, research in this area has turned into a kind of "parallel hunting": the endeavor has been to find extra-biblical parallels for biblical ideas or customs—and as soon as such a parallel has been found, all problems seem to be solved: the parallel is there, what more do we need?

It seems to me extremely important that biblical scholarship consider the methodology for the comparison of biblical and extra-biblical material, that we finally bother to ask the question: What is a parallel, and what use do we make of it? What

1. S. H. Hooke (ed.), *Essays on the Myth and Ritual of the Hebrews in Relation to the Culture Pattern of the Ancient Near East* (London: Oxford University Press, 1933); S. H. Hooke (ed.), *The Labyrinth* (London: Oxford University Press, 1935); S. H. Hooke (ed.), *Myth, Ritual and Kingship* (Oxford: Clarendon, 1958).
2. Especially *Studies in Divine Kingship in the Ancient Near East* (Uppsala: Almqvist & Wiksell, 1943; 2d ed., Oxford: Blackwell, 1967); *A Rigid Scrutiny: Critical Essays on the Old Testament* (Nashville: Vanderbilt University Press, 1969).

does it mean in its original context?   How has it found its way into the Bible?   What does it mean in its biblical context? Only when we have ascertained the original meaning and function of a certain parallel are we able to utilize it for the elucidation of a biblical passage.

The problem will be illustrated by discussing some examples from various categories of biblical literature.   The arrangement of the material is somewhat difficult, since it can be classified from many different points of view and the problems involved are manifold.

TYPES OF SIMILARITIES

First of all, there are similarities between biblical and extrabiblical texts which are not necessarily due to foreign influence. There are, for instance, similarities in vocabulary which derive from the fact that Hebrew and the other Northwest Semitic languages are closely related.   But problems arise when we deal with religious vocabulary.   The sacrificial terminology coincides to some extent with that found in the Ugaritic texts and in the Punic sacrificial tariffs.[3]   This is true, for instance, of the words *šlm* and *kālîl*. It is quite clear that the Ugaritic texts are much older than the sacrificial laws of the Old Testament, while the Punic documents are comparatively young.   However, the conclusion must be that the three languages in question draw on a common heritage of sacrificial terms which have developed differently on each side.   There is a possibility of Canaanite influence on early Israelite terminology, but it is very difficult to find out what is common heritage and what is real influence.   Other similarities exist between the sacrificial practices of Israel and those of the pre-Islamic Arabs, for example, in the use of blood.[4]   Here again, it is possible that we have to do with a common heritage, namely, from the nomadic stage.

3. R. Dussaud, *Les origines cananéennes du sacrifice israélite* (Paris: Leroux, 1921; 2d ed., 1941).
4. J. Wellhausen, *Reste arabischen Heidentums*, 2d ed. (Berlin: Reimer, 1897), p. 116; J. Chelhod, *Le sacrifice chez les Arabes* (Paris: P.U.F., 1955), pp. 173ff.

We are on somewhat firmer ground when a whole series of
words recur in two sources. In Isa. 27:1 Leviathan is referred
to as "the twisting serpent, the writhing serpent" and "the
dragon" *(nāḥāš bārīaḥ, nāḥāš 'ăqallātôn, hattannîn).* Now
Ugaritic Lotan—which is the same word as *liwyātān*—has exactly the same epithets.[5] We have to conclude from this that
the prophet has used a piece of Canaanite mythology and
adapted it for his purposes. What we do not know, however,
is whether this was still living mythology at the time of the
prophet or had simply gone into common language as a figure of
speech, which was found suitable to denote the powers of evil.

Secondly, there are narrative portions of the Old Testament
which show clear connections with extra-biblical literature but
which could not be considered to be central or essential to Old
Testament faith.

The Joseph narrative in Genesis has a very obvious Egyptian
local coloring. Egyptian words are quoted, officials are referred
to by title, customs are explained. Vergote[6] thinks that the
emerging picture reflects conditions in Egypt not at the time of
Joseph but rather at the time of the exodus. It is not necessary
to draw the conclusion that the narrative was written down by
Moses, but it might show that the narrative, so to speak, lost its
contact with real Egyptian life around 1200 B.C. and was then
handed down in the form it had when it was isolated. One
problem remains: the story of Potiphar's wife is likely to reflect
an episode in the Egyptian "Tale of the Two Brothers,"[7] but
the function of this episode is remarkably different in the two
sources. It would be premature, therefore, to conclude that the
Joseph narrative is a folktale; but there is an element of Egyptian folklore in it, which has been remodeled in the way that is
common with motifs of folklore.

The story of the Flood may be a little more essential since it

---

5. *UT* 67:I:1–3.
6. J. Vergote, *Joseph en Égypte: Genèse chap. 37–50 à la lumière des études
égyptologiques récentes* (Louvain: Publications Universitaires, 1959).
7. *ANET*, pp. 23ff.

marks a turning-point in the Yahwistic presentation of history; still it is not a major part of Israelite faith. As is well known, we now have access to three parallels in Mesopotamian literature: the Sumerian flood story, unfortunately fragmentary; the story contained in the eleventh tablet of the Gilgamesh epic;[8] and the one found in the recently published Atra-ḫasīs epic.[9] We need not dwell on the numerous details in the Gilgamesh version that correspond to the biblical narrative: the three birds that are sent out, the sacrifice by the hero after the flood, and others. It is less well known, perhaps, that the geographical background is also the same: in the Gilgamesh epic the ship lands on Mount Nisir, which is known to be one of the mountains of the country of Urartu, that is, biblical Ararat. This goes to prove that the biblical story and the Gilgamesh version have a common origin. But we have to take the two other flood stories into account, too. Unfortunately, the Sumerian version is too fragmentary to allow of a coherent interpretation. In the Atra-ḫasīs epic one detail seems to be more closely related to the biblical story than the Gilgamesh version: the reason for the flood is the noise that mankind makes which annoys the gods, while in the Gilgamesh epic the flood seems to be caused by a whim of the gods.

However, still another fact should be kept in mind with regard to the Gilgamesh story. The Gilgamesh epic is a well-planned literary composition, the sources of which we now know—in part at least—through the discovery of Sumerian literature.[10] There is, in Sumerian, a number of independent narratives about Gilgamesh, out of which the author of the epic has chosen some for his purpose, while he has left out others. It is into this Gilgamesh material that our author has inserted his flood story. That means that the flood story of the Gilgamesh epic cannot be used for comparison with the biblical story with-

8. Ibid., pp. 93ff.; Sumerian on pp. 42–43.
9. W. G. Lambert and A. R. Millard, *Atra-ḫasīs. The Babylonian Story of the Flood* (Oxford: Clarendon, 1969).
10. S. N. Kramer, *History Begins at Sumer* (Garden City: Doubleday, 1959), pp. 182ff.

out further analysis of its place in the totality of the Gilgamesh composition. In general, all three of the Mesopotamian flood stories should be submitted to a traditio-historical analysis before they are confronted with the biblical text. No such analysis has been undertaken so far, so it may suffice to point to the problem.

Thirdly, there are social institutions that must clearly be considered as imported. It has been shown that the officials of Solomon's administration had Egyptian prototypes.[11] The institution of kingship itself was imported into Israel, as the Deuteronomistic writer himself admits in making the people say: "Give us a king to govern us like the other nations." Egyptian, Sumer-Babylonian, and Canaanite documents help us to elucidate Israelite royal ideology. Details are too well known to be repeated here.[12] The five throne-names of the Egyptian king are echoed in the *four* names of Isa. 9.[13] The divine sonship of the Israelite king, his claim to world dominion, his responsibility for "righteousness," the *šālôm* that follows the enthronement of a new king[14]—all this has striking parallels in the various kingdoms of the ancient Near East, and it is quite obvious that foreign ideas of kingship have contributed substantially to forming the Israelite royal tradition.

In this connection, we should also mention the covenant concept. Since Mendenhall and Baltzer we know that the literary form of the Israelite covenant traditions exhibits striking similarities with Hittite vassal treaties. Weinfeld has added several features from Assyrian sources.[15] This is not to say that

11. T. Mettinger, *Solomonic State Officials: A Study of the Civil Government Officials of the Israelite Monarchy* (Lund: Gleerup, 1971).

12. Cf., e.g., Engnell, *Studies in Divine Kingship*; H. Frankfort, *Kingship and the Gods: A Study of Ancient Near Eastern Religion as the Integration of Society and Nature* (Chicago: University of Chicago Press, 1948).

13. G. von Rad, "Das judäische Königsritual" (1947), in *Gesammelte Studien zum Alten Testament*, ThB 8 (München: Chr. Kaiser, 1958), pp. 211ff. = "The Royal Ritual in Judah," in *The Problem of the Hexateuch, and Other Essays* (Edinburgh and London: Oliver & Boyd, 1966), pp. 229ff.

14. H. Ringgren, *The Messiah in the Old Testament*, SBT 18 (London: SCM, 1956).

15. G. E. Mendenhall, *Law and Covenant in Israel and the Ancient Near East* (Pittsburgh: The Biblical Colloquium, 1955; reprinted from *BA* 17, 1954); K. Baltzer, *Das Bundesformular*, WMANT 4 (Neukirchen: Neukirchener Verlag, 1960;

the Hebrew concept of a covenant between Yahweh and Israel is an imported idea, but it does mean that the Hebrew idea of a covenant was formed in accordance with the prevailing ideas of a treaty, or covenant, at that time—whether it be in the time of Moses or the time of Deuteronomy, which is a matter of dispute.

Thus, two of the most essential elements of Israelite tradition, kingship and covenant, have been molded in the form prepared in the thought-pattern of the surrounding peoples of the ancient Near East.

Fourthly, there are similarities with regard to literary form and style between biblical texts and extra-biblical documents. We can only give a few examples.

In Ps. 29 we read:

> Give to Yahweh, you sons of God,
> give to Yahweh glory and strength,
> give to Yahweh the glory of his name,
> worship Yahweh in holy array.

The threefold repetition of the introductory words, each time followed by new phrases, is typical of Canaanite poetry as found in the Ugaritic texts. Obviously, this stylistic device has been introduced into early Hebrew poetry from Canaanite sources— or it is part of a common literary heritage.[16] Albright even used this pattern to prove the early date of certain Israelite poetry—whether he was right or not may be left undecided. In the case of Ps. 29 the similarity in style is supplemented by a similarity of ideas: the psalm contains a description of a thunderstorm which might very well have been part of a Canaanite hymn to the god of thunder (Ba'al). It is not surprising, therefore, that many writers consider the psalm an adaptation of a Canaanite hymn.

2d ed., 1964) = *The Covenant Formulary in Old Testament, Jewish and Early Christian Writings* (Philadelphia: Fortress, 1971); D. J. McCarthy, *Treaty and Covenant* (Rome: Pontifical Biblical Institute, 1963); M. Weinfeld, "The Covenant of Grant in the Old Testament and in the Ancient Near East," *JAOS* 90 (1970), 184–203.

16. W. F. Albright, *Yahweh and the Gods of Canaan* (London: Athlone, 1968), pp. 9ff.

Even generally, the Old Testament hymns show formal similarity with other hymns, for example, the Babylonian and
Assyrian ones, as was shown by Cumming.[17] One detail is the
question of incomparability: "Who is like Yahweh?" or related
phrasing.[18] Such questions are common in Akkadian psalms,
and there is no doubt that the two traditions have common
roots. But in this case, the function of the phrase is somewhat
different. In a polytheistic religion the question has a specific
sense: there is a real comparison; the god in question is exalted
above the other gods in the pantheon. In the monotheistic
religion of Israel, part of this sense has been lost: the other gods
are not really gods; strictly speaking, the superiority of Yahweh
cannot be called in question.

There is still more impressive formal and structural similarity
between the biblical and the Akkadian psalms of lament—as is
fully clear from the work of Widengren.[19] The main parts of
the psalm: the address to God, the description of the psalmist's
suffering (with its typical imagery), the prayer for salvation,
the vow—all this has close counterparts in the Babylonian
psalms. Such an expression as *'ad-mātay, adi māti*, "till when?"
"how long?", is also common to both and, as we see, verbally
identical. Of course, such conformity can partly be explained
through the similar situation of the speaker, but the formal
similarities are so striking and so detailed that we have to
reckon with a common literary—or should we say: cultic?—tradition.

Some oracles directed to Assyrian kings begin with the words:
"Do not fear! I am Ishtar." These two formulas turn up several times in the Old Testament, especially in Deutero-Isaiah.
There is now general agreement that the existence of an Israelite *Heilsorakel* as the answer to a psalm of lament, "Do not
fear, I am Yahweh," has to be postulated in order to explain the

17. C. G. Cumming, *The Assyrian and Hebrew Hymns of Praise* (New York:
Columbia University Press, 1934).
18. C. J. Labuschagne, *The Incomparability of Yahweh in the Old Testament*
(Leiden: Brill, 1966).
19. G. Widengren, *The Accadian and Hebrew Psalms of Lamentation as Religious Documents* (Stockholm: Thule, 1937).

expression in Deutero-Isaiah.[20] The self-introduction "I am Yahweh" has another ring in Israel, since no god other than Yahweh could possibly appear in this way and no introduction would be needed, but the literary form which has grown out of the situation of the supplicant must have common roots.

The well-known Immanuel oracle in Isa. 7 contains the following formula: "Lo, the young woman is pregnant and will bear a son. . . ." In an Ugaritic text which deals with the expected birth of a divine child, there is a similar formula: "Lo, the young woman will bear a son. . . ."[21] What does such a parallel imply? In order to assess its value, we should know something about its (original) function. Is it a mythological formula that has functioned in the cult, or is it simply an everyday formula to announce the expected birth of a child? The fact that a similar formula occurs in Egyptian oracles concerning the birth of a royal child[22] could be used in both directions. As long as there is no final answer to the question of original function, it is impossible to evaluate the parallel correctly.

Fifthly, there are cases when a literary dependence seems to be at least very probable. We have already touched upon one example, namely, Ps. 29, which may represent a revised form of a Canaanite psalm. The disturbing fact is that we do not have the original. The same is true of some lines in the first half of Ps. 19. The description of the sun given there is strongly reminiscent of Babylonian hymns to the sun-god: the mythological imagery is the same.[23] However, in Ps. 19 the sun is not a god but one of Yahweh's works. Here, too, the original is missing.

Ps. 104 is another case in point. It is widely recognized that certain parts of this psalm show very close, even verbal, resemblances to the great sun-hymn of Pharaoh Echnaton.[24] The

20. J. Begrich, *Studien zu Deuterojesaja* (1938), ed. W. Zimmerli, ThB 20 (München: Chr. Kaiser, 1963), 14ff.; C. Westermann, "Sprache und Struktur der Prophetie Deuterojesajas," in *Forschung am Alten Testament*, ThB 24 (München: Chr. Kaiser, 1964), 117ff.

21. E. Hammershaimb, "The Immanuel Sign," *StTh* 3 (1949–50), 124ff.

22. G. Widengren, "Hieros gamos och underjordsvistelse," *RoB* 7 (1948), 28–29, 33.

23. O. Schroeder, "Zu Psalm 19," *ZAW* 34 (1914), 69–70.

24. *ANET*, pp. 369ff.

most important difference is on the theological level: while the
night in the Egyptian hymn quite naturally is something negative, or evil, in the Hebrew psalm it is part of Yahweh's creation
and has a positive role to play in the order of nature. The
problem is: how is it possible that Echnaton's hymn to the sun,
which as far as we know fell into oblivion, with the rest of his
monotheistic religion, shortly after his death—how is it possible
for it to influence an Israelite psalm at least four hundred or
five hundred years later? At present, no definite answer can be
given.

We are on somewhat safer ground as far as the "Teaching of
Amenemope"[25] and Prov. 22–24 ("the words of the wise") are
concerned. Since the discovery of this Egyptian wisdom book,
its close relationship with the section of Proverbs just mentioned has been an undisputed fact. There has been some
doubt, however, concerning the priority. Drioton, for instance,
thought that the language of Amenemope was to some extent
"un-Egyptian," which according to him must be explained by
the assumption that the work was a translation from a Semitic
(Canaanite) original.[26] The Hebrew collection of proverbs
would then be a revised edition of the same Canaanite work.
Two facts, however, point to the priority of the Egyptian work:
(1) there are passages in Proverbs which are best explained as
mistranslations from an Egyptian original, not vice versa; and
(2) it is easier to understand Prov. 22–24 as an abridged edition of the Egyptian work than to explain Amenemope as an
expansion of Prov. 22–24.[27] Although there are questions of
date which have not yet received a final answer, the literary
dependence of Prov. 22–24 on Amenemope seems to be beyond
dispute. This is not at all astonishing in view of the international character of the wisdom literature.

Finally, I should like to discuss two examples of a somewhat

25. Ibid., pp. 421ff.
26. E. Drioton, "Sur la sagesse d'Aménémopé," *Mélanges bibliques A. Robert*
(Paris: Bloud & Gay, 1957), pp. 254ff.
27. For a discussion, cf. H. Ringgren, *Sprüche*, ATD 16/1 (Göttingen: Vandenhoeck & Ruprecht, 1962), pp. 90ff.

different kind. They concern texts which exhibit agreement in contents, yet where the similarities are at times elusive and difficult to define.

The first example is from Ps. 74. This is a psalm of lament which describes the destruction of the temple and asks for Yahweh's intervention. F. Willesen[28] has called our attention to a parallel in a Babylonian psalm which describes the destruction of a temple in much the same words as the Hebrew psalm. His conclusion is that both psalms deal with a cultic destruction of the temple, but he does not tell us what such a destruction is like, or when or how it took place.[29] If we ask for the *"Sitz im Leben"* of the Babylonian psalm, it turns out that such laments were recited by the *kalû* priests at the rededication of a temple that had been restored after it had been polluted in some way. Very interestingly, both Ps. 74 and some Babylonian texts of this category have recourse to the creation myth in this connection. This means that the rededication of a temple marks a new beginning, which is given its mythological motivation by quoting the myth of creation. In a similar way, Deutero-Isaiah has recourse to the creation myth in 51:9–11 as a background to the new beginning marked by the expected new exodus.[30] Thus a correct understanding of the *Sitz im Leben* of the Babylonian parallel throws light on biblical ideas.

The second example is much more elusive. Brandon[31] has pointed out that there are certain details in the Gilgamesh epic which are reminiscent of the story of the Fall in Gen. 3. It is a woman (a courtesan, Eve) who "seduces the type-figure of a primitive man (Enkidu, Adam) from his original innocence . . . on the course that leads inevitably to death." The seduction involves the giving of sexual knowledge or experience, and this knowledge makes man "like God" (Gilg. IV, 34—"You are wise,

28. F. Willesen, "The Cultic Situation of Psalm lxxiv," *VT* 2 (1952), 289ff.
29. For a discussion, cf. H. Ringgren, "Israel's Place among the Religions of the Ancient Near East," VTS 23 (1972), 1–2.
30. H. Ringgren, "Die Funktion des Schöpfungsmythus in Jes. 51," *Schalom*, Festschrift A. Jepsen (Berlin: Calwer, 1971), pp. 38ff.
31. S. G. F. Brandon, *Creation Legends of the Ancient Near East* (London: Hodder & Stoughton, 1963), pp. 131–32.

Enkidu, you have become like a god"; Gen. 3:5—"You shall become like God, knowing good and evil"). The acquisition of a certain amount of civilization is involved in both cases: Enkidu learns civilized life and loses his contact with the animals; Adam and Eve discover their nakedness, and God makes clothes for them. Finally, it is a serpent who is the real culprit of the drama: in the Gilgamesh epic by snatching away the plant of life, in Genesis by setting the whole course of events in motion. The Gilgamesh epic knows a plant of life; Genesis, a tree of life. Thus there are a number of details, all connected with one specific problem of human life, which are the same in both stories but have been fitted into a context that is different in each instance based on different presuppositions. It is obvious that both the details and each of the two compositions are important if we want to make a comparative study.

The interesting point is that all these parallels are found in those parts of the Gilgamesh epic that have no Sumerian counterpart. They obviously belong to a stratum of the Gilgamesh tradition which is definitely Semitic. It is not at all certain that it is the Bible that has borrowed these elements from Mesopotamia; they could just as well be of West Semitic origin.[32]

REASONS FOR SIMILARITIES

The examples discussed above show quite clearly how complex the question of foreign influence on Old Testament tradition is. So far we have considered it with regard to various types of similarities. It can also be looked upon from a different angle: we may ask what elements are part of a common heritage, what elements are really "imported" in the course of Israelite history, and what elements of tradition are the result of a protest against foreign ideas (whereby these also are to be considered part of the impact of the Near East on Israelite tradition).

32. Cf. Ringgren, "Israel's Place among the Religions of the Ancient Near East," pp. 4–5.

The question of common heritage has two aspects. There are terms, ideas, social institutions, which must have been part of the tradition of those tribes which at the dawn of history came together to form the people of Israel. It is very difficult, however, to ascertain in detail what these elements were. We might suspect that the divine name *'ēl* was one of them; the use of blood in sacrifices might have been another. Here is the place where comparison with the pre-Islamic Arabs can occur, though it has to be done with utmost caution. What we have here is a nomadic, or semi-nomadic, tribal society, the structure of which can be supposed to be similar, in many respects at least, to the early Israelite tribes. But the distance in time and space makes a warning necessary: a similar social structure does not necessarily involve identical religious ideas. On the other hand, if we are able to discover similarities between Israelite tradition and early Arab culture, there is a certain probability that they belong to the common Semitic heritage.[33]

The other aspect of the problem concerns the existence of a unified ancient Near Eastern culture, or to use a controversial expression already alluded to, whether or not there was a myth and ritual pattern in the ancient Near East. To some extent, this is a matter of definition. If "pattern" is taken to mean an organic totality of cultural elements characteristic of one specific civilization, there can be no common pattern, but only a Babylonian, an Egyptian, and an Israelite pattern.[34] But if pattern means what Hooke took it to mean,[35] there is admittedly a common stock of mythical and ritual elements shared by all the Near Eastern cultures, just as Europe and America today share the same Western civilization without being identical.

As for the really imported elements of Israelite tradition, they

33. For a discussion of this topic, cf. S. Nyström, *Beduinentum und Jahvismus: Eine soziologisch-religionsgeschichtliche Untersuchung zum Alten Testament* (Lund: Gleerup, 1946).

34. H. Frankfort, *The Problem of Similarity in Ancient Near Eastern Religions* (London: Williams and Norgate, 1951); H. Birkeland, *The Evildoers in the Book of Psalms* (Oslo: Dybwad, 1955), pp. 17ff.

35. S. H. Hooke, "Myth and Ritual: Past and Present," in *Myth, Ritual and Kingship*, pp. 3ff.

have found their way into Israel in various epochs. The Old Testament itself insists on the Mesopotamian origin of Israel's ancestors. If there is some truth to this—and there must be—it is quite possible that some of the similarities with Mesopotamian tradition date back to this early epoch. In that case there might even be some doubt whether this is import or common heritage. On the other hand, there have been political and commercial contacts between Israel and Mesopotamia later during the centuries of Israelite history, and these have provided ample opportunity for the influx of Mesopotamian ideas and practices.

The same is true, *mutatis mutandis,* of the Egyptianizing elements. Old Testament tradition locates part of Israel's early history in Egypt, and whatever may be the exact historical truth behind this tradition, it remains very likely that during a certain period parts of what later became Israel had some very close relationship with Egypt. Nothing prevents that some Egyptian elements in Israelite tradition derive from that period. On the other hand, the reign of Solomon saw the establishment of close ties with Egypt with the likely result of Egyptian influence on Israelite institutions and education (wisdom teaching). There were also contacts in later periods.

The Hittites constitute a problem. Although Hittites are mentioned occasionally in the Old Testament, there were no direct contacts between the classical Hittite empire and Israel. The Hittite vassal treaties, which seem to have left their traces in Israelite covenant structure, must have been part of a wider cultural context which just incidentally has been preserved in Hittite sources.

Again, the Canaanite influence is of a complex nature. A long time of coexistence and the conviction that the agrarian life of Palestine was under the control of the Canaanite fertility gods must have prepared the ground for the adoption of a great many religious ideas and practices from the Canaanites. The constant and vehement struggle of the prophets against the religion of Ba'al bears witness to this fact.

However, there is also what we should like to call the indirect, or negative, influence of Canaanite religion on Israelite tradition.[36] It is hardly likely that the prophet Hosea should have put so much emphasis on Yahweh as the giver of fertility as he does in Hos. 2:10ff. [2:8ff.], if he had not had to fight the wrong idea that it was Ba‘al. Even in his picture of the future restoration in ch. 14 he is indirectly influenced by the fertility religion which he fights, for he describes the future in terms of growth, vegetation, and fertility.[37]

THEOLOGICAL IMPLICATIONS

The question that has been dealt with in this essay is primarily of historical interest: to what extent have factors from outside Israel contributed to the shaping of Israelite tradition? In this connection it is important that foreign influence is given its right place: it should neither be flatly denied, nor be exaggerated. Above all it should be stressed that foreign ideas were never taken over unchanged but were adapted to suit their new Israelite context. The important task of research in this area, therefore, is to assess the Israelite use of the foreign material and the reinterpretation it underwent in the framework of Yahwistic religion.

However, it should not be denied that this work has certain theological implications. If it is true that Israelite religion was rather heavily influenced from outside Israel, it might be asked what this means to our understanding of biblical religion as revealed by God. Here it is necessary to keep in mind that the Old Testament idea of revelation is not limited to God's speaking directly to chosen people such as Moses or the prophets. According to the Old Testament view God reveals himself not only in direct words but also through his acts in history. Amos was convinced that Yahweh had not only delivered Israel out of Egypt: he had also brought the Philistines from Caphtor

36. Cf. Albright, *Yahweh and the Gods of Canaan.*
37. G. von Rad, *Die Botschaft der Propheten* (München and Hamburg: Siebenstern, 1967), p. 114 = *The Message of the Prophets* (London: SCM, 1968), p. 117.

and the Arameans from Kir (Amos 9:7). The other nations were not beyond the reach of Yahweh's mighty arm. If Israel was right in the assumption that Yahweh had revealed himself by acting in its history, it would be presumptuous to think that this acting took place exclusively in Israel. It is conceivable, therefore, that pieces of Yahweh's revelation are to be found also among those other peoples, or to put it differently, that elements of his revelation found their way into Israel through the faiths of those other nations. If God is able to use the events of history to get across to his people, he might also be able to use the traditions of the peoples who took part in these events to make himself and his plans known to his people. Is it too bold to assume that "pagan" thinking about God could contain sparks of truth? Does not Paul say in his speech on the Areopagus that the nations might "feel after him and find him"? For "he is not far from each one of us" (Acts 17:27).

One additional observation should be made here. What was said above implies that we may have to reckon with a kind of preparatory revelation among Israel's neighbors. But this preparatory revelation was remodeled in Israel in the light of the knowledge of God present in this people. This suggests that some similar preparatory revelation might be found in other religions, too, for example, Hinduism, Buddhism, African traditional religion, and that this might be a help to interpret the Judeo-Christian message to those people. Judeo-Christian ideas might be explained by the aid of ideas in other religions, in a way similar to Israel who interpreted its faith in Yahweh in forms taken from the neighboring religions.

Part II

DEVELOPMENTS

Chapter 3

Tradition and History:
A Complex Relation*

Rudolf Smend

I

One characteristic of the Old Testament is repeatedly found
to be its "eminent relation to history."[1] G. von Rad could
even state: "The Old Testament is a history book."[2] This
assertion is intended to describe the consequence of the unusually intensive, successful historical and theological work by several generations of researchers; for him this work yielded both
results and a program. To be sure, von Rad did not remain
fixed to this position. At a later point he correctly observed
that "we are nowadays in serious danger of looking at the theological problems of the Old Testament far too much from the
onesided standpoint of an historically conditioned theology."[3]
Since then we have moved well past this danger, and not
the least by means which von Rad himself provided. In the
first place, there was a time when the attempt was made—more
supposedly than actually following von Rad—to refashion all of

---

* Translated by Douglas A. Knight.
1. Cf., recently, G. Ebeling, *Studium der Theologie* (Tübingen: Mohr, 1975),
p. 33.
2. "Typologische Auslegung des Alten Testaments" (1952/53), in *Gesammelte
Studien zum Alten Testament: II*, ThB 48 (München: Chr. Kaiser, 1973), p. 278 =
"Typological Interpretation of the Old Testament," *Interp* 15 (1961), 181.
3. "Aspekte alttestamentlichen Weltverständnisses" (1964), in *Gesammelte Studien
zum Alten Testament*, ThB 8, 4th ed. (München: Chr. Kaiser, 1971), p. 311 =
"Some Aspects of the Old Testament World-View," in *The Problem of the
Hexateuch, and Other Essays* (Edinburgh and London: Oliver & Boyd, 1966),
p. 144.

theology by means of a doctrine of "revelation as history."[4] This effort met with little approval, and it threatened to discredit even its exegetical point of departure. The result was that this base point needed to be reexamined.[5] Second, one could easily see that the Old Testament by no means contains only traditions about history; work on wisdom, which commands considerable attention at present, has made us clearly aware of that, as have other areas as well.[6] Third, it became evident that elements of historical thinking in Israel are not fundamentally different from those in Greece or even from those native to the world of the ancient Orient. In fact, both Israel and the ancient Near East conceive of divine activity in history in largely comparable categories.[7] And finally, it cannot be stated urgently enough how complex this subject is even in the Old Testament alone; it demands a cautious, discriminating consideration and evades any premature generalizations.[8] This will become obvious again in the following discussion, in which we can deal with only a few central aspects.

We agree indeed that this "eminent relation to history" is

4. W. Pannenberg, et al., *Offenbarung als Geschichte* (Göttingen: Vandenhoeck & Ruprecht, 1961, 3d ed. 1965) = *Revelation in History* (New York: Macmillan, 1968); cf. the discussion on the Old Testament by R. Rendtorff, pp. 21ff. (reprinted together with related articles in Rendtorff, *Gesammelte Studien zum Alten Testament*, ThB 57 [München: Chr. Kaiser, 1975]).

5. Cf. W. Zimmerli, "'Offenbarung' im Alten Testament," *EvTh* 22 (1962), 15–31; G. Klein, *Theologie des Wortes Gottes und die Hypothese der Universalgeschichte* (München: Chr. Kaiser, 1964), pp. 13ff., 33ff.; F. Hesse, "Wolfhart Pannenberg und das Alte Testament," *NZSTh* 7 (1965), 174–99.

6. Cf. J. Barr, *Old and New in Interpretation* (London: SCM, 1966), pp. 72ff.; R. Smend, *Elemente alttestamentlichen Geschichtsdenkens* (Zürich: EVZ-Verlag, 1968), p. 4. In recent years J. Barr has produced several important contributions to the whole subject; cf. most recently "Story and History in Biblical Theology," *JR* 56 (1976), 1–17.

7. Cf. H. Gese, "Geschichtliches Denken im Alten Orient und im Alten Testament" (1958), in *Vom Sinai zum Zion*, BEvTh 64 (München: Chr. Kaiser, 1974), 81–98 = "The Idea of History in the Ancient Near East and the Old Testament," *JTC* 1 (1965), 49–64; Barr, *Old and New in Interpretation*, pp. 71–72; B. Albrektson, *History and the Gods*, ConOT 1 (Lund: Gleerup, 1967); Smend, *Elemente alttestamentlichen Geschichtsdenkens*, pp. 33–34; H. H. Schmid, "Das alttestamentliche Verständnis von Geschichte in seinem Verhältnis zum gemeinorientalischen Denken," *WuD* NF 14 (1975), 9–21.

8. For a good compilation of the most important literature, cf. M. Weippert, "Fragen des israelitischen Geschichtsbewusstseins," *VT* 23 (1973), 416–17, n. 3. Add to this list also I. L. Seeligmann, "From Historical Reality to Historiosophical Conception in the Bible" [Hebrew], *Piraqim* 2 (1971), 273–313.

present in the Old Testament and that it plays a considerable role there and in its later after-effect. And also the double terms customarily used to refer to this relation—whether "history and tradition" or more specifically, and more problematically, "event and interpretation"—are well suited for introducing this subject matter and its problems. Anyone who is not completely unacquainted with the situation knows that theology recurringly finds itself on the offensive and on the defensive regarding the question about the extent to which tradition and history are congruous with each other. And he is also aware that the main task facing the historian is to extract history out of tradition.

II

This task meets with unusually hard difficulties in the Old Testament. So far as ancient Israel's historiographic literature is preserved, it exists in two large anonymous and undated literary blocks, each of which is a result of compilation and redaction. The younger of the two is the so-called Chronicler's History, stemming from the fourth or third century B.C. Its first part, both books of the Chronicles, is a revision of the large section in the older block dealing with the period of the monarchy. The second part, the books of Ezra and Nehemiah, was perhaps intended as an independent work; drawing on several available documents, it describes the period from the end of the Babylonian exile to the reforms of Ezra and Nehemiah. The older block comprises the Pentateuch and the Former Prophets. Component parts of the most diverse type are assembled here. The present composition probably derives from chiefly Deuteronomistic redaction, executed in several stages. Somewhat later, the Priestly document was worked into the first half, which extends from the creation until the arrival in the land of Palestine. The legal material present in this document continued to attract numerous, smaller insertions. Separating this half from the rest of the block yielded the Pentateuch. The

older materials available for this redaction were of rather diverse type. For the period until the conquest, compilations of
earlier, originally oral narrative traditions were already in existence. For the period from the conquest on it was necessary to
create for the first time a narrative context for the entirety, and
often for the individual sections as well; thus it is appropriate to
speak of the Deuteronomistic History for this half.

Given these circumstances, the historian of ancient Israel possesses almost entirely secondary sources at best, not primary
ones. Reports about the events in which he is interested come
to him second hand, and more frequently third, fourth, fifth or
even a later hand—not counting the transmission after the
canon was formed. Consequently, he tries to roll back this
tradition process as far as possible in order to reach the statements which are closest to the events. Maintaining the greatest
flexibility over against the object, he must accomplish this with
all the available means of literary-critical, traditio-critical, and
form-critical analysis, and this involves also the historian's other
two methods, analogy and inference.[9] The result is a relative
chronology of elements in the given text, and if we are fortunate this chronology will occasionally coincide at one point or
another with dates in the absolute chronology. Very often,
however, a margin of several generations at best, though frequently of centuries, remains between the reported event (the
terminus a quo) and the final redaction of the historical account (the *terminus ad quem*), and within this range the responsible historian shies away from making overly precise
determinations on the basis of scattered and unstable footholds.
The more detailed one is in discriminating within the analysis, in fixing dates in the relative and absolute chronology, and
in tying these two together, the more chance for error and the
greater the danger that the whole construction will collapse if

9. Historical work with these methods on an important subject of the Old
Testament is described in R. Smend, *Das Mosebild von Heinrich Ewald bis Martin Noth* (Tübingen: Mohr, 1959).

some of the building blocks, or perhaps even just one, prove to be unfit.[10]

If we succeed with some certainty in establishing the statement closest in time to the event, then this naturally carries tremendous weight for the historian. Nonetheless, it would be hazardous for him to set the entire burden on this datum. For one thing, he must by no means neglect those other sources of knowledge, the methods of analogy and inference. Second, statements further removed in time with which these older elements are preserved can also retain important information about the event. Due to the scantiness of the material we are often not able to free ourselves from these later views, even when we attempt to do so with all the means at our disposal. And it has been demonstrated in various ways how limited in value reports based on memory can be, in spite of their high repute, so this fact also necessarily lends considerable importance to perceptions which are gained and formulated later in time.[11] Although there is no need, if we work sensibly, to sink into skepticism,[12] these matters are especially delicate for Old Testament scholars. The historian's main points of orientation —the objective fact, the eyewitness account, and the presumed completeness of the data—have been called the "three vague concepts,"[13] and if there is any field in which the historian can lose his faith in this triad then it is the Old Testament.

Long ago W. M. L. de Wette examined the state of affairs in a very one-sided yet also very stimulating manner. He concluded that a history of ancient Israel cannot be reconstructed at all from the Old Testament and that consequently historical sci-

---

10. In my opinion, this danger is present in the ingenious attempt to reconstruct the development of the Elijah tradition in correspondence with the history of the period, as executed by O. H. Steck, *Überlieferung und Zeitgeschichte in den Elia-Erzählungen*, WMANT 26 (Neukirchen-Vluyn: Neukirchener Verlag, 1968).

11. Cf. H.-I. Marrou, *Über die historische Erkenntnis* (Freiburg and München: Alber, 1973), pp. 61–62.

12. Cf. J. Huizinga, *Geschichte und Kultur* (Stuttgart: Kröner 1954), pp. 133ff.

13. Cf. J. G. Droysen, *Historik: Vorlesungen über Enzyklopädie und Methodologie der Geschichte*, ed. R. Hübner, 7th ed. (München: Oldenbourg, 1974), pp. 133ff.

ences should forgo this part of their field.[14]   According to de
Wette, the Old Testament is inadequate as an historical source,
and not only because of the actual conditions of transmission.
More importantly for him, it is due to the intentions of the
biblical authors.   For they did not, as he perceived it, even
want to recount history; their theme was religious not historical, and their production belongs in the category of myth.
Even de Wette himself in later years did not maintain these
theses in their radical form.   However, they have proven
fruitful—not the least through applying the concept of myth.
As fascinating as this concept is and as little as several of its uses
fit the biblical circumstances, nonetheless knowledge of mythical thinking can teach us much, leaving all details aside, about
how to comprehend the structure of historical thinking in the
Old Testament.[15]

From the very outset it is questionable to assert—as has often
been done for apologetic purposes—that the biblical authors did
not even wish to write history. We may assume, rather, that
they wrote generally in good faith that the events which they
were narrating had actually happened.[16] Knowledgeable persons assure us that Israel differs from Greece at this point,
for the Greeks were less concerned about actuality.[17] In that
case we are not doing biblical narratives justice by classifying
them primarily according to their supposed reality quotient,

14. W. M. L. de Wette, *Auffoderung zum Studium der Hebräischen Sprache und
Litteratur* (Jena and Leipzig: Gabler, 1805); *Beiträge zur Einleitung in das Alte
Testament*, II (Halle: Schimmelpfennig, 1807).   Cf. also R. Smend, *W. M. L. de
Wettes Arbeit am Alten und am Neuen Testament* (Basel: Helbing & Lichten-
hahn, 1958), pp. 22ff., 49ff.

15. H.-P. Müller has produced a series of important studies on this in recent
years. For his last one and also for references to older literature, cf. J. Krecher
and H.-P. Müller, "Vergangenheitsinteresse in Mesopotamien und Israel,"
Saeculum 26 (1975), 13–44. On the diversity of the viewpoints, cf. the good
description in *Die Eröffnung des Zugangs zum Mythos*, ed. K. Kerényi, WF 20
(Darmstadt: Wissenschaftliche Buchgesellschaft, 1967).

16. Cf. M. Noth, "Geschichtsschreibung, biblisch: Im AT," *RGG* 2, 3d ed.
(1958), col. 1498; J. Hempel, *Geschichten und Geschichte im Alten Testament
bis zur persischen Zeit* (Gütersloh: Mohn, 1964), pp. 12ff.

17. Cf. E. Auerbach, *Mimesis: Dargestelle Wirklichkeit in der abendländischen
Literatur*, 2d ed. (Bern: Francke, 1959), p. 16 = *Mimesis: The Representation of
Reality in Western Literature* (Princeton: Princeton University Press, 1968), p.
14; Hempel, *Geschichten und Geschichte*, pp. 15–16.

such as in myth, folktales, legends, sagas, history writing. The claim for reality is fundamentally the same at all points, even though the reality quotient may be graduated most diversely.[18]

However, we must immediately add that, irrespective of genres, Israelite narrative is "not interested in the historical occurrences per se but in God's activity in history."[19] Perhaps such a precise material definition of the controlling interest has a rather hard ring at first. So for the moment it may suffice to assert that some other interest, however constituted, is present beyond the interest in actuality. It contributes to determining each narrative from the outset, determining it primarily or even entirely—and not seldom, from our perspective, in opposition to actuality. Without this interest there would be no narratives. This applies also to that type of occupation with history which Nietzsche called antiquarian. An incident is probably never narrated exclusively for its own sake—whether, to name two extreme cases, in poetic fiction or in an official document.[20]

Already in the initial effort to comprehend an event—and in some cases even earlier, during anticipation—this interest is playing a role, just as available categories of understanding and expression are involved at that stage. Of course we can object to the way that scholars today often state, too hastily and so to speak dogmatically, that facts in the Bible are never affirmed without interpretation.[21] Yet at the same time we must not forget that so-called objective facts in history are extremely problematic; it is not without good reason that history is called "the decidedly inexact science."[22]

18. On this, cf. the examples in Hempel, *Geschichten und Geschichte*, pp. 120–21.

19. Noth, *RGG* 2, 3d ed., col. 1499.

20. Cf. Droysen, *Historik*, pp. 124–25. Political materials and indeed even propaganda can actually appear to be objectively annalistic. The political dimension of Old Testament historiography has been rather neglected in the research of recent decades in comparison with the religious, which has of course been carried out by theologians. On this, cf. M. Buber, "Der Gesalbte," in *Werke*, vol. 2 (München: Kösel; Heidelberg: Schneider, 1964), pp. 802–803.

21. So Barr, *Old and New in Interpretation*, p. 71.

22. Huizinga, *Geschichte und Kultur*, p. 52. For various viewpoints and literature on the discussion that follows, cf. H. M. Baumgartner, K.-G. Faber, J. Rüsen, and A. Scheff, *Historische Objektivität* (Göttingen: Vandenhoeck & Ruprecht, 1975).

> [What one] calls objective facts, a battle, a council, a rebel-
> lion—have these really existed as such in reality? Are they
> not instead many, countless particulars in a single process,
> one which only the human mind comprehends as such ac-
> cording to some objective or cause or effect or something
> else common to these particulars? In truth, willful human
> acts, the deeds and sufferings of so many individuals, have
> yielded that which we identify as the fact of this battle or
> this rebellion and which results in the embracing human
> conception. The battle or the rebellion was not the objec-
> tive and real element at that moment; it was rather the
> thousands who rushed headlong against each other, shouted,
> slew each other, etc.[23]

Nothing—not even something as seemingly unequivocal as the
death of a ruler, the capture of a city, the liberation of a people
—can be perceived, narrated, and transmitted without qualifications, often a whole series of them.[24] The difference between
uninterpreted and interpreted history[25] is only a difference of
degree.[26] The incontestable fact of advancing theologization is
juxtaposed with the other equally incontestable fact of advancing objectification due to historical distance, and indeed no firm
laws can be formulated at these points.

III

"History is the thought-form of faith for the Old Testament
person."[27] This statement expresses pointedly, yet not incor-
rectly, why tradition about history holds such rank, according to
both quality and quantity, in the Old Testament. It is a very
specific expression of common human mythical thinking which
grasps and mediates data less through defining and describing

---

23. Droysen, *Historik*, pp. 96–97; cf. also pp. 134ff.
24. Cf. Marrou, *Über die historische Erkenntnis*, pp. 172ff., and the examples
given there; also Hempel, *Geschichten und Geschichte*, p. 25.
25. Cf. G. von Rad, *Theologie des Alten Testaments*, vol. 2, 5th ed. (München:
Chr. Kaiser, 1968), pp. 382–83= *Old Testament Theology*, vol. 2 (New York and
Evanston: Harper & Row, 1965), pp. 359–60.
26. That must be the case even for the contrast between "Historians and
Prophets" in P. R. Ackroyd's study in *SEÅ* 33 (1968), 18–54.
27. I. L. Seeligmann, "Menschliches Heldentum und göttliche Hilfe: Die dop-
pelte Kausalität im alttestamentlichen Geschichtsdenken," *ThZ* 19 (1963), 385.

than through narrating. It places *mythos* before *logos*; it perceives being in events, reinterprets it into events, presents it as events. In this, the events serve partially as etiology, partially as paradigm. To be sure, the verb "serve" must not stir up any false notions: narratives are not manufactured ad hoc, as it were; they are neither arbitrary nor interchangeable; they have beauty, worth, and power, can even become overwhelming.

Etiology provides the *aitia* or the *aition*, that is, the reason, the cause for an actual phenomenon. This can include actualities of the most diverse type. Almost nothing of importance is without an etiology or even several of them—occasionally competing ones, in which case the narrators and compilers regard and treat this competition in a way apparently similar to how they dealt with, for example, the disagreements between the Yahwistic and the Priestly accounts of the Flood. The classical treatment in Old Testament research, that of H. Gunkel, distinguishes between ethnological, etymological, cultic, and geological motifs in legends.[28] Examples from Genesis are the most familiar: the primeval history in many of its details and as a whole is an etiology of the human condition in this world; the patriarchal history is an etiology for the existence and theoretical structure of the people Israel; the latter group of narratives in turn contains numerous individual etiologies: for a pillar of salt at the Dead Sea (Gen. 19:26); for the existence and names of the two neighboring peoples, Moab and Ammon (Gen. 19:36–38); for Bethel, the holy place, its sacred stone and its name, presumably also for a sacral custom practiced there (Gen. 28:17–19); for the names Penuel and Israel as well as for a dietary custom (Gen. 32:29–33 [32:28–32]). The list could be much longer; indeed, the search for etiological motifs in Old Testament narrative literature can be pursued almost like a sport.

In the Old Testament discipline etiologies constitute a fre-

28. H. Gunkel, *Genesis*, 8th ed. (Göttingen: Vandenhoeck & Ruprecht, 1969), pp. XXff. = *The Legends of Genesis: The Biblical Saga and History* (New York: Schocken, 1964), pp. 25ff.

quently discussed and quite controversial subject, although no one fully contests their existence or even their importance.[29] Gunkel considered etiologies as answers to the child's question "Why?" and thus as the beginnings of human learning. Since then we have perceived more and more clearly that etiologies were to satisfy, besides the need for knowledge and in fact more significantly than this, also an elementary need of life—the need for legitimacy and security, ranging from the legitimacy of a sanctuary on the basis of some divine relation, to that of a prophet on the basis of his call, to the security of existence and order of the world on the basis of the creation (cf. also Gen. 8:22). An etiology can, on the other hand, also serve to contest legitimacy, as in the story about the origin of the idol and priesthood in Dan (Judg. 17–18).

It is questionable whether we should speak of a regular genre of etiological narratives. The etiological motif can constitute a whole narrative, but it can also be affixed to a narrative which originally was not etiological. Therefore when examining etiologies we must proceed carefully and differently from case to case. That is true also with regard to drawing conclusions about the historicity of what is narrated. As a rule, the point of departure for an etiology is the *explicandum*, the actuality to be accounted for. The historian can generally consider that this was real at the time of the narrative. In contrast, the *explicatio*, the etiology, is subject to the suspicion of being fictional. As is well known, this suspicion was very impressively confirmed for the stories about the capture of the cities of Jericho and Ai in Josh. 6 and 8, which archaeology proved to be unhistorical; both stories presuppose the ruins of the cities and attribute

29. The most important specialized literature on this is: I. L. Seeligmann, "Aetiological Elements in Biblical Historiography," *Zion* 26 (1961), 141–69 [Hebrew, with English summary]; S. Mowinckel, *Tetrateuch—Pentateuch—Hexateuch*, BZAW 90 (Berlin: Töpelmann, 1964), pp. 78ff.; B. O. Long, *The Problem of Etiological Narrative in the Old Testament*, BZAW 108 (Berlin: Töpelmann, 1968); F. Golka, "Zur Erforschung der Ätiologien im Alten Testament," *VT* 20 (1970), 90–98; B. S. Childs, "The Etiological Tale Re-examined," *VT* 24 (1974), 387–97.

them to the Israelites' conquest of Palestine.[30]   In the phrase "until this day," which frequently concludes etiologies,[31] the present time of the narrative stands out explicitly as the goal. Thereby, a connecting line is drawn between the past and the present, between the inaugurating act and that which is seen to be its ongoing effect.

Yet one does not narrate only in order to re-present causes and beginnings.   Alongside the etiologies are the paradigms, perhaps more widespread and interwoven with the whole tradition, including the etiological narratives.   The link between the narrated occurrence and the narrative purpose (*"Skopus"*) is not "because—therefore," but "as—so."   As the coalition of Canaanite kings failed and finally its army commander Sisera was killed, "so may all your enemies perish, Yahweh, but your friends are like the rising of the sun in its might" (Judg. 5:31). The purpose is seldom formulated so explicitly; because we are not usually familiar with the location and interests of the narrators and their audience, as a rule this purpose can be determined with relative certainty only if it is similarly general. Yet we can assume that it is present nearly everywhere—even at those places where we observe occurrences arranged only stiffly together, or at other points where we detect pure, masterful narrative art, for precisely such indirectness can be the product of special artistic abilities.   Moreover, paradigms are often less easily separable from etiologies than would seem logically to be the case.   Paradigms involve by no means only illustrative examples and analogies, but also binding, obligating precedents. Consider again the case cited above: it should and will always be as it was in Deborah's battle, and one reminds God and Israel of this by reciting and transmitting this song.

30. On this, cf. especially A. Alt, "Josua" (1963), in *Kleine Schriften zur Geschichte des Volkes Israel*, vol. 1, 4th ed. (München: Beck, 1968), pp. 176–92; M. Noth, *Das Buch Josua*, 3d ed. (Tübingen: Mohr, 1971), pp. 21ff., 49ff.; Noth, *Aufsätze zur biblischen Landes- und Altertumskunde*, vol. 1, ed. H. W. Wolff (Neukirchen-Vluyn: Neukirchener Verlag, 1971), pp. 8ff., 23ff., 43ff.

31. This phrase, however, is not evidence that a given text is an etiology; an overview of its occurrences is found in B. S. Childs, "A Study of the Formula 'Until this Day,'" *JBL* 82 (1963), 279–92.

We do not have to search hard for paradigms. The Old Testament is full of them, for almost nothing is narrated that is not
paradigmatic in some sense. Israel's life as a people or the life
of its members is presented as it was, is, should be—or even as it
should not be. It deals with primordial situations of human
coexistence and conflict: Cain and Abel, Abraham and Lot,
Jacob and Esau, Jacob and Laban, Joseph and his brothers, Job
and his environment, priest and prophet, prophet and prophet,
prophet and king, prophet and people, Israelite and non-
Israelite. The list could be broadened and greatly lengthened,
even more so than the list of etiologies. And at that the most
important characteristic is not even mentioned: human relations are, as a rule, viewed *sub specie Dei*. In fact often enough
the God of Israel is participating not just indirectly but directly. Most stories in the Old Testament are covertly or
overtly stories of Yahweh, and as such they are canonical standards for measurement—long before there is a canon as such.

IV

In view of the diversity and complexity of the material, no
firm rules about the forming of narratives can be established.
Nonetheless, several basic principles are distinguishable.

As we have already discussed, one fundamental feature on the
whole is the thinking in terms of events, and this often, but not
always, involves rethinking or transforming the object into
events. Thus the psalmist describes Yahweh's kingship with
the act of ascending the throne,[32] and Deuteronomistic historiography issues a general opinion on Israelite royalty by
recounting its origin, the stories about Samuel and Saul.[33]
One example of this, impressive precisely because of its dry
character, is the way that geographical lists in Josh. 13–19 are

---

32. Cf., e.g., Ps. 47:6, 9 [47:5, 8], and on this O. Eissfeldt, "Jahwe als König"
(1928), in *Kleine Schriften*, vol. 1 (Tübingen: Mohr, 1962), pp. 190–91.
33. 1 Sam. 8–12.

changed into descriptive sentences and set into the act of distributing the land.[34]

Rethinking something over to an event, just like retaining an event, usually goes hand in hand with considerable concentrating and condensing, particularly in oral transmission.[35] Thus in Josh. 1–11 the protracted process of taking the land became a single dramatic military effort under the leadership of a single man, Joshua. What took a long time to occur is narrated as an individual happening, compacted into a short time, so that it in turn will be intelligible and relevant for a long time to come. An important factor is already present here in this individualizing manner of comprehending and describing: the nearly consistent personalization. Just as powers are experienced as a "Thou,"[36] so also collectives are embodied in individuals,[37] and developments are understood and presented in individual human decisions. Of course, while many of these men and women may become ever so real characters for us, and while they may be pictured in ever so lifelike form—just consider the first human couple in Gen. 3 and the royal couple in 1 Kgs. 21—still there is no character portrayal in our sense nor even a real tendency toward biography.[38] In the place of historical portraits we find pictures which often diverge decidedly from each other and which are affected by different perspectives and different interests; all of this can conceal the original picture

34. On this, cf. O. Bächli, "Von der Liste zur Beschreibung: Beobachtungen und Erwägungen zu Jos. 13–19," *ZDPV* 89 (1973), 1–14.

35. Cf. Droysen, *Historik*, p. 63; and R. C. Culley, "Oral Tradition and Historicity," in *Studies on the Ancient Palestinian World*, ed. J. W. Wevers and D. B. Redford, Toronto Semitic Texts and Studies 2 (Toronto: University of Toronto Press, 1972), pp. 102–16.

36. Cf. H. and H. A. Frankfort, J. A. Wilson, T. Jacobsen, and W. A. Irwin, *The Intellectual Adventure of Ancient Man* (Chicago: University of Chicago Press, 1946), pp. 4ff.

37. Cf., e.g., S. Mowinckel, *He that Cometh* (Oxford: Blackwell, 1956), pp. 214ff., and the literature discussed there; also G. von Rad, *Theologie des Alten Testaments*, vol. 1, 5th ed. (München: Chr. Kaiser, 1966), pp. 120–21 = *Old Testament Theology*, vol. 1 (New York and Evanston: Harper & Row, 1962), pp. 108–109.

38. Cf., instead of many, S. Mowinckel, *Zur Komposition des Buches Jeremia* (Kristiania: Dybwad, 1914), pp. 25–26. Of a different opinion: K. Baltzer, *Die Biographie der Propheten* (Neukirchen-Vluyn: Neukirchener Verlag, 1975).

more than bring it into focus. It suffices to mention the two main figures, Moses and David. The case is similar with the great scenes in which Israel, challenged by Joshua, Elijah, or Ezra, has to respond with a "yes" or a "no" and, binding all time to follow, does respond. And at that we are not even mentioning countless smaller scenes in which an endless wealth of experience took on form.

The most important element of content during the development of Old Testament narratives is the reference to Israel and to its God Yahweh. This is not equally strong and equally direct in all areas of the tradition, but it is never absent. This reference leaves its imprint on the narratives and, even more so, on the entire tradition. "Israel was ready to see herself embodied in the most out-of-the-way traditions of one of her component parts, and to include and absorb the experience there recorded in the great picture of the history of Israel."[39] Thus Abraham, Isaac, and Jacob are the fathers of all Israel; all Israel was delivered out of Egypt, received Yahweh's revelation at Sinai, conquered the promised land, fought under leaders in the period of the judges. In historical reality, all of this was completely different. Particular figures and events were involved, and rather frequently we can catch glimpses of them themselves in the tradition, for example, in individual stories about the judges. Israelitizing the traditions contrary to history, a procedure that is presupposed already in the forming of Pentateuchal tradition at a stage available to us,[40] is not simply a matter of antedating the national unity gained later. More importantly, belief in the one God enters into this—the One who is Israel's God, just as Israel is his, Yahweh's people. Israelitizing is closely connected with "Yahwehizing," which characterizes the entire tradition as well. This or that other

---

39. Von Rad, *Theologie des Alten Testaments*, vol. 1, pp. 131–32 = *Old Testament Theology*, vol. 1, p. 118.
40. Cf. M. Noth, *Überlieferungsgeschichte des Pentateuch* (Stuttgart: Kohlhammer, 1948), pp. 45ff., 274 = *A History of Pentateuchal Traditions* (Englewood Cliffs: Prentice-Hall, 1972), pp. 42ff., 254.

numen before or beside Yahweh, such as one that appeared in earlier forms of individual patriarchal stories, has long since disappeared in the God of Israel, been eliminated or replaced by him.

The statement that Yahweh is the God of Israel and Israel is the people of Yahweh was not formed as such until relatively late, perhaps barely in the pre-exilic period; at any rate it presupposes the great crisis which the prophets recognized and interpreted.[41] But what this sentence signifies is much older— something which exists already at the beginning of Israelite history and which, as the fundamental theme in the Old Testament witness, becomes fully conjugated, as it were, throughout the centuries. Stated somewhat schematically: an initial and relatively unreflective manner of thinking develops intellectually all the way to a fully evolved theology with its propositions. Of course this development does not move along a straight line, any more than is the case elsewhere in intellectual history. Even if the religious element intensifies through the progressing relation to Yahweh, this does not at all allow us to posit that the beginnings were profane. It may suffice to point to what is probably the oldest reaction to the miracle at the Reed Sea, the Song of Miriam (Exod. 15:21). Already at that point it was a hymn to Yahweh, an interpretation of an event in terms of belief in Yahweh; it is a rather idle enterprise for us to want to reconstruct some "profane" original form out of this song and out of the further narrative interpretations in Exod. 13–14. As is well known, the final stage in forming the state under Solomon, which G. von Rad even described as a period of enlightenment,[42] constitutes a turn to relatively profane conceptions and descriptions. Recently E. Würthwein exposed sharply the secular character of the superb literary work of that period, the extensive narrative about the succession to

41. Cf. R. Smend, *Die Bundesformel*, ThSt 68 (Zürich: Evangelischer Verlag, 1963).
42. *Theologie des Alten Testaments*, vol. 1, pp. 62ff. = *Old Testament Theology*, vol. 1, pp. 48ff.

David's throne (2 Sam. 9–20; 1 Kgs. 1–2); according to him, this is political, not theological historiography.[43]   Although these alternatives are perhaps drawn too sharply and although the religious element plays from the outset a greater role in this narrative than Würthwein supposes, still it is certainly true that the real theological highlights were drawn in later.   As elsewhere, this was chiefly the work of the Deuteronomistic school, for nearly all pre-exilic tradition known to us passed through their hands.

This school did not interpret solely by means of formulating new theological statements—whether lengthy as in Josh. 23 or very short as in 1 Kgs. 17:24b—but also, indeed perhaps more significantly, by means of composing the narrative material as such.   There were precedents for the former, but even more so for the latter.   It is enough for us just to mention the Yahwist, who for that matter was not the first one though certainly the most important one to fashion a larger whole out of existing individual traditions.   This procedure, which was related more or less closely to Israelitization, had great significance for the narratives.[44]   Often enough, in order to fit the new context their original point was modified or replaced by another. Local etiologies lost their own thrust which they had had from the beginning; their narrative purpose was subordinated to the usually paradigmatic sense of an entire composition, like the Jacob cycle, in order to retain some of their function as a sign. This development could not be arrested, and it is very seldom possible for us to reverse it in such a manner that we can with certainty reconstruct the original independent narrative and determine its meaning.

But tensions within a narrative, beyond those which are natural to a good narrative progression, do not arise initially or only at the point when it is fitted into a larger context.   Such

43. E. Würthwein, *Die Erzählung von der Thronfolge Davids—theologische oder politische Geschichtsschreibung?* (Zürich: TVZ-Verlag, 1974).
44. On this, cf. especially I. L. Seeligmann, "Hebräische Erzählung und biblische Geschichtsschreibung," *ThZ* 18 (1962), 305–25.

tensions are most commonly expressed in deviations from the historical reality, for reality as such rarely or never expresses exactly what the narrative intends. Scholars have referred to the tension between an impressionistic and an expressionistic impulse[45] or to the tension between a primary experience and a secondary experience;[46] in the second case narrators are considered more passive than in the first, but both mean basically the same thing. This tension actually forms the narratives, usually not just at the first conception but in a reciprocal action often lasting through many generations, an action in which the past is related to the given present (and future) and the given present (and future) is projected back into the normative past.[47] The most productive periods are when something is not yet self-evident or when something is no longer self-evident but is perhaps threatened by loss or even lost already. It is no accident that the great crisis around the Babylonian exile left its tracks most distinctly in the tradition; it is no accident that that period saw the most comprehensive composition and theologization of the material.[48]

V

The deeper we penetrate into the development of the tradition, the more difficult the task of the tradition historian, but of

45. Hempel, *Geschichten und Geschichte*, pp. 25–26 and elsewhere.

46. G. von Rad, "Offene Fragen im Umkreis einer Theologie des Alten Testaments" (1963), in *Gesammelte Studien zum Alten Testament: II*, pp. 304–305. With respect to the relationship between these elements of tension, it would be possible to discuss the types of relationship between event and interpretation all the way to the extent of obliterating the event in its real sense, so that only "secondary experiences" or "expressionistic impulses" remain as real phenomena. On this—and with not unfounded skepticism about the whole schema—cf. J. Barr, "Some Old Testament Aspects of Berkhof's 'Christelijk Geloof,'" in *Weerwoord: Reacties op Dr. H. Berkhof's Christelijk Geloof* (Nijkerk: Callenbach, 1974), pp. 9–19, especially pp. 10ff.

47. As an aside, we might call attention to the important fact that the manner of treating history (or tradition) is indeed determined also by this very history (tradition). The historian's question, "How does history emerge from the activities?" (Droysen, *Historik*, p. 322), should always be set side by side the other question: "How do the activities emerge from our own history?" On this, cf. especially Huizinga, *Geschichte und Kultur*, pp. 130ff.; Huizinga, *Mein Weg zur Geschichte* (Basel: Schwabe, 1947), pp. 73ff.

48. This basic question of continuity and discontinuity is discussed below by P. R. Ackroyd, Chapter 9.

course also that of the historian of ancient Israel; actually these two are cutomarily one and the same person. If he succeeds in recovering those primary and secondary experiences in the course of history (and these may divide further into tertiary and quaternary experiences and even more), then he has gained the most both for history as well as for tradition history. At the beginning of our discussion we intimated that this is an enterprise full of risks;[49] in the meantime this has probably become more obvious.

But we do tradition an injustice if we use it only as a source of history or if we consider tradition history merely as an important component of history. Tradition has more to say. Not as if we should adopt its picture of history and thus return to "mythical" thinking with its grandeur, but also with its abyss.

> History adequate for our culture can only be scientific history. In the modern Western culture the form of knowledge about occurrences in this world is critical-scientific. We cannot surrender the demand for the scientifically certain without damaging the conscience of our culture. Mythic consolidations of the past can still have literary value for us as a form of play—but for us they are not history.[50]

Yet there is a truth here for our type of history also: it is "always a moulding of the past, and it cannot pretend to be more."[51] With all temporal distance and all scientific objectivity we are no less exposed to the overgrowth of "expressionistic" factors and secondary experiences than were the people who produced the ancient traditions. Actually, almost any term or concept which we use and which is taken from our social and political world of experience is necessarily a source of misunderstandings.[52] Stated pointedly: we can still learn more about ancient

49. Cf. above, pp. 52–53.
50. Huizinga, *Geschichte und Kultur*, p. 13.
51. Ibid., p. 8.
52. Ibid., p. 73.

Israel, including her history, from reading the historical books of the Old Testament than from reading the best textbook today on this subject matter; and a textbook is perhaps at its best when its author knows that.

G. von Rad asserted that until the sixth century Israel "was unable to dispense with poetry in drafting history" and that "[she] only finally went over to the prosaic and scientific presentation of her history with the Deuteronomistic history."[53] Setting such temporal periods is as questionable as are the attempts to date a beginning of historiography in Israel (usually in the period when the state was being formed). One would almost prefer to agree with W. Vatke, who contested altogether the existence of real historiography in the Old Testament.[54] Yet what von Rad specifies in this context about poetry remains important: "In those times poetry was, as a rule, the one possible form for expressing special basic insights," and above all "the faith needed" these historical expressions. Old Testament narratives "appeal for assent; they address those who are prepared to ask questions and receive answers along like lines, that is, those who credit Jahweh with great acts in history."[55] Here we see the indispensable priority position of tradition over all our historico-critical history, and under present conditions this latter history is inherently obliged to be silent at that point. This priority position also settles the controversy over whether theology is concerned foremost with the former or with the latter picture of history.[56] Actually we are

53. Von Rad, *Theologie des Alten Testaments*, vol. 1, p. 122 = *Old Testament Theology*, vol. 1, p. 109.

54. W. Vatke, *Die biblische Theologie wissenschaftlich dargestellt, I: Die Religion des Alten Testaments* (Berlin: Bethge, 1835), p. 716.

55. Von Rad, *Theologie des Alten Testaments*, vol. 1, pp. 121–22 = *Old Testament Theology*, vol. 1, p. 109. J. Wellhausen was not far removed from this position when he stated with respect to Elijah: "Legend—but not history—was able to preserve a picture of him"; *Israelitische und jüdische Geschichte*, 7th ed. (Berlin: Reimer, 1914), p. 73.

56. Cf. the literature mentioned in Weippert, "Fragen des israelitischen Geschichtsbewusstseins," pp. 414–15, n. 1. In addition, R. Hanhart, "Kriterien geschichtlicher Wahrheit in der Makkabäerzeit," in his *Drei Studien zum Judentum* (München: Chr. Kaiser, 1967), pp. 7ff.

not faced with a strict alternative here; one reason is that pictures of history in the earthly, human sphere, where they can be compared, are possibly not really so incompatible with each other,[57] but the primary reason is that the historico-critical picture of history renders essential assistance in interpreting that other picture, the older one which contains God's word not only to the Israelites but also to us as well.

57. So Weippert, "Fragen des israelitischen Geschichtsbewusstseins," p. 416.

Chapter 4

Prophetic Proclamation and Reinterpretation*

Walther Zimmerli

THE PROPHETIC "NO" TO ISRAEL'S TRADITIONS

In response to various attempts to anchor Amos' message within certain traditional institutional spheres,[1] R. Smend selected as title for his article the phrase "Amos' No."[2] With this key-word "No!" he has undoubtedly struck a characteristic note not only of Amos but also of the other great literary prophets of the pre-exilic period. Indeed, this "No" is found explicitly in the negative expressions by which Hosea names his children: *lō' 'ammî*, "Not-my-people," for his youngest child, and *lō' rūḥāmāh*, "Not-pitied," for his second child.[3] Isaiah's utterances about "this people" (*hā'ām hazzeh*),[4] even though the explicit negative particle is lacking, approximate the Hoseanic *lō' 'ammî*.

This "No" negates ancient elements of tradition. It is Israel's heritage from antiquity to be the people of Yahweh. This tradition contains also confidence in Yahweh's love and mercy—precisely that which is countered in the name given Hosea's second child. The same "No" to an ancient religious

* Translated by Douglas A. Knight.

1. As in E. Würthwein, "Amos-Studien," *ZAW* 62 (1950), 10–52 = his *Wort und Existenz: Studien zum Alten Testament* (Göttingen: Vandenhoeck & Ruprecht, 1970), 68–110; and more distinctly in H. Graf Reventlow, *Das Amt des Propheten bei Amos*, FRLANT 80 (Göttingen: Vandenhoeck & Ruprecht, 1962).
2. R. Smend, "Das Nein des Amos," *EvTh* 23 (1963), 404–23.
3. Hos. 1:6, 9.
4. Isa. 6:9–10; 8:11; and elsewhere.

tradition can be recognized in Mic. 3:12 where the coming devastation of Zion and of the mountain of the temple is proclaimed,[5] as also in Ezek. 15 where the picture of Israel as the noble vine, fetched from Egypt by Yahweh, is destroyed from within by treating it with insult as a useless vine branch. And how effectively they shatter the tradition of the loving relationship between Yahweh and his people when Hosea, after him Jeremiah, and, most gruesome of all, Ezekiel speak of Israel or Jerusalem with the picture of a whoring, faithless wife (or, in Ezek. 23 concerning the two kingdoms, two such women at the outset in Egypt). In all of this, it is time-honored tradition, that which bore Israel's identity as the people of Yahweh, that is destroyed.

Thus in such a volume as this one on the "theology of tradition," one could close the cover on the pre-exilic prophets with the verdict: "Old Traditions—Non-Applicable!"

However, this impassioned and unmistakable "No" does not sufficiently describe all prophetic speech, not even just that of the great pre-exilic prophets—and in fact not even regarding only the question of their stance toward older Israelite traditions. Their "No" is the reverse side of an equally impassioned "Yes." We would be misunderstanding the prophets if we regarded them as revolutionary nihilists who rejected the entire heritage of pious Israel. Their polemic occurs, in the final analysis, on the basis of what they held in common with Israel's confessions and cultic traditions—although they could issue only a vehement "No" to what qualified as worship in their days.

We can begin with a very elementary matter that is obviously presupposed in all of their utterances and that links their speech fully with that of the people. When all of these prophets refer to God, they use the same name that is invoked in Israelite

5. Cf., e.g., E. Rohland, "Die Bedeutung der Erwählungstraditionen Israels für die Eschatologie der alttestamentlichen Propheten" (dissertation in theology, Heidelberg, 1956), pp. 119–208; H.-M. Lutz, *Jahwe, Jerusalem und die Völker*, WMANT 27 (Neukirchen-Vluyn: Neukirchener Verlag, 1968). Differently, G. Wanke, *Die Zionstheologie der Korachiten in ihrem traditionsgeschichtlichen Zusammenhang*, BZAW 97 (Berlin: de Gruyter, 1966).

worship and that was handed down from generation to generation—the name Yahweh. It is not merely common religious language which could be immediately generalized world-wide. Rather, they are speaking about the One who is known by this proper name, the personal One who is designated unmistakably in this name, the One who under this name entered into Israel's history.

We would be in error to think that this is really only a self-evident matter and that no special significance is to be given this traditional element of the "Name" since it is only a casual cipher without specific content. To be sure, it is correct that this name is not used as a signifier, something that decodes the secret of God, with which also the prophets dealt.[6] It is not a predicative statement that reduces God to a concept and subjects him to certain categories of understanding. The name remains a proper name, with all the irrationality of a proper name which in the first instance designates the unmistakable identity of a person.

There is a specific rhetorical form which Ezekiel uses that shows precisely how this name is bound to an inner fullness, not to a void or to an easily interchangeable substance. This form of speech, which I have termed a "proof-saying" (*"Erweiswort"*),[7] was not coined by Ezekiel but was appropriated from older, preclassical prophets. We find it exclusively in connection with prophetic proclamation of impending divine activity. For example, a rhetorical unit proclaiming the coming "end" concludes in Ezek. 7:4 with the following statement: "My eye will not spare you, nor will I have mercy; but I will cause your

---

6. Exod. 3:14 attempts to "decode" the name and its etymological meaning, yet it is striking how in this passage itself the expression "I am who I am" defies any possibility of grasping who the Lord is. H. W. Wolff's suggestion of finding in Hos. 1:9 a reference to Exod. 3:14 is questionable; cf. his *Dodekapropheton 1: Hosea*, BK 14/1 (Neukirchen: Neukirchener Verlag, 2d ed. 1965), ad loc. = *Hosea*, Hermeneia (Philadelphia: Fortress, 1974), ad loc.

7. W. Zimmerli, "Das Wort des göttlichen Selbsterweises (Erweiswort), eine prophetische Gattung," in *Mélanges Bibliques rédigés en l'honneur de André Robert* (Paris: Bloud et Gay, 1957), 154–64 = *Gottes Offenbarung: Gesammelte Aufsätze zum Alten Testament*, ThB 19 (München: Chr. Kaiser, 1963), 120–32.

ways to come upon you, . . . and you will know that I am Yahweh." Thus it is Yahweh's imminent activity itself that is the locus and documentation for this very Yahweh. There is no predication in use here—not Yahweh as the powerful one, or as the exalted one, or as the wrathful one, who seeks to prove himself and to be known to Israel in his proof. Rather, all is expressed through the straightforward use of the proper name: the one recognizable in this activity is the one called by this name; through this very activity he will be identified and proven to be Yahweh.[8] "You will know that I am Yahweh."

The above discussion brings something else into focus as well. The name Yahweh has been characterized chiefly as a traditional element of the Israelite language of worship. Tradition is, *per definitionem*, oriented toward the past. The hand and the mouth carry on that which has been received, delivered over. In this element of prophetic speech, however, the transmitted material is related to that which is yet to come. In his coming activity Yahweh demonstrates who he is—namely, that he is Yahweh. The name Yahweh is thus completely opened up to the future.

In saying this, moreover, we have touched upon the essence of prophetic speech. In its primary and true pathos it is announcement of the imminent—and thus not chiefly retrospection, nor primarily penitential sermon.[9] This can be seen in Amos' report about his call. Yahweh took him away from his flock and commissioned him to preach against Israel and to announce the future judgment, for which the high priest in Bethel denounced him before the king: "By the sword Jeroboam will die, and Israel will be led into exile, away from his land" (Amos 7:11, 15). In like manner, Hosea is sent to proclaim, through the names of his children, that Yahweh will soon

8. This assertion remains valid even in light of the fact that the "recognition formula" ("*Erkenntnisformel*") can later be subject to expansions. The material is gathered in W. Zimmerli, *Erkenntnis Gottes nach dem Buche Ezechiel*, ATANT 27 (Zürich: Zwingli, 1954) = *Gottes Offenbarung*, ThB 19, 41–119.

9. Contra, e.g., H. W. Hoffmann, *Die Intention der Verkündigung Jesajas*, BZAW 136 (Berlin: de Gruyter, 1974).

punish the blood-guilt in Jezreel, Jehu's murdering when he seized power (1:4–5), and that the "merciless" and the "not-my-people" will be manifest in history. Isaiah is dispatched with a message that will make the people obdurate and thus will effect the devastation of the land (6:8–11). Jeremiah sees in the second vision connected with his call (1:13ff.) how disaster will spill over the land from the North like boiling water out of a pot held over fire. Thus his early message deals with the announcement of an unnamed foe from the North. In a strikingly formal speech of commission, Yahweh charges Ezekiel simply to proclaim: "Thus says the Lord Yahweh" (2:4; 3:11) —regardless of whether the people will listen to it or ignore it. However, he is then ordered to eat the scroll written on front and back with lamentations, groans, and woes (2:9–10), and in this we recognize the coming disaster which Ezekiel was to utter against Jerusalem.

The great pre-exilic prophets proclaim Yahweh as the One who comes—the same One who since antiquity has been invoked with this name. This "coming" of which they must speak, however, is the unexpected, that which runs counter to all familiar tradition. In Mic. 3:11 we can observe how Micah's proclamation collides with what tradition said of Yahweh and what was cherished so by prophets opposing the classical pre-exilic prophets: "Its [Jerusalem's] prophets divine on payment [literally: for money]; they lean on Yahweh by saying: 'Is not Yahweh in our midst? No evil will come upon us.'" Tradition says that Yahweh lives in the midst of the people. This is interpreted as Israel's great security against all danger. In contrast to this, Micah discerns the freedom of Yahweh in his coming. Yahweh cannot be domesticated by knowledge oriented toward the past, nor can he be attached, like some predictable element, to a pious view of existence. Rather, he shatters the fixed conception that Israel developed in her tradition, and in this, his new and terrifying coming, he proves himself to be Yahweh—the One invoked by the people as Yahweh.

Before we proceed with our examination of the extent to which the great pre-exilic prophets were influenced by traditional material, by memory of the past as it was transmitted in Israel's worship, we must be entirely clear about this central element of the prophetic proclamation. Whenever this prophecy does in fact take up traditional materials, it does not regard these as simple elements of tradition, as *traditum* in the neutral sense of material that can be conveyed from one person to another—like a plot of inherited land or other property that is handed down and then used by the new inheritor. Whatever the prophets appropriated from traditional language about the God of Israel, whatever they reiterated of this or fit into their own utterances—it is attached to the name of Yahweh. This latter, however, cannot in its true content be considered neutrally as *"traditum."* It is the suggestive appellation of the One who, for all that is said about him, remains a personal subject and decides himself, in his freedom, what he will do when he comes. And as certainly as he once came to Israel, as "tradition" tells of him in Israel's worship and apart from this, he is never at the disposal of humans like earthly property.

To be sure, there are unmistakable future-oriented elements already present in the tradition at the disposal of the prophets. However, the way in which these elements are appropriated by the great pre-exilic prophets shows how the Lord, who approaches his people freely and who is known by the name of Yahweh, weighs upon the prophets to make these elements into vehicles of new proclamation about this same Lord.

This can be elucidated with the help of a traditional element which from the outset corresponds structurally to prophetic discourse about the One who is approaching, yet which experiences a specific, innovative application at the hands of the prophets. I have in mind the discourse about the "Day of Yahweh." Amos 5:18–20, the earliest passage where we find this traditional element, verifies clearly that among the people to whom Amos was sent there was talk about the Day of Yahweh. We have had little success in finding a fully satisfactory answer to the question of the ultimate origin of this element. While Gressmann[10] thought he could discern in its background a mythical *Weltanschauung* that conceived of an alternation between evil and good times, Mowinckel[11] on the other hand pointed to the Israelite cult as the place of origin. According to him, in the Israelite tradition of worship the great victory of Yahweh over the opposing forces was celebrated in every New Year festival. Thus the expectation of an approaching Day of Yahweh as a day of light and salvation would be the future projection of Yahweh's victory as recited and ritually enacted in the cultic practice of Israel. In contrast to this view, G. von Rad[12] thought that he could derive this image from the tradition of the Holy War; thus this expectation of the day of salvation would be, in concentrated form, the future projection of old tradition stemming from the days of Yahweh's deliverance in battle.

However these lines are to be drawn, we are in any event obliged to see in the expectation of a Day of Yahweh, such as in the people's anticipation in Amos 5:18–20, the future projection of previously experienced salvation, which Israel remembered in her tradition.

Amos detaches the expression "the Day of Yahweh" from its association with the transmitted salvation tradition, and he preaches Yahweh as the One who in his freedom draws near to judge. The Day of Yahweh is not light but darkness. It is "as if a man runs from a lion, and a bear meets him. And he enters the house and rests his hand against the wall, and a snake bites him."

All further utterances by other prophets about the Day of Yahweh have a similar meaning, except that we no longer find,

10. H. Gressmann, *Der Ursprung der israelitisch-jüdischen Eschatologie*, FRLANT 6 (Göttingen: Vandenhoeck & Ruprecht, 1905).

11. S. Mowinckel, *Psalmenstudien II: Das Thronbesteigungsfest Jahwäs und der Ursprung der Eschatologie* (Kristiania: Dybwad, 1922). In this same direction, though also with reference to Ugaritic texts, cf. now J. Gray, "The Day of Yahweh in Cultic Experience and Eschatological Prospect," *SEÁ* 39 (1974), 5–37. The latter contains also recent literature on this subject.

12. G. von Rad, "The Origin of the Concept of the Day of Yahweh," *JSS* 4 (1959), 97–108.

as in the Amos text, a contrary expectation current among the people.[13] In each case the reference to the Day of Yahweh is accentuated anew. What is appropriated is the traditional element about a day which is characterized entirely by Yahweh's presence. But the way in which Yahweh approaches breaks all traditional expectations; it is the nearness of the One who is free, the One who shows himself as the Lord, the One who cannot be restricted by past-oriented discourse.

It has just been stated that, unlike Amos, later prophets were not provoked to speak about the Day of Yahweh directly by the reassured expectation of the people. Rather, this concept was transmitted from one prophet to another, and this fact brings into view a problem of "tradition history" that has been scrutinized too little in the past. To the degree that, as their utterances about the Day of Yahweh show, the prophets oppose secure, traditional expectations of salvation and that they do this by announcing the sovereign freedom of Yahweh to destroy such expectations—to this degree we can see that there is also an inner-prophetic "process of tradition." Isaiah in his early preaching takes up elements from Amos' proclamation.[14] The connections between Hosea and Jeremiah have been isolated by Gross.[15] Miller[16] has worked on the question of the relationship between Jeremiah and Ezekiel, and Baltzer[17] has exposed ties from Ezekiel to Deutero-Isaiah, whereby the latter was not without influences from Proto-Isaiah as well.

THE PROPHETS' CONCRETE USE AND TRANSFORMATION OF HISTORICAL TRADITIONS

We need now to turn our attention to the question of how

---

13. Isa. 2:12ff.; Zeph. 1–2; Ezek. 7; 30:1ff.; Joel; Mal. 3; and elsewhere.

14. R. Fey, *Amos und Jesaja*, WMANT 12 (Neukirchen: Neukirchener Verlag, 1963).

15. K. Gross, *Die literarische Verwandtschaft Jeremias mit Hosea* (Borna-Leipzig: Noske, 1930); idem, "Hoseas Einfluss auf Jeremias Anschauungen", *NKZ* 42 (1931), 241–56, 327–43.

16. J. W. Miller, *Das Verhältnis Jeremias und Hesekiels sprachlich und theologisch untersucht* (Neukirchen: Verlag der Buchhandlung des Erziehungsvereins, 1955).

17. D. Baltzer, *Ezechiel und Deuterojesaja*, BZAW 121 (Berlin: de Gruyter, 1971).

pre-exilic and later also exilic literary prophets treat the tradition of Israel as the people of Yahweh.

In his study on "The Form-Critical Problem of the Hexateuch,"[18] G. von Rad found that the elements relevant for Israel's faith, the confessional underpinnings for their special relationship to Yahweh, were gathered together in the "short historical credo" which spoke of the exodus, the wilderness wanderings, and the gift of the land. The patriarchal history and the primeval history came later, independently of each other, as frontal extensions to the rest, while the narrative of the Sinai events, traditio-historically different in origin, is an insertion into this complex. M. Noth[19] has distanced himself theologically from this by speaking of "themes" which are treated in Pentateuchal tradition. He investigated five themes in the following order:

(a) Guidance out of Egypt
(b) Guidance into the Arable Land of Palestine
(c) Promise to the Patriarchs
(d) Guidance in the Wilderness
(e) Revelation at Sinai

At this point we will need to ask how these elements, so important for the tradition of Israel, are appropriated, modified, or simply ignored in prophetic proclamation.

(1) *Amos* makes no recognizable reference to the patriarchal tradition or to the Sinai tradition. The guidance out of Egypt is appraised positively in 2:10 and 3:1, although the authenticity of both passages is contested. However in 9:7, a saying which surely stems from Amos, this same tradition is depreci-

18. G. von Rad, *Das formgeschichtliche Problem des Hexateuch*, BWANT 4/26 (Stuttgart: Kohlhammer, 1938) = his *Gesammelte Studien zum Alten Testament*, ThB 8 (München: Chr. Kaiser, 1958), 9–86 = "The Form-Critical Problem of the Hexateuch," in his *The Problem of the Hexateuch and Other Essays* (Edinburgh/London: Oliver & Boyd, 1966), 1–78.
19. M. Noth, *Überlieferungsgeschichte des Pentateuch* (Stuttgart: Kohlhammer, 1948) = *A History of Pentateuchal Traditions* (Englewood Cliffs: Prentice-Hall, 1972).

ated and set on a par with the guidance of the Philistines out of
Caphtor (Crete?) and the Arameans out of Kir. It is impossible to miss the polemic here against a false security derived
from Israel's relation to Yahweh; it is a radical "No" to Israel's
retreat into revered tradition. But Amos also knows and
acknowledges the special connection between Yahweh and Israel (although he draws quite unexpected conclusions from it);
this can be seen in the surely genuine utterance in 3:2: "You
only have I known of all the families of the earth;[20] therefore I
will punish you for all your iniquities." Whenever their appeal to the guidance out of Egypt gives this sinful people cause
to relax, not only will this misguided rhetoric about their history with Yahweh be struck from them, but also in light of
Yahweh's special nearness to Israel they will face exactly the
opposite consequence of this intimacy. It is dangerous to come
near to Yahweh, who even in his "intimacy" with Israel remains
the free Lord who is resolved to bring its sins to judgment.

Amos mentions in a special manner the tradition of the wilderness period and the conquest. In both cases he turns them
in accusation against the people. In 5:25 the time of Israel's
wandering in the wilderness appears in polemic against the
present: that earlier period was free of the cultivated sacrificial
system, replete with sacrifices and gift offerings, of the present
day.[21] The remembrance of the time of conquest in 2:9 confronts Israel in a different manner. Here the prophet has in
mind the tradition, found also in the story of the spies (Num.
13–14), about the people of great stature who once occupied
the land but then were destroyed by Yahweh. For the prophet,

---

20. This "knowing" includes on the one hand intimacy, but beyond this also
election. Jer. 1:5 uses it parallel to the one who "consecrates" whomever he will.
21. However, there may be some question whether this statement, which has a
parallel in Jer. 7:22 with its explicit reference to burnt offerings and sacrifices,
belongs to the original text of Amos. On this, cf. J. Vollmer, *Geschichtliche
Rückblicke und Motive in der Prophetie des Amos, Hosea und Jesaja*, BZAW
119 (Berlin: de Gruyter, 1971), who links Amos 5:25 with 5:26 and thus considers
it only as a polemic against burnt offerings and sacrifices that are connected
with idolatry. Cf. also H. W. Wolff, *Dodekapropheton, 2: Joel/Amos*, BK 14/2
(Neukirchen-Vluyn: Neukirchener Verlag, 1969), ad loc. = *Joel/Amos*, Hermeneia
(Philadelphia: Fortress Press, 1976), ad loc.

this tradition becomes the occasion to make manifest the ingratitude of the people who repay Yahweh's great deed with disobedience.

(2) *Hosea,* who is obviously much better versed in Israel's ancient tradition and cites it copiously, also makes no explicit reference to the Sinai tradition. In its stead, however, the patriarchal tradition appears here for the first time. Moses, the unnamed "prophet" in 12:14 [12:13] through whom Yahweh effected the exodus from Egypt, is contrasted with the patriarch Jacob in 12:4, 13 [12:3, 12] who possessed the same traits of untruthfulness and dishonesty that later on characterized Israel. While still in the womb he cheated his brother, and later he fought with God. It is striking to note this sharp antithesis between, on the one hand, the valuation of Moses and the exodus, which also emerges distinctly elsewhere in Hosea,[22] and, on the other hand, the assessment of the figure of Jacob, who despite all his questionable aspects is nonetheless one of the bearers of promise in Genesis. According to the prophet, the patriarch represents the present people in their sinfulness. Thus this time-honored tradition becomes a subject of polemics.

In comparison, Moses and Israel's trek through the wilderness are bright memories for Hosea (12:14 [12:13]; 13:5). On closer analysis, though, we can see that this clear picture is painted not in order to provide in Hosea's day a firm foundation, here in its cultically guarded tradition, on which Israel could recline undisturbed. Rather, as in Amos 5:25 and Jer. 7:22 the prophet introduces the wilderness recollection as a picture contrasting with his present age. Unlike Amos, Hosea does not have in mind solely the previous lack of contact with contemporary sacrificial practices. With more historico-theological insight, he contrasts, on the one hand, the wilderness period as a time of poverty with, on the other, the period beginning with the entrance into the land when the people became wealthy, opulent, and forgetful of God. While in the creedal formula-

22. Cf. Vollmer, *Geschichtliche Rückblicke.*

tion the remembrance of the divine guidance in the wilderness and the divine gift of land merge together in a positive emphasis, Hosea puts the two periods, wilderness wandering and settlement of the land, in radical contrast with each other. It is obvious how existing tradition does not retain and develop its own momentum here, but is rather fashioned anew by the prophetic preacher and thus becomes material, a plastic structure, for the prophet's specific proclamation about Yahweh's imminent assault against Israel. Would Hosea have known nothing of the acts of rebellion in the wilderness?[23] We can detect nothing of this in Hosea's view of history. With his preaching the prophet intended for the people who had sinned with the powers (the Baals) in the land to be confronted with the full impact of Yahweh's coming to set things aright. This led him to use the key-word "wilderness" (= area away from the land of Baals) as an extremely colorful contrast to the key-word "land" (= territory of the Baals).[24] We will see in Ezekiel that also the elements "exodus from Egypt" and "guidance through the wilderness" experience a new shift in character in the context of a yet more sharply radicalized accusation of sin.

Another development occurs in Hosea that has great significance for later prophecy. As we already mentioned, this prophet proclaims Yahweh not, in the first instance, as the One who encountered Israel in antiquity, but as the One who is prepared to come anew. Consistent with this, Hosea takes the traditional elements that appeared questionable in retrospect and thrusts them into his announcements of the future. Thus we find that references to Egypt, to the guidance in the wilderness, and to the conquest receive surprisingly new use in the prophet's future-oriented utterances. While Yahweh once

23. G. Coats, *Rebellion in the Wilderness: The Murmuring Motif in the Wilderness Traditions of the Old Testament* (Nashville: Abingdon, 1968).

24. Nevertheless, Hosea was not at all unfamiliar with the positive element of tradition, "Yahweh's gift of land"; cf. 2:9ff. [2:7ff.].

called his son out of Egypt,[25] now the pronouncement of imminent judgment declares: "Now he [Yahweh] remembers
their iniquity and punishes their sins; they will return to
Egypt" (8:13). In 9:3 it is connected with the simultaneous
threat of exile in Assyria: "They will not remain in Yahweh's
land; but Ephraim will return to Egypt, and in Asshur they will
eat unclean food."[26] The same double threat is also to be
found in the original text of 9:6: "For behold, they will go to
Asshur; Egypt will gather them, Memphis will bury them."[27]
Both can also be linked together in an utterance that looks
beyond the judgment to a future pardon: "Like a bird they will
come trembling from Egypt, and like a dove from the land of
Assyria; and I will return[28] them to their houses, says Yahweh"
(11:11). Here the language of the period, with the antipodal
powers being Assyria and Egypt, is connected with the singular
idea, seen clearly in 8:13, about Israel's "return" to Egypt—in a
sense, the removal of the *Heilsgeschichte* back to its beginning,
from which point a new start can then occur. We find a more
obvious allusion to a traditional element of salvation history in
the passage where the approaching judgment is pictured as the
fetching of Israel back into the wilderness: "But I, Yahweh,
your God from the land of Egypt—again I will make you dwell
in tents, like in the days of the [initial] encounter" (12:10
[12:9]).[29] Yet here in Hosea the wilderness period is also
esteemed as the time of Yahweh's special closeness and pristine
love to his people, and as such it is inserted into an announcement about the future. For in 2:16–17 [2:14–15] the threat

25. "When Israel was young, I became fond of him; out of Egypt I called my
son" (11:1). Alongside of this and rather incongruously, 9:10 states that Yahweh
found Israel in the wilderness. It is perhaps too extreme to suggest, as does
R. Bach ("Die Erwählung Israels in der Wüste," dissertation in theology, Bonn,
1951), that this and a few other texts give evidence of a separate discovery-tra-
dition.

26. Cf. Amos 7:17.

27. Cf. also 11:5 (according to the LXX).

28. The MT reading, "cause to dwell," is probably a scribal error.

29. There is a strong threat similar to this in 2:5 [2:3].

of being fetched back into the wilderness joins with a statement about a new effort by Yahweh to woo Israel, to "speak to her heart"; and then this is followed by a new gift of land, the renewed bestowal of vineyards from the desert. Here it is not only old tradition as the heritage from the past that is "interpreted," but the transmitted remembrance is also turned antitypically into promise that is to be validated when Israel truly returns to her God.

(3) In *Isaiah* we can also observe the same transformation of transmitted proclamation into announcements about the future. Recent scholarly effort has determined clearly that Isaiah moves within a different sphere of tradition than does Hosea. To be sure, Isaiah is concerned with no other Lord than the *one* Yahweh. Called the "Holy One of Israel," Yahweh is considered to be associated in a special way with Israel, which at the time of the prophet's early preaching existed politically as "both houses of Israel" (8:14). But Isaiah is a Jerusalemite. As such he is not so preoccupied with Yahweh's activity in the exodus from Egypt, wilderness wandering and conquest, as much as with Yahweh's dwelling in Jerusalem.[30] It was here during his call that he had a direct experience of the presence of Yahweh, the Holy One. Thus it is no accident that the messianic expectation of a savior-king from the house of David breaks forth in the prophecy of this resident of the City of David, for this promise made to the house of David belongs to his background of tradition.

Yet Isaiah preaches the Coming Lord as well. The category of the Holy One, who alone is exalted and who humbles everything on earth that becomes haughty, is central for him, and for this reason his announcement of the coming Day of Yahweh issues also into the image of a tumult which devastates everything that is lofty in the natural and human world.[31] From his

30. For more details on this stream of tradition, see below, Chapter 8 by O. H. Steck, especially pp. 193, 199ff.
31. Isa. 2:11ff.

own call he is familiar with the burning power of the Holy One wherever he encounters uncleanliness. Thus for Isaiah the account of the judgment against Jerusalem, the city that became a harlot,[32] does not take the form of a story about a return to Egypt or to the wilderness or about a new conquest. Rather, it is a report about a consuming fire that will smelt the base metal, purge the impurities, and thereby create the future for a city that will again deserve the name "faithful city" (1:21–26).

Among the traditions in Jerusalem associated with the Holy One of Israel, in whose presence Israel had believed since the time of David and Solomon, was apparently also one about the nations that assaulted the mountain of God and were dashed to pieces on it.[33] The people of Jerusalem spoke perhaps in mythical language about this guarantee of security at the place where God resides. Pss. 46, 48, and 76 give evidence that this security of the place was praised in light of past assaults, and that it was confidently expected for the future as well. One is inclined to connect this with the security which Jeremiah, a century after Isaiah, found so objectionable in the people who came to the temple: not only did they emphasize it liturgically in triplicate form—"This is the temple of Yahweh, the temple of Yahweh, the temple of Yahweh" (Jer. 7:4)—but they also drew from this a comforting conclusion—"We are safe" (7:10).

Just like Micah (3:12) in the time of Isaiah, Jeremiah responded to this comfortable security by proclaiming a catastrophe that would bring the same fate of the temple in Shiloh to the Jerusalem temple as well. Both Micah and Hosea stem from a background of tradition other than that of Isaiah. Therefore it is instructive for us to see how this Jerusalemite

---

32. This image, referring here not to the people but to the city of Jerusalem, shows clearly how close—yet with differences as well—Isaiah is to Hosea.

33. Cf. Rohland, "Die Bedeutung der Erwählungstraditionen," and Lutz, *Jahwe, Jerusalem und die Völker*; also F. Stolz, *Strukturen und Figuren im Kult von Jerusalem*, BZAW 118 (Berlin: de Gruyter, 1970); and J. Jeremias, "Lade und Zion," in *Probleme biblischer Theologie*, Festschrift G. von Rad, ed. H. W. Wolff (München: Chr. Kaiser, 1971), 183–98.

Isaiah in his prophetic message transforms the traditions that come down to him. This is most obvious in the Davidic promissory tradition as well as in the Zion tradition.

Concerning the promise to the Davidic house, we might first conclude from the account in 7:1ff. that Isaiah permits this promise to remain valid and completely unbroken into the present. In his earlier preaching he had proclaimed that judgment would soon come upon Jerusalem—the consequence of the burning wrath of the Holy One of Israel against all arrogance and all unrighteousness in this city. Then in the so-called Syro-Ephraimite War in the year 733, two kings from the North, Rezin the king of Aram-Damascus and Pekah the king of Northern Israel, went to battle against Jerusalem for the sole military purpose of setting a man on the Jerusalem throne who would have leanings in favor of their anti-Assyrian coalition efforts. Because of his father's Aramean name Tabeel, it seems likely that the new king was to be an Aramean. In this situation with cold fear gripping Jerusalem, Isaiah is charged to approach King Ahaz and to announce to him in the indicative mood: "That will not happen, nor will it come to pass" (7:7). It is striking that the "house of David" is expressly mentioned several times in the account in 7:1ff. So Würthwein is surely correct in assuming that behind Isaiah's utterance and assurance can be perceived the Davidic tradition reflected in the promise of Nathan in 2 Sam. 7.[34] In this does not Isaiah simply join the ranks of the ones who through retrospection take refuge wholly in the old tradition esteemed so highly in David's court?

The conclusion to the episode in 7:1–9 and its continuation in 7:10ff.[35] are informative at this point: "If you do not believe (*ta'ămînû*), you will not remain (*tē'āmēnû*.)" The first scene ends with this polished word-play, an exhibit-piece of all the

---

34. E. Würthwein, "Jes. 7, 1–9. Ein Beitrag zu dem Thema: Prophetie und Politik," in *Theologie als Glaubenswagnis*, Festschrift K. Heim (Hamburg: Furche, 1954), 47–63 = his *Wort und Existenz*, 127–43.

35. For the present discussion it is unimportant whether this second scene was connected immediately with the first or separated from it by a time difference.

splendor of Isaianic diction.[36]   The simple indicative assurance, which seemed to impart so much certainty, is thereby set into the context of prophetic openness toward future conduct. Its truth and validity will hold good if "belief" is present—and that means only at those points where people do not presume that their refuge and security lie simply in their possession of the *traditum* from the past, but where they open themselves in expectancy and obedience to God's approaching activity and set their whole security in him who is speaking here.

The episode that follows in 7:10ff. shows clearly how reluctant King Ahaz is to accept this assurance, which is to be confirmed by a sign. He declines the offer of a sign and attempts throughout to preserve his own freedom of action over against what is expected from Yahweh. So Isaiah holds indeed to his promise that the immediate danger will not be fatal. But after this comes a judgment against David's house that is all the more ominous: there will come "days the like of which have not existed since Ephraim broke from Judah" (7:17).

We can detect a similar treatment of the *traditum* revered in Jerusalem about the invulnerability of Zion. Probably at a later historical period when the Assyrians had already come dangerously close to Judah, the authorities in Jerusalem relied on their secret negotiations with allies, rather than on protection by Zion. In this situation comes the puzzling divine utterance of 28:16–17a in which the prophet seems to take up the belief about Zion without disrupting it: "Behold, I am laying in Zion a stone, a tested stone, a precious cornerstone for a firm foundation." But again he turns to the future and makes the additional observation that in all of this Yahweh has in mind not simply the empirical Jerusalem, but his just city: "I will make justice as the plumb-line and righteousness as the level." Yet above all there is again a demand for faith here: "He who be-

36. W. Zimmerli, "Verkündigung und Sprache der Botschaft Jesajas," in *Fides et communicatio*, Festschrift M. Doerne (Göttingen: Vandenhoeck & Ruprecht, 1970), 441–54 = *Studien zur alttestamentlichen Theologie und Prophetie: Gesammelte Aufsätze II*, ThB 51 (München: Chr. Kaiser, 1974), 73–87.

lieves will not waver." Again there is no simple reliance on "tradition." Again mention of the tradition about unshakable Zion empties into the free future of God. The declaration of "tradition" can retain its validity only if there is complete, open trust in Yahweh. The same point is formulated somewhat differently in another passage. Isa. 14:28–32 indicates that messengers from the Philistines were in Jerusalem at the time of a change in rules in Asshur, and with confidence and even joy because of the opportune situation they wanted to include Jerusalem in their planned security network. To this Isaiah states: "What should one answer the messengers of this people? This, that Yahweh has founded Zion. The poor among his people will take refuge there" (vs. 32). Again in this utterance all obvious security is shattered. The tradition about Zion as the place of safety is not cast aside, but is reestablished with a divine proviso. One cannot simply flee into this shelter. Zion is a refuge only for the "poor." This is to be understood as the "believers," as used elsewhere. The prophet has in mind those people who do not rely, with firm security perhaps quite piously expressed, on the salvific tradition about Zion, but rather who are sure only of their own poverty—yet thereby also of the certain future of Yahweh. It is stated that Zion will be a shelter only for these "poor."

The Ariel prophecy in 29:1–7 illustrates this declaration from yet another perspective. The city that celebrates its feasts where David once encamped is told of its greatest degradation. All details remain in the semi-darkness of intimation. This arrogant, festal city must sink deep into the dust even though it bears the name Ariel, "Hearth," after the altar of God that is found in it. But then, when it has reached the lowest point of degradation (might we interpret this according to 14:32—"will have become poor"?), then God will turn its fate and will cause the foes encamped against it to be scattered like a nocturnal apparition, a dream in the night.

For all of this, Isaiah clearly appropriates more of pious tradition than does, for example, Amos. But nowhere does he regard tradition simply as self-evident *traditum* that is to be honored because of its origin. In all of these passages the freedom of Yahweh, who desires that his personal will be recognized in everything, is reckoned into the element of tradition. As long as Yahweh remains true to character, he will always show himself to be the One who is free, who holds all future in his hands. This will not simply sweep aside a promise handed down in tradition—but it may well transform it.

The same thing can be said of the messianic statements in (8:23aβb?) 9:1-6 [9:1aβb?, 2-7] and in 11:1-9. Bright light breaks over the greatest need of the people who sit in darkness, who have become poor; the king appears in whom the righteousness demanded by Yahweh will be fully realized. According to 11:1ff. this new king of righteousness is a shoot growing out of the chopped-down stump of Jesse. In this case also, Yahweh prepares his new thing only for a later period, after judgment has caused the people to despair of their own power.[37]

Isaiah's language, just like the place from which his traditions stem, is quite different from that of Hosea. While Hosea spoke of a return to the wilderness, Isaiah speaks of the poor, of faith, as the only way by which the promises in received tradition can attain reality.

(4) *Ezekiel* leads us into yet another world. Although he was probably from Jerusalem, it is no longer possible for us to assign him exclusively to the Israelite or the Jerusalemite sphere of tradition. His preaching is a blend of tradition streams. The allegorical speech in ch. 16 refers to Jerusalem as the unfaithful wife. To describe her origin, vs. 3 seized upon elements remembered from Jerusalem's Canaanite prehistory. On the other hand, it is Israel in its entirety, during its Egyptian ori-

---

37. Mic. 5:1ff. [5:2ff.] has the messianic king stemming from Bethlehem and not from Jerusalem. It may be asked whether this utterance presupposes judgment on Jerusalem and Yahweh's return to the origins of the Davidic dynasty in Bethlehem.

gins, that is the subject of the metaphorical speech about the two whoring women in ch. 23, as also in the nonmetaphorical theology of history in Ezek. 20. The location of the city and the temple is not identified by the name of Zion, a word which appears nowhere in the whole book, but as the "high mountain of Israel" (*har měrôm yiśrā'ēl,* 20:40). The same name is given the place where, according to 17:23, the messianic twig will be planted anew.

But especially impressive is the relentless daring with which Ezekiel is able to shatter revered elements of tradition in their original meaning and instead make them serve the prophetic message.

Of the five themes identified by Noth, the patriarchal history never occurs in a positive way in Ezekiel's own words. We have evidence that it was not unknown to him: he cites a statement current among the people remaining in the land after 587, a statement in which they looked to Abraham for consolation. Although Abraham was only one man, he received the land. "But we are many, and the land is given us as a possession" (33:24). The prophet sharply rejects such efforts of the still sinful people to comfort themselves by remembering the promise to the Fathers.[38]

However, we can observe Ezekiel's radical transformation of revered tradition most clearly in his use of the other Pentateuchal traditions. In Ezek. 23 the element of the exodus from Egypt is shriveled into the assertion that Yahweh had taken as wives two young women with Bedouin (tent) names who, while yet in Egypt, had been promiscuous and evil and who later continued to play the whore with foreign lovers—Asshur, Babylonia, Egypt. "Egypt," the element remembered from the past, is reassessed in terms of Judah's impious politics of coalition during Ezekiel's time. Judah refuses to learn anything

---

38. Both Ezek. 28:25 and 37:25, referring to Yahweh's giving land "to my servant Jacob," surely do not stem from the hand of the prophet himself but from a later editor; cf. W. Zimmerli, *Ezechiel,* BK 13/2 (Neukirchen: Neukirchener Verlag, 1969), ad loc. = *Ezekiel,* Hermeneia, vol. 1 (Philadelphia: Fortress, 1977).

from the fiasco that resulted when her elder sister Northern Israel whored after Asshur. Rather, the Southern kingdom whores first with the Babylonians, turns then to renew her old, illicit love-affair with the Egyptians, and so incurs the vengeance of her older lovers. What remains intact of the good assertions in the credo?

There is analogous poignancy in the literal description of Israel's early history in 20:1–31. This passage treats the themes of the exodus from Egypt and the wilderness period, with allusion as well to the giving of the commandments. But what is left of the creedal statements? In Egypt Yahweh swore to the house of Israel that he would lead them out from there, and he commanded them to abandon the Egyptian gods. Yet even at that point they would not let themselves be separated from the gods of Egypt. Nevertheless, Yahweh led them out of Egypt "for the sake of his name, that it might not be profaned in the sight of the nations." And he gave them his commandments in the wilderness, but the people in turn disregarded them, with the result that God refused to allow the first wilderness generation to enter the land.[39] Despite renewed appeal for obedience to the laws, the next generation remained rebellious also, so that Yahweh, while not destroying them in the wilderness for his name's sake, nonetheless decided then to scatter the people later into all the world—and in fact gave them commandments on which they could only run aground.[40] At this point the account breaks off.[41] Quite clearly it jumps over additional historical phases in order to get to the immediate motivation in the fate that is coming to pass in Ezekiel's days.

39. Here we can recognize the transformed tradition about the reconnaissance of the land in Num. 13–14.

40. The reference is to child-sacrifice. On this problem, cf. W. Zimmerli, "Erstgeborene und Leviten: Ein Beitrag zur exilisch-nachexilischen Theologie," in *Near Eastern Studies in Honor of W. F. Albright*, ed. H. Goedicke (Baltimore and London: Johns Hopkins, 1971), 459–69 = *Studien zur alttestamentlichen Theologie und Prophetie*, 235–46.

41. Vss. 27–29 were added later when one missed any reference to the conquest or to life in the land; cf. *Ezechiel*, BK 13/1, ad loc. = *Ezekiel*, Hermeneia, vol. 1.

The old *heilsgeschichtliche* themes in the tradition—exodus, Sinai events, guidance in the wilderness, conquest—are all completely recast in the service of the divine "No," which combats firmly any of Israel's self-assurance of her creedal tradition. The same history that confirms salvation and is esteemed in tradition is here transposed into history that confirms disaster.

Ezek. 16 demonstrates the same process with the Jerusalem/Zion tradition, which is recapitulated in 5:5–6 at the conclusion of Ezekiel's symbolic actions to announce the fall of Jerusalem: "This is Jerusalem: I have set her in the center of the nations, with countries around her.[42] But she rebelled against my ordinances, becoming more wicked than the nations, and against my statutes more than the countries around her." Ezek. 16 shows Jerusalem's ignoble origin: "According to your ancestry and your origin you stem from the land of the Canaanites. Your father was an Amorite, your mother a Hittite" (vs. 3). Lacking nobility, she acts thereafter with the unfaithfulness of a foundling whom Yahweh had picked up, raised, made honorable, and married but then who became proud of her beauty and gave herself to foreign lovers. In the behavior of this woman we can recognize the essence of Baalism for which Hosea had reproached the Northern kingdom and with which later Jeremiah in his early preaching had also charged Judah/Jerusalem.

However in Ezekiel we can also see how old tradition in altered form is introduced, after the catastrophe of 587, into the announcement of future salvation. In a new supplementary passage (20:32ff.) formulated after 587, the prophet confronts a people who think that theirs is the lot of assimilation to the idolatrous cults of their neighbors (20:32). With exodus terminology and in oath form Yahweh announces his royal reactions, the new exodus, the new encounter with Yahweh in the wilderness, and the new conquest, at the center of which will be

42. This election to be the "city at the center" results from the omphalos notion (explicit in 38:12). This notion is transformed here into a new adoption statement.

the new cult on the "lofty mountain of Israel." The *heilsge-schichtliche* message, handed down as *traditum* from Yahweh's previous salvific actions, is formulated in the future mood as the anticipation of things yet to come for Israel—the community's tradition transformed into hope. In chs. 40ff. the new temple constitutes the object of the last great visionary description in the book of Ezekiel. It undoubtedly contains significant secondary additions, and in its present form the concluding section describes a new, ideal division of the land—a fully righteous allotment corresponding antitypically to Josh. 13ff.

In the second half of the book of Ezekiel, in chs. 34 and 37, the *traditum* "David" occurs within a promise about the future. Ch. 34 is a retrospective condemnation, sharply polemical, of previous "shepherds of Israel." Somewhat in tension with this, the new situation promised by Yahweh includes the name of David, familiar from the past: "I will set over them one shepherd to tend them, namely, my servant David. . . . And I, Yahweh, will be their God, and my servant David will be a prince among them. I, Yahweh, have spoken" (34:23–24).[43] In this passage the old traditional promise to David is thrust intact into an announcement of the future.

(5) *Deutero-Isaiah*, the prophet during the final years of the exile, appropriates to the full the promissory theme of the new exodus, treated earlier in Ezek. 20:32ff. He makes use of a typological correspondence between old and new in his descriptions of the path through the wilderness where water flows forth from the rock (48:21), and Yahweh himself accompanies his people (40:10–11). As in Ezek. 20, these traditions about exodus, wilderness wandering, and new conquest are transposed into anticipation of the coming acts of Yahweh, and in this they are conjoined with an expected glorification of Zion. Thus it is impossible for us to distinguish sharply between traditional backgrounds or "streams," as we could between Hosea and Isaiah.

43. The same promise is found in 37:25 immediately following the promise of reunification of the two kingdoms.

Yet in comparison with Ezek. 20, there is something novel in Deutero-Isaiah's reflection on the category old/new—tradition about the past and announcement about the future. In connection with this, we need also to direct attention to Jer. 31:31–34, certainly a post-Jeremianic piece. This pericope contrasts the two covenants: the old covenant stemming from the exodus from Egypt, with the law mediated in imperative form to Israel; and the new covenant, replacing the old, with the law to be written upon the people's hearts so that imperative instruction is no longer needed. Thus the new will do away with the old, that which had been handed down in tradition. In Isa. 43:16ff. the old exodus from Egypt is compared to the new exodus, with the words: "Do not think about the former things; behold, I am doing something new." However, this is not to be understood as a polemical invalidation of the old. Rather, the greater "new thing" simply surpasses the old, and this renders unnecessary any "remembrance," that is, the process of transmission of old tradition in the cultic "memory."[44]

Nonetheless, we can see elsewhere that Deutero-Isaiah sets aside the previously intended import of ancient traditions and boldly recasts them in terms of the "new." While he appropriates the patriarchal tradition (Abraham in 41:8 and 51:1–2) in its old sense as narrated in Genesis, and while he appeals to the Noah tradition as an example (54:9–10), he does not deal similarly with the Davidic tradition. In a daring manner, the latter tradition in 55:3–5 is redirected toward the future and widened to include the whole people. The David of the past is no longer esteemed as the founder of a great kingdom to which the people, newly liberated and guided back to Zion, can return; rather, he is Yahweh's "witness." In the imminent future the promise given to David (*hasdê dāwid*) will now be fulfilled for the people; their political liberator Cyrus is even given the title "Yahweh's anointed one" (45:1). The people will then

44. This might be compared with the parallel passages Jer. 16:14–15 = 23:7–8.

be "Yahweh's witness" among the nations and will increase "Yahweh's empire" in that other persons will come running to give glory to Yahweh. This would also be the sense of 44:1–5, a description of how, through Yahweh's poured-out spirit, that is, his blessing, the people will be increased, persons will come and say, "I am Yahweh's," will call themselves by the name of Jacob and will tattoo Yahweh's name (as a sign of belonging) on their hand.

There is another matter that we can only present in the form of a question here: Deutero-Isaiah's preaching is characterized by copious flashbacks to Israel's older traditions about salvation. Aside from the creation statements, it begins with the Noah tradition, which is mentioned in 54:9–10 for comparative purposes; its connection with the statement about the covenant seems to suggest that the prophet had in mind a narrative form related to the Priestly source tradition. He appropriates the tradition about Abraham (and Sarah) in a positive way (41:8; 51:2), whereas he seems to refer to Jacob in 43:27 in the same critical fashion as Hosea does. In Deutero-Isaiah the exodus, wilderness wandering, conquest, and Zion appear, in part antitypically, thrust into the future. We spoke also of the way he recast the Davidic tradition. In light of all of this, we might well ask whether the Mosaic tradition also reverberates in Deutero-Isaiah. Might such a correspondence be concealed behind the mysterious figure of the Servant of Yahweh, the one who brings forth justice to the nations (42:1, 3–4), after he had first been charged with the prior task of leading Israel home? Deutero-Isaiah's own office is perhaps also delineated behind this assignment. This question about a Moses typology hidden here deserves serious consideration, but since the problem remains unresolved it will not be reckoned into our final evaluation of the matter of prophetic proclamation and interpretation.[45]

45. Cf., e.g., A. Bentzen, *Messias, Moses redivivus, Menschensohn*, ATANT 17 (Zürich: Zwingli-Verlag, 1948), 62–66.

THE THEOLOGICAL IMPORT

By way of conclusion, we must now attempt to summarize what we have observed in concrete texts. In terms of the main title, "Tradition and Theology," our task is to reflect on discernible features of the phenomenon of "interpreting" pregiven tradition especially in the area of prophetic proclamation, as seen in the examples treated.

To begin with, it is obvious that one can speak of "traditions" on a narrower and on a wider horizon. In the *narrower sphere*, clear relations among the individual prophets came to light. Prophetic proclamation about the Day of Yahweh, the origin of which as a confrontation with popular faith can be recovered in the work of Amos, is transmitted through later periods as a special prophetic *theologoumenon*. The image of the destroyed marriage between Yahweh and Israel, which finds its roots in the symbolic act demanded directly of Hosea, becomes part of the prophetic message in the preaching of Jeremiah and Ezekiel.[46] And reference to the "Holy One of Israel," for which Isa. 6 seems to be the place of prophetic origin, reoccurs in Deutero-Isaiah.[47]

What does it mean for the understanding of the great prophets that they live like this within an inner-prophetic "tradition"?[48] Does this lead to the picture of a specific "office" with

---

46. It is especially evident that the speech about the two faithless women in Ezek. 23 is dependent on Jer. 3:6ff.

47. On Trito-Isaiah's dependence on Deutero-Isaiah, cf. W. Zimmerli, "Zur Sprache Tritojesajas," Festschrift Ludwig Köhler, *STU* 20 (1950), 110–22 = *Gottes Offenbarung*, ThB 19, 217–33.

48. This inner-prophetic transmission can be considered in terms of two further, different aspects. We have been treating above the way one prophet's proclamation may be dependent on that of another, but in addition to this there is also a path from a prophet's utterances to the prophetic book itself. We must consider that prophetic utterances were transmitted, in part along school-lines, within circles of traditionists who in turn sought to affect the "thrust" of a prophet's message by the way they collected his utterances together into a whole and added further elements to them—such as in the addition of the salvation prophecy at the end of Amos' words in 9:11–15. Redaction-critical analyses attempt especially to trace such later stylizations of an entire prophetic collection. However, such an interpretative posthistory can be discerned even for individual prophetic utterances. An example is the way in which the original symbolic act in Ezek.

an "officially" regulated sermon, and do the great literary prophets fit also into such a picture?[49] Does not even such a prophet as Jeremiah refer to this when he opposes Hananiah with the reproach: "The prophets who were before me and you from ancient times—they preached of war, famine and pestilence against many countries and great kingdoms" (28:8)? Does not this presuppose a prophetic norm of preaching, a "tradition" in which each prophet stands?

There is opposition to this as early as Amos' hefty protest against Amaziah, who wanted to fit him into a "school": Amos contradicts him by referring to the commission he received directly from Yahweh. Jeremiah's polemic against the prophets who steal each other's words (23:30) is also opposed to this. Moreover, this same Jeremiah, who reflected on the legitimacy of prophetic proclamation more intensively than any other prophet, was the very one to accentuate "Yahweh sent me" (26:15; cf. 1:7) as well as the polemically defensive charge, "Yahweh did not send you" (28:15 and elsewhere). This itself counsels against our tying prophetic legitimacy with a general office which in turn would be bound to a specific tradition.

Jer. 28 is an especially impressive text for elucidating the prophet's peculiar freedom from "school ties"—while still being demonstrably determined by "older prophetic tradition." Isaiah preaches (in 14:25) that Asshur will be broken and its yoke and burden eliminated from the people. Isa. 9:3 [9:4]

12:1ff. was later reinterpreted in light of the historical fate of King Zedekiah (cf. 2 Kgs. 25:1ff.). Such "interpretative posthistory" can occasionally lead to extensive overpainting of the original texts (cf., e.g., my *Ezechiel*, BK 13/1, on Ezek. 1). This phenomenon has not been treated in the above discussion and is therefore not considered in this summary. For an example, cf. the analysis of the book of Nahum in J. Jeremias, *Kultprophetie und Gerichtsverkündigung in der späten Königszeit Israels*, WMANT 35 (Neukirchen-Vluyn: Neukirchener Verlag, 1970), 11–55. On fundamental matters, cf. S. Mowinckel, *Prophecy and Tradition: The Prophetic Books in the Light of the Study of the Growth and History of the Tradition* (Oslo: Dybwad, 1946); and discussions in D. A. Knight, *Rediscovering the Traditions of Israel*, rev. ed., SBLDS 9 (Missoula: Society of Biblical Literature, 1975), part II, passim.

49. For the most pronounced position on this, cf. H. G. Reventlow, *Das Amt des Propheten bei Amos*, FRLANT 80 (Göttingen: Vandenhoeck & Ruprecht, 1962).

formulates it with corresponding language: "The yoke that burdens him, the rod that strikes his shoulder [or: the collar on his shoulder?], the rod of his oppressor, you shatter as on the day of Midian." Jer. 28 then reports that in the fourth year of Zedekiah Jeremiah put a yoke upon his neck and proclaimed the necessity of surrendering to Babylonia. The prophet Hananiah confronts him in the temple. He tears the yoke from Jeremiah's neck and smashes it to pieces while declaring solemnly in Yahweh's name: "Thus will I break the yoke of Nebuchadnezzar, the king of Babylon." With these words Hananiah is standing fully in the tradition of Isaiah and simply repeating what his predecessor had said before him. Yet, so we are told, Jeremiah departs without a word, although he had just previously warned Hananiah by referring to an opposing prophetic tradition (quoted above). Could it be in the end that Hananiah's actualization of the tradition from Isaiah is truly legitimate? The text then reports tersely that Jeremiah receives a new message from God to tell Hananiah: "Within the year you shall die"; and the account ends without commentary: "And the prophet Hananiah died in the same year, in the seventh month." This episode shows clearly how little shelter a prophet can actually find in tradition, even where this happens to be a previously valid prophetic message. It demonstrates well how little the prophet, even within the inner-prophetic process of tradition, can dispense with the fact that Yahweh in his freedom can utter his word anew.

Such ties in view of inner-prophetic transmission of the prophetic message are paired with, on the other hand, the great freedom with which a prophet, despite considerable dependence on the proclamation of another prophet, can nevertheless treat the message handed down from this predecessor. Such sovereignty is perceivable, for example, in the use made by Ezekiel of the tradition about the exodus-wilderness period: whereas Hosea and Jeremiah sketched this in brilliant colors as the time of Israel's closeness to her God, Ezekiel (in chs. 20 and

23) transforms this into an exactly opposite picture of total recalcitrance.

This last example leads us into the *wider sphere*: ancient pre-prophetic tradition about Israel's salvation, and its treatment in the context of prophetic proclamation.

The entire discussion in this essay took its starting-point in Amos' "No" to all revered tradition in which the people of his day sought shelter. Alongside Amos, Hosea issued a "No," formulated in the name given his third child, against the central affirmation of Israel's "covenant formula," the awareness that Israel is Yahweh's people; this "No" thus exceeds the warning in Amos 3:2.

However, it also became clear right at the beginning that this "No" stems from an equally impassioned "Yes"—a "Yes" to Yahweh, known by this name in Israel's pious tradition, the God who had now mobilized against his people. Amos' "No," like that of Hosea, is to be understood in terms of Yahweh's uprising against Israel, against the people "known" by Yahweh (Amos 3:2) and identified by him as "my people" in Amos 7:8 and 8:2 within a proclamation of judgment, indeed within a message about the "end." In speaking of Yahweh, whose name they knew from Israel's tradition, these prophets were not expounding a neutral *traditum* but rather the personal God designated in his very name, the One who lives, who comes.

Yet this One, whose ominous approach is proclaimed, became also the subject of all that was commonly recounted from older Israelite tradition—that which occurred in the exodus from Egypt, in the wilderness wandering, in the conquest (the patriarchal tradition recedes well into the background), in dwelling on Zion, in David's kingdom with the promise associated with him. But Israel's faith sought refuge in these as declarations of assurance, of historical promise, and of Yahweh's gracious presence in the midst of his people. And for this reason all of these traditions had to take on a different complexion.

We could see that the individual prophets spoke very differ-

ently about these *tradita*. The memory of Yahweh's gift of land
could become an illustration of Israel's current deep ingratitude
toward the God whose will for justice was known well, yet was
disregarded (Amos). With perceptible sublimation of actual
recollection, the wilderness period could become a time of
virtuous poverty and full loyalty to Yahweh—in sharp contrast
to the neglect of the present, when Baalistic opulence in the
land had eclipsed the knowledge of Yahweh (Hosea). When
Yahweh's people relied more on current political agreements
than on the Holy One in their midst, then the fact that Israel's
Holy One dwells on Zion could become a threat, and deliverance was to be expected only for those who relied on and
believed in Yahweh and who recognized their own deficiency
before the One who alone is exalted. Insolent assault against
the statutes of the Holy One in the Davidic house established by
him could, though, also spell the ruin of an external power
(Isaiah). For Ezekiel, however, the entire tradition from the
people's past merged, in light of their present rebellion against
Yahweh, into a single history of disobedience. The initial
events during the exodus from Egypt and the wilderness period
were declared to be the true cause of the immediately impending catastrophe.

For all of this, is it appropriate to speak of "interpretation" of
historical traditions? To be sure, old traditions emerge
throughout. Yet in terms of the actual function which "tradition" should serve, namely, the function of wholesome assurance for the present in "memory" and in "actualization"[50] of
past events, the *traditum* crumbles to pieces wherever the great
pre-exilic prophets take hold of it. In their preaching it becomes the accuser of the present. And even at the price sometimes (especially in Ezekiel) of radical recasting with all

---

50. M. Noth, "Die Vergegenwärtigung des Alten Testaments in der Verkündi-
gung," *EvTh* 12 (1952/53), 6–17 = *Gesammelte Studien zum Alten Testament, II*,
ThB 39 (München: Chr. Kaiser, 1969), 86–98 = "The 'Re-Presentation' of the Old
Testament in Proclamation," in *Essays on Old Testament Hermeneutics*, ed.
C. Westermann and J. L. Mays (Richmond: John Knox, 1963), pp. 76–88.

beneficial aid eliminated, the *traditum* is made to serve entirely the prophets' immediate proclamation of judgment, the sole locus of emphasis. The God who comes in judgment emerges from the entire pious tradition. He is to be known in his impending judgment, and no longer in tradition about previous deeds (*"Erweiswort"*). Alongside this, the old traditions have nothing of their own to emphasize. "Tradition," in the salutary sense of the word, shatters and becomes an empty shell of mere historical recollection, over which a completely different word of God is proclaimed.

But then something else happens. The ancient tradition can experience a peculiar transformation that one cannot properly call "interpretations of traditions": in an antitypical fashion it can express what Yahweh pronounces as judgment (return to Egypt, a new period in the wilderness) and as the sequel to judgment (new exodus, new covenant, new conquest, new presence of Yahweh, new kingdom on Zion). Israel's old tradition offers the vocabulary with which the impending action can be described. Yet as such it is still more than just a graphic illustration. Tradition discloses the constancy of the One who is free, who remains committed to act "for his own sake" (Ezek. 36:22; Isa. 43:25; 48:11), who "takes pity on his own name," as Ezek. 36:21 formulates it with sober objectivity.

These summarizing comments have not attended adequately to points of connection or to distinctions that could be made between, for example, Amos and Isaiah. Israel's great prophecy does not speak with one voice—and especially not in terms of the traditions available to it and treated by it. Yet it happens that upon every historical tradition that may be cultically transmitted as revered *traditum* the prophets, despite all individual differences, impose their message about the One who is known by the traditional name of Yahweh and who is about to rise up again within Israel's history. He cannot be captured in some citation about a past event—and thus be put at our disposal. "Tradition history" must not be evaluated unthinkingly as "theology."[51]   The "No" of such as Amos remains firm and relentless.   Nevertheless, God is the One who is free—free then also to begin anew after the great catastrophe.   Since old material in new form seems to reappear in the proclamation of this new beginning granted freely by Yahweh, it becomes evident that the One acting in Israel remains unchanged.   In proclaiming this new deed Ezekiel declares: "You will know that I am Yahweh when I open your graves and lead you up, my people, out of your graves" (37:13).   The *traditum* "Yahweh," which is more than just a *traditum*, becomes an indicator, pointing to the One who, in freedom and yet also in faithfulness, can begin anew—and desires to begin anew.

Prophetic proclamation thus shatters and transforms tradition in order to announce the approach of the Living One.

51. Cf. W. Zimmerli, "Alttestamentliche Traditionsgeschichte und Theologie," in *Probleme biblischer Theologie*, ed. Wolff, pp. 632–47 = *Studien zur alttestamentlichen Theologie und Prophetie*, ThB 51, 9–26.   In my opinion, R. Albertz's treatment of Deutero-Isaiah's statements on creation (*Weltschöpfung und Menschenschöpfung, untersucht bei Deuterojesaja, Hiob und in den Psalmen* [Stuttgart: Calwer, 1974], pp. 1–90), is an example of such an inadmissable dogmatization of tradition history.   After a useful and surely accurate analysis of the traditio-historical background of statements about creation of the world and creation of humanity, Albertz postulates that, although Deutero-Isaiah joins the two tradition strands, which use similar terms in speaking of Yahweh's creative activity, the two must be assessed separately, not intertwined.   Thus for him, the *traditum* which he ascertains traditio-historically assumes more importance than the fact that now by the time of Deutero-Isaiah both *tradita* are the domain of the single living Lord, who acts in both and who in his personage under the name of Yahweh makes both into a *single* event, to be sure with two directions.   It is as though the *traditum* prevails over the personage who emerges under this name, and degrades him into serving two separate spheres.

Chapter 5

Tradition and Worship:
The Role of the Cult in
Tradition Formation and Transmission

Arvid S. Kapelrud

THE CULT—THE FERTILE SOIL

O God, when thou didst go forth before thy people,
  when thou didst march through the wilderness,
the earth quaked, the heavens poured down rain,
  at the presence of God;
yon Sinai quaked at the presence of God,
  the God of Israel.[1]

In these lines from the ancient hymn several different features are blended together, all of them characteristic elements in Israelite worship. Here is praise of God, a dominant part of so many psalms—praise because he acted with his people in history, in the exodus from Egypt, the march through the wilderness, and the events near and at Sinai. Here are ancient mythological traits, known from the theophany of the Canaanite rain-and-storm god: the earth quaked, the heavens poured down rain. Furthermore the presence of God is emphasized: it is no incidental God, but he who had chosen his people Israel.

In these few lines are gathered elements which were constitutive in the Israelite cult, and it may be useful to systematize them preliminarily already at this stage. They are found in the following order: (a) mythical feature: God's marching at the head of his people; (b) historical element: Israel's march

---

1. Ps. 68:8–9 [68:7–8]. This translation, like most others in this chapter, is from the RSV.

through the wilderness; (c) theophany in the ancient style of the rain-and-storm god, with strong reactions in nature; (d) the presence of the God of Israel, here at Sinai (later at Zion).

These elements are not accidentally combined in a few lines of an ancient hymn. They are found again and again in the psalms and also in the preaching of the prophets, and they indicate that these elements were continually used and reused in the cult. They represented traditions which received their form— probably without ever reaching a "final form"—in the cult. And they surely received more than just their form. As Weiser expresses it: "Here the study of the history of the traditions and of the cultus is of greater assistance in that it takes us right back to the cultus as the common original foundation of the tradition and as the fertile soil out of which the parallel traditions of the different types of literature have grown."[2] Independently of Weiser the present author wrote at about the same time: "The cult was the fertile soil in which ideas were born—and lived. There the ancient traditions were given their form and handed down to posterity; there the psalms were composed and used. In it the hope, the joy, the fear, the anxiety, and the desperation of the people were expressed; in it Yahweh's answers came to them. The cult was nothing accidental; it was a living core in the relation between Yahweh and his people."[3]

Decisive in ancient Israel was the fact that the individual did not exist first and foremost as an isolated phenomenon. He was part of his family, of his tribe, of his people, and of the covenant with Yahweh, the God of Israel. He was accustomed to channeling his relationship with God through the official cult, and actually it was no question of ancient "custom"—it *had* to be so. The cult had thus a dominating place in the life of the Israelite people. That was even more the case because the cult was the medium through which most spiritual and cultural life

2. A. Weiser, *The Psalms: A Commentary*, OTL (Philadelphia: Westminster, 1962), pp. 25–26.
3. A. S. Kapelrud, "The Role of the Cult in Old Israel," in *The Bible in Modern Scholarship*, ed. J. P. Hyatt (Nashville and New York: Abingdon, 1965), p. 55.

was expressed. It was not alone in handling these important factors in the life of a nation, but its two counter-poles had certain limitations. The popular culture was operative in the daily life, especially in early times and in primitive communities, but it was not powerful enough to seize and maintain the lead.

The situation was otherwise in what may be called the royal culture, thriving mainly in and around the king's court. It seems to have been dominated by the king's scribes, who made the annual reports and wrote the victory reports in wartime and who were personally interested in the international wisdom patronized also by the kings. The wisdom literature was not always available to the common people, nor were its ideas relevant for all. If it was really to reach the people it needed to be transformed, and such a transformation was effected through the cult. The wisdom literature, its ideas and terminology, was appropriated by writers who were more closely connected with the temple circles than the authors at the king's court tended to be. They set this literature into a new context and gave it a new ideological color. The result of their work can be seen demonstrated in Proverbs, where the ancient royal and international wisdom has been transformed so that it would fit into an Israelite context. The Proverbs speak of one's relationship with God and with other persons, and the dominating ideas are adjusted to accord with a Yahwistic view.

Who did this adjustment? "Wise scribes" are supposed to be the authors of the Proverbs. These scribes were not, however, those at the king's court. In ancient Ugarit the scribes had their place in the house of the high priest, and there was also a school of scribes in the same house. They were servants of the temples (probably also of the king), and it was their task to take care of the ancient traditions and to transmit them to the following generation, as can be seen from the manuscripts found in the house of the high priest.

In Israel the temple scribes (who were also royal scribes) had to take care of the ancient traditions that were used in the temple cult and in the teaching of the priests. The information given in 2 Chr. 34:13, "some of the Levites were scribes, and officials, and gatekeepers," was most probably true not only for a late time, as is usually supposed, but also for previous periods in the history of Israel-Judah.

That priestly authors and scribes were not only interested in handing down to posterity the traditions as they had received them from their predecessors, but that they also would write new passages reflecting their own view, can be seen clearly in the Priestly Code. In this work the Priestly authors fashioned a new framework for the ancient collections of traditions and thus actually created an important new tradition, which was taken over by their successors, new generations of scribes.

Especially in Gen. 1 can this be seen clearly.[4] Here the Priestly author exposed his method in a more direct way than was customary for him. He needed a creation narrative which used ancient, well-known elements but at the same time was characteristic of the Yahweh religion and superior to previous creation descriptions. The author did not hesitate to fashion a new creation narrative, and an analysis shows how complex this chapter actually is, being composed of features from other narratives. But every one of them is fayed into the framework devised by the author. And the framework had an obvious cultic character: to emphasize the importance of the seventh day of the week as a holy day, a sabbath instituted by God himself as the final crown of his creation work.

The creative work of the cultic traditionists comes to a point in Gen. 1. Here it can be seen how they re-formed ancient material for cultic purposes. That there is also an intellectual moment here shall not be denied. It shows that even if the traditionists were conscious that they were working for a well-

---

4. A. S. Kapelrud, "The Mythological Features in Genesis Chapter I and the Author's Intentions," *VT* 24 (Fasc. 2, E. Hammershaimb-Festschrift, 1974), 178–86.

defined purpose they also had their eyes open for other important demands.

WHAT DID THE CULT FORM AND TRANSMIT?

As already mentioned, it was in the cult that a new creation narrative was formed. It was also there that the ancient proverbs assumed a new shape, as indicated above. It might be helpful at this point to widen our perspective of the activity within the cult, specifically with respect to the diversity of traditions which were preserved there.

Laws

The laws and rules which regulated the whole life of Israel in her covenantal relationship with Yahweh were connected with the cult, and this can be seen clearly from Exod. 19 and the following chapters, where the rules for those living in the covenant are found. A connection between laws and cult is widely accepted today, although its exact nature and extent are still under discussion. For example, Albrecht Alt considered the apodictic (categorical) laws unique to Israel and at home in the cult, especially important because they were proclaimed in the name of Yahweh every seven years at the Feast of Booths to renew the covenant. New interest in these questions was aroused through G. Mendenhall's thesis that the Old Testament covenant was patterned after the form of the Hittite suzerainty treaty. Further modifications of Alt's theses were indicated by other scholars, for example by E. Gerstenberger who tried to connect apodictic laws with "clan-ethos."[5] However this question about origins is to be answered, later contact between cult and laws was inevitable.

---

5. A. Alt, "Die Ursprünge des israelitischen Rechts" (1934), in *Kleine Schriften zur Geschichte des Volkes Israel,* vol. 1 (München: Beck, 1953), pp. 278–332 = "The Origins of Israelite Law," *Essays on Old Testament History and Religion* (Oxford: Blackwell, 1966), 79–132; G. E. Mendenhall, *Law and Covenant in Israel and the Ancient Near East* (Pittsburgh: Biblical Colloquium, 1955); E. Gerstenberger, *Wesen und Herkunft des "apodiktischen Rechts,"* WMANT 20 (Neukirchen: Neukirchener Verlag, 1965).

That rules could be formulated according to changing situations and views becomes clearer when we compare the Decalogues rendered in Exod. 20:1–17 and Deut. 5:6–21. The former, in its ordinance about the Sabbath, alludes to the creation narrative given by the Priestly author in Gen. 1. The latter Decalogue does not mention this feature when observance of the Sabbath day is ordered; instead Israel is reminded of its situation when the people were slaves in Egypt (Deut. 5:15). Both Decalogues were intended to be used in the cult, in the great annual festival when Yahweh revealed himself to his people and the covenant was renewed. The contents of the Decalogues were fixed, but some accompanying circumstances could obviously be changed, in order not to cause too much trouble for the audience.[6]

History

Gerhard von Rad suggested that the historical narratives in the Pentateuch had their origin in certain brief statements which he preferred to call "credos," for example, as found in Deut. 6:20–24; 26:5b–9; Josh. 24:2b–13.[7] He indicated that these credos were composed in accordance with an ancient scheme which allowed few deviations. What is also important, according to him, is the lack of any mention of Sinai and the events connected with it. This is also the reason why he considers the credos to be very old, representing their own line of traditions.

---

6. For recent traditio-historical studies of the Decalogues, cf. E. Nielsen, *Die Zehn Gebote: Eine traditionsgeschichtliche Skizze*, AThD 8 (Copenhagen: Munksgaard, 1965) = *The Ten Commandments in New Perspective: A Traditio-Historical Approach*, SBT 2/7 (London: SCM, 1968); J. J. Stamm with M. E. Andrew, *The Ten Commandments in Recent Research*, SBT 2/2 (London: SCM, 1967); and W. H. Schmidt, "Überlieferungsgeschichtliche Erwägungen zur Komposition des Dekalogs," VTS 22 (1972), 201–20.

7. G. von Rad, "Das formgeschichtliche Problem des Hexateuch" (1938), in *Gesammelte Studien zum Alten Testament*, ThB 8 (München: Chr. Kaiser, 1965), 9ff. = "The Form-Critical Problem of the Hexateuch," in *The Problem of the Hexateuch and Other Essays* (Edinburgh and London: Oliver & Boyd, 1966), pp. 1ff.

Nevertheless, von Rad has approached the problem from the wrong angle. His credos are not really elements standing at the beginning of a tradition, but at the end.[8] Traditions do not begin in that way. They commence in a far more chaotic way, and some of them need centuries to reach their final form, especially the kind of fixed form that von Rad has isolated.

There are also features connected with them which von Rad has overlooked. They all have a prominent trait in common. They speak first and foremost of Yahweh's salvaging operations for his people, how he promised them their land and gave it to them, how he saved them from the Egyptians. The covenant obligations are also mentioned (e.g., Deut. 6:24), but what is more important is the fact that all "credos" are found in narratives actually used in the covenantal cult, that is, in passages used at festivals when the covenant was renewed. And in these cases the point was not to emphasize the Sinai event, but to underline the fact that the covenant is enacted here and now. It is now that we are under the obligations, now that Yahweh, who saved us from the Egyptians, is present and gives us his commandments. The traditions were living traditions, doing their work here and now. That is also the reason why they were given a form in the cult which could appeal to the audience. In one of the passages pointed out by von Rad as a credo it can be seen easily how the ancient traditions were cut and tailored in order to make them emphasize in the strongest possible way how Yahweh took care of those who lived in his covenant. Therefore the conclusion, which von Rad seemed to overlook, must be that the people had only one possibility: to fear Yahweh and to serve him in sincerity and faithfulness (Josh. 24:14). The traditions played an active role here; therefore it is wrong to separate Josh. 24:2–13 from the following passages, which tell about the renewal of the covenant be-

8. Cf. also the discussion in E. W. Nicholson, *Exodus and Sinai in History and Tradition* (Oxford: Blackwell, 1973), pp. 20ff.

tween Yahweh and his people. In his discussion of the credos von Rad has broken up a unity which was most important for the author.

The so-called credos of von Rad (Deut. 6:20–24; 26:5b–9; Josh. 24:2b–13) are brief narratives which transmit and summarize ancient history, previously told in a less condensed way by skilled narrators and authors. They must not, however, be cut off from their context. If so, their role in living tradition gets lost, and the pieces that remain fall dead to the earth.

The Song of the Sea, in Exod. 15, has been the object of much discussion.[9] This song, which is probably old and has recently been dated to the late twelfth or early eleventh century B.C.,[10] tells the story of the victory over the Egyptians in the Reed Sea in terminology and images that are obviously taken from ancient cult—not from Israelite but, as the images reveal, from Canaanite cult.

In this song it is demonstrated how historical facts have been taken up in poetry, with selected features used in the hymn to glorify Yahweh and the whole material placed into a new context, colored by the ancient Canaanite terminology and imagery. What emerges clearly here is the feature that it was not the actual history as such that was decisive, but rather the *interpretation of history* as Yahweh's deeds for his people. This interpretation was relevant not only in historical context, but also here and now, in the acts and texts of the cult, and through them also for the future. Traditions were created not so that they might become rigid and fixed but so that they could live on in the cult. How these traditions grew and were changed

9. Cf., e.g., H. Schmidt "Das Meerlied, Ex. 15,2–19," *ZAW* 49 (1931), 59–66; F. M. Cross, *Canaanite Myth and Hebrew Epic* (Cambridge: Harvard University, 1973), pp. 112–44; P. D. Miller, Jr., *The Divine Warrior in Early Israel* (Cambridge: Harvard University, 1973), pp. 113–17; and F. M. Cross and D. N. Freedman, *Studies in Ancient Yahwistic Poetry*, SBLDS 21 (Missoula: Scholars Press, 1975).

10. Cross, *Canaanite Myth and Hebrew Epic*, p. 124; cf. also D. A. Robertson, *Linguistic Evidence in Dating Early Hebrew Poetry*, SBLDS 3 (Missoula: Society of Biblical Literature, 1972).

can be seen in Exod. 13:17–14:30, where the Priestly author has underlined strongly the miraculous features in the event.

As was argued emphatically by Johannes Pedersen, Exod. 1–15 was the text used by the Israelites at their spring feast, the Pesach.[11] Again and again the wonderful story of Yahweh's deliverance of his people from the archenemy, the Egyptians, was recited and interpreted. Some scholars hold the opinion that the original story is found in one single verse: "And Miriam sang to them: 'Sing to Yahweh, for he has triumphed gloriously; the horse and his rider he has thrown into the sea' " (Exod. 15:21). The "minimum principle" used here is, however, no real, living principle. It is a scholarly construction.

It is more likely, as Frank M. Cross has recently emphasized,[12] that the point of departure may be found in Exod. 15, the Song of the Sea. It is also a hymn to Yahweh, who "has triumphed gloriously, the horse and his rider he has thrown into the sea." The description of the events is simple and sober and well built into the hymn. It can easily be seen that it forms the grid into which the narrative of the Priestly work is built, Exod. 13:17–14:30. To the ancient poet it was the victory that was most important, won with the help of Yahweh, the "man of war" (15:3). In the Priestly narrative, however, it is the miracle of Yahweh that stands out: "And the people of Israel went into the midst of the sea on dry ground, the waters being a wall to them on their right hand and on their left. The Egyptians pursued, and went in after them into the midst of the sea, all Pharaoh's horses, his chariots, and his horsemen" (Exod. 14:22–23). The pattern followed can be discerned in Exod. 15:8–9: "At the blast of thy nostrils the waters piled up, the floods stood up in a heap; the deeps congealed in the heart of the sea. The enemy said, 'I will pursue, I will overtake, I will

---

11. J. Pedersen, *Israel: Its Life and Culture*, III–IV (London: Oxford University; Copenhagen: Brunner, 1940), 393ff., 726ff.
12. See above, note 9.

divide the spoil, my desire shall have its fill of them. I will draw my sword, my hand shall destroy them.' "

The poetical language used in the Song of the Sea was substituted by the rather dry prose of the Priestly writer. But in his prosaic way he heightened the importance of Yahweh's work. His God was not only "a man of war"; he was Lord of the Universe, who could "make the sea dry land and divide the waters" (Exod. 14:21).

It is important here to emphasize that Exod. 1–15 was used in the central festival cult. The text was recited to the people, and the Priestly author found it necessary to underline certain features which in his eyes had not been sufficiently pointed out in the old songs and narratives. What was happening in worship needed a text where these features had their "right" weight, according to this author.

If we have a look at the Deuteronomistic text in Josh. 24 for the Covenant Renewal Feast (or whatever designation may be deemed appropriate for this festival), there are also certain features worth noticing. The writers of the Deuteronomistic History have not followed the same line as the Priestly author but have adhered to the view found in the Song of the Sea—that the important event was the victory over the Egyptians: "Then I brought your fathers out of Egypt, and you came to the sea; and the Egyptians pursued your fathers with chariots and horsemen to the Reed Sea. And when they cried to Yahweh, he put darkness between you and the Egyptians, and made the sea come upon them and cover them" (Josh. 24:6–7).

The interchange between "your fathers" and "you" is interesting, showing that we are here in a cultic sphere. Important is also Josh. 24:9: "Then Balak the son of Zippor, king of Moab, arose and fought against Israel; and he sent and invited Balaam the son of Beʻor to curse you." Now the fact is that in the ancient narrative about Balak and Balaam in Num. 22–24 nothing is told about a war between Balak and the Israelites.

That does not mean that we have in Josh. 24 an older, more reliable narrative (a credo) than in Num. 22–24. On the contrary, there can be no doubt that the story in Num. 22–24 is older than that in Josh. 24. And it can easily be seen why this is so. The narrative in Josh. 24 is adjusted to the Deuteronomistic doctrine that the Israelite tribes did really fight the people they met on their way into Canaan and that they had no friendly relations with them. Here a new tradition was created, and also this "tradition" was intended for use in a cultic event, intended to tell the people, gathered in worship, how to behave in life as well as in the cult.

Prophets and Poetry

As has been demonstrated above, both law and history played an active part in the Israelite worship, where they were transmitted to posterity in forms which changed through the centuries. It is evident that this was even more the case with prophetic and poetic traditions. The words of the prophets were taken care of by the disciples and followers of the prophets. In the case of some of the prophets of doom they may have been met with suspicion by the temple authorities, and it may have been difficult to have the words integrated into the official body of religious material used in worship. But most of the prophets, if not all, ended their preaching—or at least the collections of their words ended—in a tone of hope which in the situation of Israel-Judah was of great significance and of necessity for life. Whether this tone of hope was a product of tradition or was genuinely prophetic cannot be discussed here, but it was surely decisive for the use of the prophetic collections in worship. This use was an important factor in the transmission of the prophetic words to posterity. Even more than was necessary in popular transmission, the prophetic words used in worship had to be transmitted without changes and were therefore well preserved. However, what happened was that passages could be added which might change the original meaning or trend of a prophetic word.

In their use in worship the prophetic utterances came to their full effect, for that was the forum where they could be used again and again without losing their edge. Indeed, throughout much of Israel's history we have to reckon with the existence of prophets who were attached to the cult as permanent functionaries there. S. Mowinckel was one of the first to point to such cultic prophets, and he was followed by others, for example, A. Haldar, A. R. Johnson, H. G. Reventlow and E. von Waldow, who emphasized that the prophetic forms and their background were closely connected with the rituals of the covenant people.[13] From all of this we have to conclude that the transmission of the words of the prophets was an important task in cultic circles. Even for prophets who did not themselves work in close contact with the cult and whose utterances were not preserved there from the outset, at some later point— perhaps after their predictions were fulfilled—the cult took over their transmission.

Concerning poetry there is no doubt that all religious poetry in Israel-Judah was concentrated in the cult, where it was composed, attained its final form, and was transmitted to new generations. Days are gone when scholars tried to ascribe them to small circles outside the temple and the official cult. Some psalms may have been written by wise scribes or theologians, more learned than poetical, but also these psalms were intended for use in the cult, if not for singing.

In a later section, there will be opportunity to treat in more detail such psalmic transmission and traditions.

13. S. Mowinckel, *Psalmenstudien III: Kultprophetie und prophetische Psalmen* (Kristiania: Dybwad, 1923; reprinted 1961); A. Haldar, *Associations of Cult Prophets among the Ancient Semites* (Uppsala: Almqvist & Wiksell, 1945); A. R. Johnson, *The Cultic Prophet in Ancient Israel* (Cardiff: University of Wales, 1944; 2d ed., 1962); H. G. Reventlow, *Das Amt des Propheten bei Amos*, FRLANT 80 (Göttingen: Vandenhoeck & Ruprecht, 1962); idem, *Liturgie und prophetisches Ich bei Jeremia* (Gütersloh: Gütersloher Verlagshaus, 1963); and E. von Waldow, *Der traditionsgeschichtliche Hintergrund der prophetischen Gerichtsreden*, BZAW 85 (Berlin: Töpelmann, 1963).

FACTORS AFFECTING THE CULTIC PROCESS
OF TREATING TRADITIONS

A series of different factors influenced the cultic process of selecting, developing, altering, and preserving traditions. In some of the examples indicated above it is not difficult to discern some of the factors at work.

Ancient tradition material, like the Decalogue and other legal collections, had its basic home in the cult, which actually seems to have been built around this material, as may be seen in the book of Exodus. This is ancient Israelite kernel material, which we cannot always isolate easily but which has directed the reactions of Yahwistic circles throughout ages.

Closely connected with this material goes the interpretation of historical events as saving deeds of Yahweh. Again Exod. 1–15 is a typical example, painting the basic deeds of Yahweh in establishing his covenant with his people, after having saved them from slavery and a mighty enemy. This historical background, in its special interpretation, was a dominating feature in Israel's religion, a constant corrective against foreign influences which threatened to lead the cult into new tracks.

This corrective was necessary at all times. From the very beginning and practically without ceasing, Canaanite and other foreign elements slipped in. Some features were accepted and amalgamated; others were rejected. Somewhat schematically it may be said that features connected with the ancient Canaanite high god El were accepted without trouble, while those known to be bound to Ba'al were generally rejected. But not even this latter statement is quite true. In certain periods several Ba'al-colored features were used in descriptions of Yahweh.

An example of this can be seen in the central passage in Exod. 19 where the theophany of Yahweh at Mount Sinai is described: "On the morning of the third day there were thunders and lightnings, and a thick cloud upon the mountain, and a very loud trumpet blast, so that all the people who were in the camp trembled. . . . And Mount Sinai was wrapped in smoke, because Yahweh descended upon it in fire; and the smoke of it went up like the smoke of a kiln, and the whole mountain quaked greatly" (Exod. 19:16, 18).

Yahweh is described here as coming to his mountain in the same way as the rain-and-storm god Ba'al-Hadad used to do. But in 1 Kgs. 19 there is a reaction against this description of Yahweh's theophany (which was the usual one, cf. Ps. 29), and there it is said expressly that when Elijah visited Mount Horeb Yahweh was not in the wind, or in the earthquake, or in the fire, but in a still, small voice (1 Kgs. 19:11–13). This is one of the cases where the reaction against an ancient, long-accepted feature from the Ba'al worship comes into the open. However, this reaction from a Deuteronomistic historian may have been a single cry against a theophany description which had become part and parcel of the Yahweh cult.

Other influences, however, strengthened the view of the history writers. The terrible experience of the destruction of both Israel and Judah led to a reaction which placed the prophets in the center of the cultic interest, together with the ancient historical traditions and the psalms. The reaction against the foreign conquerors also made the ideas of the Deuteronomists into dominating features in the world view of those who lived through the destruction and the deportation. How this affected traditions has been indicated in some of the examples given above.[14]

In the case of the Israelite psalms the picture is rather multicolored. In ancient Israel-Judah, as even today, the poetic literature very often represents a conservative tendency. That means that ancient poems, with imagery and terminology no longer in use or for some reason considered unsuitable, still can be found in the collection used in services or festivals in the Jerusalem temple. On the other hand, and that has also to be emphasized, some late poems are included—of a wisdom type

14. Cf. also the discussion by P. R. Ackroyd, below, Chapter 9.

like Ps. 1, or in praise of the law, like Ps. 119, a psalm which uses stylistic devices taken from the wisdom literature.

A rich variety of impulses and influences has determined the composition of the Psalter, from ancient times down to a rather late period. This makes it possible to discern different trends of traditions in the collection. Actually, each single psalm deserves a special investigation, although this obviously cannot be considered necessary or possible in our discussion. A series of examples will serve the purpose.

HOW THE CULT USED AND FORMED TRADITIONS: THE PSALMS

As shown above, the cult used, formed, and transformed traditions of a varying kind: law, history, prophetic words, poetry, wisdom. A few indications have been given in order to show how this influence on the traditions worked. Our main interest will, however, be concentrated on the psalm material, where the choice of traditions is unusually rich. In the long use of the psalms through changing ages and situations different elements were blended together and transmitted to new generations, undergoing certain changes in the process. Several motifs were current and were treated differently in the transmission, according to dominating trends among the transmitters. They are only roughly structuralized in the following presentation, as a thorough discussion would be beyond the scope of this study.

Theophany

The psalms often speak about the theophany of Yahweh, and this is quite natural as it was in the cult that Yahweh used to meet his people. In a special way this is done in the so-called *Thronbesteigungspsalmen*[15] (Pss. 47; 95; 97–100; 104), psalms that were used at the great annual festival, the New Year

---

15. Cf. S. Mowinckel, *Psalmenstudien II: Das Thronbesteigungsfest Jahwäs und der Ursprung der Eschatologie* (Kristiania: Dybwad, 1922; reprinted 1961).

Feast, when Yahweh was greeted by his people as king, creator, and victorious warrior. The ideology, imagery, and terminology in these psalms, as well as in related ones like Pss. 19; 29; 48; 74:12ff.; 144, have been preserved in a form sometimes only so slightly changed in Israelite use that the ancient Canaanite background can well be seen behind them.

Worship in Israel, first in the tribes and later in the kingdoms, was built upon the people's meeting with Yahweh, their God. In the psalms homage was paid to him, and his mighty theophany was described. The description was given along traditional lines, as they had been adopted from the Canaanites. Even if the composition took place in Israelite circles there were ancient patterns for describing a god's theophany. As can be seen very clearly from the Ugaritic texts, these patterns were found especially in the descriptions of the theophany of the rain-and-storm god Ba'al-Hadad.

A clear demonstration of the way this was done can be seen in Ps. 29: "Ascribe to Yahweh glory, ye sons of gods, ascribe to Yahweh glory and might! Ascribe to Yahweh the glory of his name; worship Yahweh when he appears in his sanctuary! The voice of Yahweh resounds over the waters; the God of glory thunders, Yahweh upon the mighty ocean." The whole psalm goes on in this way—in its form a homage to the voice of Yahweh, but with an ideology and terminology well known from the Ras Shamra texts where they are used to describe the appearance of Ba'al-Hadad.[16] The name of the Canaanite god is changed to that of Yahweh, and this change is also a declaration: Yahweh is the true rain-and-storm god, who crushes cedars of Lebanon (vs. 5).

Interesting also is vs. 8: "The voice of Yahweh shakes the wilderness, Yahweh shakes the wilderness of Kadesh." Here not only the name of Yahweh has been substituted for that of the Canaanite god, but Kadesh is also mentioned. That is no

16. See, e.g., *UT* 51:V:68ff.

coincidental change. The psalm, speaking of the voice of Yahweh, actually revolves around the theophany of the god, and for this theophany Kadesh was the right place to be mentioned.

What can be seen here, then, is a method of transmission where the ancient Canaanite material is used, with slight changes (actually only that of the god's name), but where a first intrusion of historical material from Israel's own experiences can be observed. This latter fact represents a tendency in tradition that is found also in other psalms whose character is not so very different from Ps. 29. The hymn Ps. 97 is an example of this, with the same elements except that Zion and "the daughters of Judah" are mentioned instead of Kadesh. Vs. 7 probably has an addition colored by Israelite theology: "All worshipers of images are put to shame, who make their boast in worthless idols"; but then the psalm continues with the ancient words, rather astonishingly: "all gods bow down before him." The tradition process can hardly be demonstrated more clearly than in this verse where contrary ideas are so loosely connected.

Another example is found in Ps. 47: "For Yahweh 'Elyôn is terrible, a great king over all the earth. He subdued peoples under us, and nations under our feet. He chose our heritage for us, the pride of Jacob whom he loves" (Ps. 47:3–5 [47: 2–4]). The psalm was used at the great festival in the temple when Yahweh revealed himself to his people, but there can be no doubt that the pattern was ancient Canaanite, and very little is changed in it. The name of Yahweh was necessary, as was also Jacob in the context, but the theophany ideology and terminology are those of the rain-and-storm god.

The same unevenness that was found in Ps. 97:7 is present also in Ps. 47:10 [47:9]: "The princes of the peoples gather, people of the God of Abraham," where the name of Abraham is obviously substituted for another one, for example, 'Elyôn.

Other examples of a related kind could be given, but it may be more useful to have a look at a psalm where some other trends are found. Ps. 99 begins in the same way as the ancient

hymns: "Yahweh reigns; let the peoples tremble! He sits en-
throned upon the cherubim; let the earth quake! Yahweh is
great in Zion; he is exalted over all the peoples" (Ps. 99:1–2).
The psalm describes the theophany of Yahweh in the usual way,
and when he is praised for executing justice and righteousness
in Jacob there is nothing unexpected in that. But in vs. 6 the
psalm takes an unexpected turn: "Moses and Aaron were
among his priests, Samuel also was among those who called on
his name. They cried to Yahweh, and he answered them. He
spoke to them in the pillar of cloud; they kept his testimonies
('ēdōtāw), and the statutes that he gave them." Here, in describing the theophany of Yahweh as king on Mount Zion, the
author suddenly introduces three human figures, well known
from the history of Israel, and connects their attitude to
Yahweh with his theophany.

What does that mean? A new note has come in. It was
considered necessary to legitimate Yahweh as more than the
ancient rain-and-storm god. He was, first, a god of history.
Secondly, he was a god who had chosen his own people, among
whom were outstanding figures like Moses, Aaron, and Samuel.
Thirdly, he was a god who placed certain demands on his
adherents, and these were expressed in his testimonies and his
statutes.

A conscious choice of traditions can be discerned here. The
psalm is an old one, and the author picked out some features
which he thought would underline the connection between
Yahweh and historical events and persons. These features were
in line with some dominating traits in Israelite religion. One
may say that there is nothing directly creative in this psalm. It
represents a kind of transmission where a few features from a
broader tradition are concentrated in order to indicate a tendency.

How this broader tradition could be formed is discussed
above in the case of Exod. 15, the Song of the Sea. That song
had a central position in the Pesach feast, during which the

exodus events and the covenant were celebrated. The central position of the song made it part of the Exodus text used at the Pesach, and only this fact kept the song out of the Psalter, where a doubling was unnecessary and unwanted.

But even if it may be said that there was nothing directly creative in Ps. 99 when analyzed feature for feature, it is certain that this psalm, also Exod. 15, and other psalms as well represent a creative feature of high distinction: the firm connection between ancient mythological imagery and historical traits. This is by no means an Israelite invention, as has been convincingly shown by Bertil Albrektson.[17] It is, however, not only a question of invention but also of use. In Israel-Judah this intimate combination of mythological terminology and indications of historical events is a standing and dominating attitude, one that lived through ages.

It seemed to have been called forth by a strong and vivid experience of the presence of Yahweh in the religious cult, but necessarily also by other elements. According to Albrektson, the element of revelation was found in the oracle proclaiming the event rather than in the event itself, in the word about history rather than in history.[18] He may be right in this, but it does not explain the combination pointed out above. The explanation must be found in a decisive experience of a theophany which expressed itself through an historical event. There can be no doubt about that event: the wonderful exodus from Egypt, later interpreted again and again.

Historical Elements

As demonstrated above, historical features were interwoven into the ancient theophany and thus given a sacred tinge which they might not otherwise have received. Historical features became part of the cultic texts and were transmitted also in this way, not only in the more detailed narratives.

17. B. Albrektson, *History and the Gods*, ConOT 1 (Lund: Gleerup, 1967).
18. Ibid., p. 121.

As is well known from Exod. 20:2, decisive historical features may be used as legitimation: "I am Yahweh your God, who brought you up out of the land of Egypt" (Ps. 81:11 [81:10]). This was some kind of a repeated designation, intended to underline the fact that Yahweh was a God who acted in history, but also to point him out as a God who was not identical with the Canaanite rain-and-storm god. It also served to emphasize the importance of the historical traditions, and this transmission in the cult worked as a constant tonic for the historical narratives.

One may indicate that the legitimation also contains an element of motivation. The people had to listen to Yahweh who had saved them from slavery in Egypt. This may be seen clearly, for example, in Ps. 66:5–6: "Come and see what God has done; he is terrible in his deeds among men. He turned the sea into dry land; men passed through the river on foot." Here the motive is obvious: come and see God's deeds. The cult audience is called to praise God, and his deeds in the life of the people are mentioned. In this psalm they are not given in historical terms but are shrouded in mythological terminology, as occurs so often and so characteristically in the cult.

More direct speech is found, for example, in Ps. 81: "In distress you called, and I delivered you; I answered you in the secret place of thunder; I tested you at the waters of Meribah." Here are concrete details from history, together with mythological remnants.

With direct historical reference the author of Ps. 83 speaks in a prayer: "Do to them as thou didst to Midian, as to Sisera and Jabin at the river Kishon, who were destroyed at En-dor, who became dung for the ground. Make their nobles like Oreb and Zeeb, all their princes like Zebah and Zalmunna, who said, 'Let us take possession for ourselves of the pastures of God' " (Ps. 83:10-13 [83:9-12]). Here events related or only indicated in Judg. 4–8 are mentioned as examples of God's help, and the author of the psalm leaves no doubt that all the events reveal God's saving his people. This view serves as a motive for the praying person. So as you have helped us before you must help us again!

In some psalms, like Pss. 78; 105 and 106; 136, the great events in the history of Israel-Judah are recapitulated in detail. When we take a closer look at these psalms it is soon observed that the historical interest is concentrated to a very strong degree on the significant and decisive events during and immediately after the exodus from Egypt. These psalms demonstrate that the historical examples are not chosen at random. They have been consciously picked in order to motivate prayers or praise, and for both these purposes God's great deeds during the exodus events have been considered as the right media.

The miraculous events were emphasized in the psalms, just as was done by late transmitters of the prose narratives: "He divided the sea and let them pass through it, and made the waters like a heap. In the daytime he led them with a cloud, and all the night with a fiery light" (Ps. 78:13–14).

The psalms show better than any other medium how the different tradition elements were welded together and combined in a way which actually created a new set of traditions. These traditions formed the final picture of Israelite-Judean religion, the same picture taken over by Judaism and Christianity. But there is reason to maintain that this picture was formed very early, probably earlier than is usually supposed.

This welding of traditions and forming them into a new one may be observed in several psalms, also in psalms of an early date, for example, Ps. 18. In this psalm Yahweh is described as the great warrior who saved his people from the enemies. He is also depicted in the ancient terminology used about the rain-and-storm god (vss. 8–16 [7–15]), but also as the god who took care of his statutes and ordinances (vss. 21–27 [20–26]). Here is royal ideology built on the special relationship between Yahweh and his representative (vss. 32–51 [31–50]). This ideology is closely connected with David and his descendants (vs. 51 [50]), and a central line in the religion of Israel is thus brought to the fore and underlined.

This fusing of traditions of different origin is also found in other psalms. One of them is Ps. 89, which begins as a magnificent hymn and ends as a psalm of lamentation. Here Yahweh is pictured as the creator, who crushed Rahab (vs. 11 [10]) and ruled the raging of the sea. Righteousness and justice are the foundations of his throne (vs. 15 [14]). He had chosen David and made his covenant with him: "I will establish your descendants for ever and build your throne for all generations" (vss. 4–5, 20ff. [3–4, 19ff.]).

Also Ps. 144 combines ancient features connected with the rain-and-storm god (vss. 5ff.) with praise of Yahweh's support of "David, his servant" (vs. 10). The ancient idea of God as a fertility god springs out in full flower in vss. 12–15. This is a combination of traditions, performed in the cult, which may be characterized in the words of Ps. 133: "It is like the dew of Hermon, which falls on the mountains of Zion. For there Yahweh has commanded blessing and life for evermore" (vs. 3). Mythological traditions from Canaan, connected with the rain-and-storm god and the fertility cult, were taken up in Yahwistic circles, given a new subject and bound together with historical traditions among the Israelites, partly built up around the exodus from Egypt and the covenant events, partly around the kingdom and the person of David.

CONCLUSION

The psalms have been the great melting-pot of traditions in ancient Israel. That is no wonder, as all currents, whatever their origin, seem to have met in the cult. Therefore the picture which the psalms give of Israelite religion is multicolored and rich in interesting details from different traditions. The psalms constitute a true quarry, and from this source diverse traditions can be dug.

That means that no investigation of Israelite traditions can be done without a discussion of the material found in the psalms. The theological implications are obvious: a detailed scrutinizing of traditions must make a full use of the psalm material, as the psalms reflect the influence of the cult on the development of the traditions. Furthermore, it has to be acknowledged that a picture of the religion of ancient Israel is not complete, not even correct, if it does not make a comprehensive use of the psalms. There the traditions were welded together in a theological form which was directive in Israelite religion.

Indeed, the situation was reciprocal. Just as the cult formed tradition, tradition also formed the cult. The heritage from the past and the rituals celebrating it carried weight. Changing situations and the influx of new materials and ideas affected the life of the cult, and it is only to be expected that traditions preserved there might also be adjusted to reflect new situations —whether through an innovative combination of elements or through formation of new traditions. Yet for all its internal changes the cult represents a certain stabilizing element, a scarlet thread running throughout Israel's history. In light of this as well as the cult's multiplex, responsive nature as we have described above, perhaps it would be appropriate to picture it as a "fluid orthodoxy." Most elements converged there, but the cult itself was not in the hands of everybody. Its rituals and its texts were guarded and controlled by the priests, the temple singers, the temple prophets, and other cult personnel. They took care of the official religion, and the Old Testament speaks with their voice. They formed the Yahwistic theology and drew the lines into the future. However, this very formation was a process that continued at all times in response to new elements. It is impossible to give a complete picture of Israelite religion by focusing on any single stage of the cult. Furthermore, beyond the cult a more popular form of religion was alive, as may be seen, for example, in some of the wisdom literature or in Genesis where the ancient popular narratives are shining through. Yet in the cult there was a stability— though not monolithic and rigid—and a desire to preserve— though not without creativity. For the very existence of the Old Testament we have the Israelite cult to thank. In the long run, its theological reworking of the traditions was victorious.

Chapter 6

Tradition and Language: The Import of Oral Expression

Roger Lapointe

Without tradition, man would not be man. Man would not be man because he would not develop any culture. It is indeed due to a gradual buildup, involving successive generations' keeping constantly in touch with each other through a chain of unbroken transmission, that culture appears among mankind.

When it is given such a broad definition, the word "tradition" covers as much ground as the associate words "culture" and "language." If culture is a child of tradition, as we just argued, it is no less clearly and necessarily related to language.

The title of this essay on "Tradition and Language" would seem, then, to open an extremely broad perspective. What it seems to intend is as a matter of fact intended. But only as a background. The precise matter to be handled has to do with "tradition" in a narrower sense, the sense, namely, with which the word occurs in the context of various scientific discussions. In the said contexts, "tradition" is no longer equivalent to culture or to language in general. Its meaning is restricted to a particular type of culture, a culture which may be called variously: primitive, popular, oral, etc., and which is characterized by the fact that the technique of written communication is either nonexistent or at least not utilized to its full potential.

In theological circles, for example, scripture has commonly been opposed to tradition. And even though the traditions concerned could be either written or not written, the fact that they were globally distinguished from the Holy Writ tended to link them up with the oral mode of communicating the faith.

Within modern folkloristic studies, folklore has been regularly opposed to literature. On the one hand, literary works are defined in terms of being written as to their mode of linguistic existence, devised by individual authors for individual readers, relatively detached from concrete situations, and finally patterned according to forms and structures that eventually cease to be alive. On the other hand, folkloristic productions have been stamped with the opposite characteristics, namely, orality, social or communal origin, close connection with a particular situation, and the implementation of functional forms. H. Bausinger warns against hardening the distinction separating folklore and literature.[1] This notwithstanding, it would appear that folklorists set apart popular or traditional works from literary or written compositions.

The same is true on the biblical scene. The middle of this century has seen the emergence of a new exegetical approach, usually labeled "traditio-historical." Sharply distinguished by some of its proponents from literary criticism,[2] although not from form criticism,[3] the traditio-historical method was applied with enormous success by G. von Rad and M. Noth in Germany.[4] It is in the hands of Scandinavian exegetes that it attained its purest form—in the sense that the correct interpretation of the biblical text now involved transcending the

---

1. "Folklore and literature approach each other"; quoted by E. Güttgemanns, *Offene Fragen zur Formgeschichte des Evangeliums*, BEvTh 54 (München: Chr. Kaiser, 1970), 135.

2. ". . . the break with the literary-critical method must be radical; no compromise is possible. The old method must be replaced by a new one. And the only possible alternative is . . . the traditio-historical method" (I. Engnell, "Methodological Aspects of Old Testament Study," VTS 7 [1960], 21).

3. "The form-literary investigation still is of an outstandingly great value and holds a central position also within the traditio-historical method" (ibid., p. 28).

4. Cf. D. A. Knight, *Rediscovering the Traditions of Israel*, rev. ed., SBLDS 9 (Missoula: Society of Biblical Literature, 1975), chap. 8.

limitations of a bookish attitude and attempting to reach beyond the written text toward the oral stages of its transmission.[5] On these three counts, then, tradition does not have to do with language in general, but with a definite form of it, namely, oral language. Consequently, we will focus on orality in our discussion of the topic "Tradition and Language."

LINGUISTIC PROLEGOMENA

To start with, a few points taken from profane linguistic studies could be in order.

Let us point out, first, that modern linguists define the prime and specific object of their inquiries as being oral or spoken language. There are all sorts of good reasons to justify such a stance. For one thing, spoken language is more universal than written language. Also, it lends itself better to an historical or diachronic description of any particular tongue. But most of all, written language seems to be a simple transcription of oral language and is as such secondary and relatively accidental. F. de Saussure, the father of structuralist linguistics, entertained an opinion of this kind.[6] J. G. Herder had held a comparable view.[7] This, indeed, has been the bias of the whole Western culture, according to the French philosopher J. Derrida. The temptation was great for the West to downgrade the written text, when compared to its spoken counterpart, since in truth the Western scripts are alphabetical, that is, composed of signs that refer immediately to sounds and only mediately to the objects of the world. But, in falling prey to this temptation, says

5. Cf. ibid., part II.
6. "Language and writing are two distinct systems of signs. The second exists for the sole purpose of representing the first. The linguistic object is not both the written and the spoken forms of words; the spoken form alone constitutes the object" (F. de Saussure, *Course in General Linguistics* [London: Owen, 1964], pp. 23–24).
7. "For him [J. G. Herder] written language represents, for one thing, a diminishing of the potency of orality and, second, actually a divine endowment and a support of the intellect" (Güttgemanns, *Offene Fragen*, p. 120).

Derrida, the Western culture has yielded to the logocentric prejudice. It has emphasized presence and identity, instead of following the longer route through absence and difference. Language, claims Derrida, is difference, and, as such a *"trace"* and a *"graphème"* destined to an absent interpreter, not a word or a phrase spoken within hearing distance of a listener.[8]

Here is another point. Language does not operate in isolation from extra-linguistic circumstances. It is completely meaningful in the midst of the situation where it belongs. And this is particularly true of spoken language, as B. Malinowski has clearly and forcefully stated: "A statement, spoken in real life, is never detached from the situation in which it has been uttered. . . . Exactly as in the reality of spoken or written languages, a word without *linguistic context* is a mere figment and stands for nothing by itself, so in the reality of a spoken living tongue, the utterance has no meaning except in the *context of situation.*"[9] The job of describing the relevant situations Malinowski assigns the ethnologist, not the philologist. By the way, that kind of distinction should not bother the exegete, for he wears nearly all the hats that grace the scientific profession. Another ethnologist, J. Vansina, insists, in line with our present contention about the situational dimension of language, that "traditions always serve some particular interest. . . ."[10] By "traditions," Vansina means oral traditions. Let us take careful note of the general relation of language to situations, and of the specific dependence endured by spoken language with regard to relevant factual circumstances.

From a third point of view, that of style, linguists have been wont to distinguish between spoken and written language.

8. Cf. J. Derrida, *De la grammatologie*, Coll. "Critique" (Paris: Éditions de Minuit, 1967).

9. B. Malinowski, "The Problem of Meaning in Primitive Languages," in C. K. Ogden and I. A. Richards, *The Meaning of Meaning* (New York: Harcourt, Brace & Co., 1953), p. 307.

10. J. Vansina, *Oral Tradition: A Study in Historical Methodology* (Chicago: Aldine, 1965), p. 50.

When confronted with a text, ordinarily a literary work, they have asked themselves whether the language of the text wore the marks of the spoken or of the written form.   They thus implied two things: first, that oral and written communication differ in style; second, that a given piece of writing, although normally couched in the written style, could for some reason, for example, a conscious effort at imitating or the redaction of minutes, employ the oral style; for that matter, a spoken utterance could conversely be couched in the written style.   Now, precisely what separates the two styles in principle is not so easy to determine.   J. Vansina feels that "the only marked difference between written and oral literature . . . is that repetition is more frequently employed in oral literature."[11]   To this trait, A. B. Lord, followed by R. C. Culley, would add the constant use of formulas or stock phrases.[12]   Let us also take into account the paratactic style mentioned by E. Nielsen,[13] who, in this matter, would have the support of a linguist like A. Sauvageot.[14]   Granted that spoken and written modes of language are distinguishable from each other, we are still confronted by the almost insurmountable difficulty of diagnosing orality in the Bible.   To the extent, indeed, that the Bible is a literary work and not a straight record of words uttered, it has the written form, it is artificial, it does not present us with the Hebrew and Greek that were spoken at the time.[15]

11. Ibid., p. 55.

12. Cf. A. B. Lord, *The Singer of Tales* (Cambridge: Harvard University Press, 1960); and R. C. Culley, "An Approach to the Problem of Oral Tradition," *VT* 13 (1963), 113–25.

13. ". . . a monotonous style, recurrent expressions, a fluent, paratactic style, a certain rhythm and euphony which are especially noticeable when one hears the account, and finally anacolutha which a literary writer would hardly have let pass . . ." (E. Nielsen, *Oral Tradition*, SBT 11 [London: SCM, 1954], p. 36).

14. "One can even make it into a principle that the spoken style is often nothing else than a series of clauses without connection, or better: of clauses the connection of which depends entirely on inflection ('*moyens modulatoires*')" (A. Sauvageot, *Français écrit, français parlé* [Paris: Larousse, 1962], pp. 39–40).

15. "In their present state the biblical texts are of course 'literary.' We can recover their 'preliterary' state solely through reconstruction by means of inference from analogies (thus through *indirect* empirical means)" (Güttgemanns, *Offene Fragen*, p. 149).

The fourth and last element to be borrowed from the field of linguistics has to do with the notions of *"texte"* and *"inter-texte."* In its common use, "text" means something like a copy, that is, a piece of writing authentically performed or presented. As undertood by R. Barthes, a text is a network of words, and as such a structure and a form, but considered as resulting from the active interplay of the various aspects pertaining to a particular field called "intertext." The intertext comprises elements such as anonymous formulas, unconscious quotations, and other items—more generally the complete mass of linguistic data present at the time of making the text and thus accessible to the writer (or speaker).[16] My only comment, at this point, will be to say that the approach to the text by way of the intertext seems to bridge the gap opened earlier between oral and written language, to the extent at least that it stresses the social and traditional dimension of the written work.

ORAL EXPRESSION IN THE OLD TESTAMENT

To go one step further, let us now take a sweeping look at the biblical scene, more particularly at the Old Testament, in line of course with our main concern, namely, tradition as it relates to oral language.

It is to be noted that Hebrew, as a written language, is phonetical, even alphabetical. This means that it reflects directly its oral state and, through this only, the objects of experience. Contrariwise, the Egyptian script was ideographical. This situation has all sorts of implications, ranging from the logocentric proclivity mentioned above in connection with J. Derrida's speculations, to the simple and constant possibility for written texts to be read aloud and, in this guise, returned to oral communication. How many people were in fact literate at any moment of Israel's history is a relevant question in that context.

16. Cf. R. Barthes, "Texte (théorie du)," in *Encyclopaedia Universalis* 15 (1974), 1015.

It is antecedently clear that the inner logic of written language (Hebrew) will have been felt in proportion to the number of people actually making use of this technique—always taking into consideration, of course, that printing did not yet exist. J. van der Ploeg, for one, feels that even before exilic times many Israelites, particularly priests, merchants, and civil servants, were able to read and to write.[17]

Next, how does written biblical Hebrew relate to spoken Hebrew, apart from being a visual transcription of the same? The answer can only be that the said relation is multiple. For a devotee of the traditio-historical method, the reflex is to state that the present written text has gone through an anterior oral stage, at least in most cases. One should not fancy that the redactor (or copyist) of the present text is its real or complete author. The reverse is true. In a number of cases, certain psalms for example, as R. C. Culley and H. Ringgren have shown,[18] the text would have been produced and transmitted orally prior to being put in writing. This transmission could have taken the channel (1) of a fixed text's being memorized by disciples of a master, or successors to a given officer, or (2) of a fluid text's being recreated anew on the occasion of performances by trained artists. J. Vansina, as well as A. B. Lord, distinguishes sharply between these two modes of transmission. In the biblical field, B. Gerhardsson has made much of the first mode in connection with the rabbinic schools and the New Testament,[19] while, according to R. C. Culley, the composition

17. Cf. J. van der Ploeg, "Le rôle de la tradition orale dans la transmission du texte de l'Ancien Testament," *RB* 54 (1947), 23. The actual extent of literacy in Israel and its effect on the recording of traditions are questions much debated; cf. Knight, *Rediscovering the Traditions of Israel*, passim.

18. Cf. R. C. Culley, *Oral Formulaic Language in the Biblical Psalms*, Near and Middle East Series 4 (Toronto: University of Toronto Press, 1967); H. Ringgren, "Oral and Written Transmission in the Old Testament", *StTh* 3 (1949), 34–59.

19. Cf. B. Gerhardsson, *Memory and Manuscript: Oral Tradition and Written Transmission in Rabbinic Judaism and Early Christianity*, ASNU 22 (Lund: Gleerup, 1961).

of quite a few psalms would have involved the implementation of the second mode.[20]

But this is not the whole story of the relationship between written and oral Hebrew. We have already alluded to the possibility for a written text to smack of spoken utterances. One could argue, for example, with L. Koehler, that the dialogues reported by the biblical text reflect conversations held in real life.[21] Or one could insist that the Deuteronomic style is strongly rhetorical and, as such, harks back to actual speeches delivered by priests for the instruction of the people. But, of course, a written text exhibiting oral features does not lose the status of a written text.

Still concerning the spoken mooring of the written text, one cannot escape stressing the obvious fact that speaking characters are quoted as to the very words they supposedly have uttered. These words may be entirely fictitious, or they may correspond in part to what has been really said, or finally they may be verbatim transcriptions. Whatever be the case, in principle they constitute oral intrusions in the flow of the written text.

Before we come to the main issue, the broad question has to be raised concerning the passage to the written medium—a passage probably as important as the passage through the Sea of Reeds. Why were oral compositions put into writing? How do we account for the first appearance of the Bible as a whole? These questions are of vital interest and belong in the present inquiry, except that, in considering the focus given above to our discussion of tradition and language, the special problems connected with writing as such must remain tangential. Short then of a direct treatment, let us mention the converging opinions of E. Nielsen and A. Paul on the subject. In Nielsen's words, "the change from oral to written literature does not take

---

20. ". . . oral formulaic language is traditional language" (Culley, *Oral Formulaic Language*, p. 116).
21. Cf. L. Koehler, *Hebrew Man* (London: SCM, 1956), p. 78.

place because cultural summits have been reached, nor because the ability to read and write has become common property, but because the culture itself is felt to be threatened. . . ."[22] Note the function assigned the written word, the function of a rampart against potential destruction. A. Paul suggests something similar when, in connection with the biblical phenomenon as a whole, he points out how the Jews of Alexandria, the Qumranites, and the Christians, all three groups more or less at the same time, reacted to the dangers threatening their existence through the transformation of their traditions into a Sacred Book, a Bible, that would enshrine until the last days their particular conception of history.[23]

Now to the main issue. We have, as well we thought we should, linked tradition with oral language and popular culture. How does such an approach fit the requirements of Old Testament study? Concerning the Bible, we are not in the position of A. B. Lord or J. Vansina, who had the opportunity of recording oral compositions still in the process of being transmitted. We are dealing with written documents, with literature. *How does one resurrect tradition on the basis of written evidence?* If the transition from oral to written language involves a qualitative jump, does not the reverse path involve a similar switch or break?

All of this means that there is a real discontinuity between the spoken and the written word, in spite of their close relationship, particularly in the case of phonetic languages like Hebrew and Greek. Such a gap or discontinuity serves well the traditio-historical method. It underscores, in fact, the usefulness of unearthing the oral stage of the Old Testament. On the other hand, it shows the limitations of the same method, since the possibility of reaching beyond the written text is bound to appear as debatable.

22. Nielsen, *Oral Tradition*, p. 60.
23. Cf. A. Paul, "Testament," in *Encyclopaedia Universalis* 15 (1974), 997.

It would seem, then, that to account for all the data without supposing that we can keep the cake while eating it as well, we should both attempt to restore as much of the oral stage as we can, but realistically also accept that this has to be achieved by way of the written stage. Since language in general is intimately connected with situations and since spoken language in particular refers to concrete situations, a search of this type will consist, for all practical purposes, in reestablishing the diverse and successive situations in the midst of which the texts have been produced.

From this point of view, strong similitudes will appear among the historico-critical, the form-critical, and the traditio-historical methods. The common element uniting them into a complex whole will be no less than the *situation*—social, economical, political, cultural, personal, and others—in which biblical language has to be set to be fully meaningful; in other words, the introductory questions as handled by historical criticism (author, time, place . . .), the *"Sitz im Leben"* of the *Formgeschichte*, or the setting required by oral transmission. Given all these strictures, the study of Old Testament tradition will amount to the description of the situations in which the biblical text has been successively read, recited, or simply uttered.

WRITTEN INFORMATION ABOUT SITUATIONAL CONTEXT IN THE OLD TESTAMENT

Where shall we get the relevant information concerning the situations of the biblical text? Since this text is written, the answer is bound to be: *in the text itself.* Over against oral language which can leave many elements of the situation unmentioned because they are self-evident to those who communicate—for example, who is speaking, when, where—written language must feed supplementary information; it must describe linguistically the situation which prevails in connection with a given text. For instance, the author of a letter will identify himself. To quote Malinowski again: ". . . written statements are set down with the purpose of being self-contained and self-explanatory."[24]

Of course, the literary description of the relevant situation can be more or less sketchy. In a sense, it will always be very sketchy. But as sketchy as it may be, and even supposing it is reduced to only one datum (for example, a name or a date), it provides an anchorage for other information to be attached and thus for a more detailed description to be drawn.

It is no less clear that the situation provided by the written text can be fictitious. Pseudonymity is a good case in point. The task of unmasking and unraveling false information belongs to the critical interpreter. And there is no reason not to claim that right in the field of biblical studies.

What is, then, the general picture offered us by the biblical text as to the situations it verbalizes? Five possibilities must be distinguished:

(1) Some texts bear a signature or quasi-signature, that is to say, the one who holds the pen introduces himself. See, for example, Ezek. 1:1–3; Sir. 50:27; 2 Macc. 2:19–32. The situation of writing is more or less fully described, but it is firsthand and unmistakable.

(2) Frequently, we are not provided with a self-presentation of the redactor. The redactor introduces a writer, but does not identify himself. The situation is consequently twofold. One of the two situations is described and thematized, but the other one is not, the one, namely, that surrounds the redactional activity as such. See, for example, Isa. 1:1; Jer. 1:1–3; Hos. 1:1; Joel 1:1; Amos 1:1; etc.; Prov. 1:1; 10:1; 22:17; Ps. 90:1; Cant. 1:1; Deut. 1:1; 5:1; 28:69 [29:1]; Neh. 1:1; Tob. 1:1–2.

(3) Often no presentation at all is found in the text. The one who writes does not identify himself, and he does not intro-

24. Malinowski, "The Problem of Meaning," p. 306.

duce anyone else. A voice is simply heard. We are assured that someone is speaking by the mere fact that speech indeed is taking place. This third possibility reminds one of the omniscient narrator who is generally heard in the classical novels. See, for instance, Job; Pss. 2; 33; 71; 91–100; Wis.; Gen.; Exod.; Lev.; Num.; Josh.; Judg.; Ruth; Sam.; Esth.; 1 Macc. In such cases, the situation underlying the text has to be deduced from the observation and analysis of relevant indications.

(4) It may also happen that the reader quotes a speaker or a document. See, for instance, 2 Sam. 1:17 (David mourns Saul and Jonathan); Judg. 5 (Deborah and Barak's song of victory); 1 Macc. 12:5, 19 (letters to and from Sparta). Yahweh is often quoted addressing a prophet or the people. Concerning Yahweh, it is logical to suppose that speeches attributed to him by the prophets and their listeners will have been transmitted orally in a fixed form, and eventually put down in writing in view of preserving them without blemish.[25] Be that as it may, the speeches introduced in this way by the redactor enjoy *ipso facto* a literary situation. The text tells the reader by whom, where, etc., they have been uttered.

(5) Lastly, it may happen that the redactor really quotes a speaker or a document, but does not warn the reader about it. The notion of "intertext" here comes to mind, as does also the formulaic style of bards reciting an epic poem. The permanent pride of literary criticism as applied to the Bible lies precisely in the magnificent results obtained in this area. The critical acumen of rational exegetes has exercised itself on the various suggestive inconsistencies of the Old Testament and has allowed them to imagine sources, traditions, documents, etc., about which the text says nothing explicitly, but which can be shown nonetheless to have been utilized by the redactor. Instances are innumerable. Let us mention Gen. 12 and 20; 2 Sam. 21:19 and 1 Sam. 17.

25. Cf. G. W. Ahlström, "Oral and Written Transmission: Some Considerations," *HThR* 59 (1966), 81.

These five classes of literary situations seem to offer a complete picture of what is to be found in this regard in the Old Testament. How should one go about tapping this huge reservoir of information?

It bears repeating, first of all, that we can either believe or disbelieve what the text says about its own production. That is to say, the literary situations can either be thought to reflect historical facts, or they can be assessed as being legendary, mythical, fictitious, or whatever. For instance, we may take as literal truth, and thus as pointers to a real situation, that Moses taught the people in the way he is shown doing in Deuteronomy, or that Yahweh addressed prophets exactly in the manner he is pictured addressing them in various parts of the Old Testament. We may conversely think that things must have happened differently, that Moses could not possibly have been so explicit concerning life in Palestine, or that Yahweh could not possibly have uttered the Hebrew speeches attributed to him. We must then undertake the task of reconstructing hypothetically the real situations within which Moses or Yahweh related to Israel. Such a reconstruction may require the multiplication of situations in order to account for the gradual formation of the biblical text.

Even if we believe the text, at least in part, we are still confronted with the task of filling the picture sketchily drawn, through resorting to all the available documentation, whether archaeological, social, psychological, ethnological, philological, or otherwise.

But we should not be deluded into thinking that past situations can ever be reconstructed in full. J. Derrida makes the point that context or situation cannot be saturated, especially when they are attached to written language.[26]

Of the situations so reestablished, some will be individual and

---

26. Cf. J. Derrida, "Signature, événement, contexte," in *La communication II*, Actes du XVème congrès de l'ASPLF (Montréal: Éditions Montmorency, 1971), pp. 72–73.

singular—for example, the literary activity of J according to G. von Rad, or the writing of Daniel's prophecy around the year 160 B.C. Others will be so to say recurrent, that is, typical or repeatable—for example, the periodical renewal of the covenant with Yahweh during which the creed was recited, or the temple ritual with the various formulas it included. The method called form criticism is tailored to this type of situations.

One facet of the situational problem is, of course, the use of oral language. If a close scrutiny of the text can lead to the conclusion that a longer or shorter part of the Old Testament has gone through a stage of oral transmission, important conjectures can at once be made as to the historical context or situation in which they have been carried. Without any further ado, it becomes possible to assert that such pieces have no assignable author, at least when the mode of transmission does not involve a fixed determination of the text. It can also be concluded that professional transmitters (a guild of prophets, for example) have been active. It seems that professionals are those who do the best job, not amateurs.[27] Another aspect of the situation that can be imagined has to do with the group or public to whom the text is delivered. We may imagine an active group, an audience that is both knowledgeable and interested. Without being deeply interested, the group would not take the pains of listening to sometimes long and protracted recitations. On the other hand, once it has repeatedly heard the same text, it eventually knows it rather well, well enough even to correct the professional singer whenever he would falter.

Undoubtedly, the more we will know in general about the modalities of oral transmission, the better equipped we will be

27. "If the tradition of psalm composition was like the other oral traditions that have been studied, the bearers of the tradition were probably 'professional' poets, well trained in their craft, whose function it was to compose psalms on behalf of people who desired a psalm to be offered" (Culley, *Oral Formulaic Language*, p. 113).

to picture for ourselves the situation in which the text of the Old Testament has been composed and handed down. The only added requirement consists in identifying the passages which would have undergone a spoken stage of transmission before having been put in writing.

It will appear, then, that orality is not the whole, not even the specific trait of tradition, although it belongs in it with an indisputable right. *Tradition is rather the complex network of situations that underlie the biblical text.*

The study of tradition is thus proclaimed to be of utmost necessity and importance. It is as necessary to biblical exegesis as extra-linguistic situations are necessary to language. In the same way that language (spoken or written) is normally and completely meaningful when related to real situations, similarly the biblical text needs to be reset in the historical context that produced it in order to attain true intelligibility.

The preceding comments have made clear that, to achieve that much, various methods have to be combined, especially historical criticism, the history of forms, and the history of traditions. All of these have something to contribute toward describing and defining the immensely varied situations within which the text of the Old Testament has been communicated.

It goes without saying that tradition and situation have a dimension that has not been touched upon in this brief discussion, namely, the *hermeneutical.* Old Testament tradition does not extend only until the final composition of the texts; it reaches beyond these as far as the New Testament and, beyond the New Testament, as far as our own time—in other words, as far as the situation of all Bible readers, past and future. This aspect has been voluntarily left aside for the sake of simplicity. More precisely, it has not been thematized, even though it was perforce operative—since what we said about Old Testament situations was indeed said within the contemporary situation in which we live.

CONCLUSION

Recapitulating briefly the ground covered until now, we started with the idea of tradition as related to culture and language. Tradition was then restricted to oral language and to cultures making a predominant use of this medium. Since spoken language operates in the context of live and concrete situations, tradition was therefore related to situations. Such situations as surround oral communication are not, however, attainable anymore so far as biblical texts are concerned, that is, they are not directly observable; yet they have not entirely faded out, but somehow survive in the written word of the Bible. It is well known, on the other hand, that written language can verbalize the situation or situations in which it belongs. The Old Testament is true to type on that score: it informs the reader about the circumstances that surrounded the production of such and such a text. Taking his cue from indications of this kind, the exegete is confronted with the task of defining the innumerable situations that underlie the Old Testament text. The chain of these situations constitutes Old Testament tradition, without the knowledge of which Old Testament language would be ultimately meaningless.

The gist of this circuitous discussion is then simply that Old Testament tradition, as indeed any tradition, anchors the text in real life and, in this way, provides it with the referents and situations without which it would make no real sense.[28]

Such an understanding of tradition has broad theological implications. Let us mention some of them, to round off the present study.

---

28. This view is shared by B. O. Long in an article which I read after the present study had been written. Note his summarizing statement: "They all [recent studies in oral literature] deepen the general picture drawn by Culley without changing it fundamentally. But with ever increasing sophistication, the recent studies emphasize the fact that social and cultural factors are among the most important things to be considered when studying oral tradition" ("Recent Field Studies in Oral Literature and Their Bearing on OT Criticism," *VT* 26 [1976], 187).

First is the question of biblical truth or inerrancy. If there is validity in our contention that Old Testament language conveys its meaning in close relationship with the historical situations within which it has been produced, it follows that the biblical text cannot enjoy indisputable meaningfulness and truth since the situations which it reflects are, at best, known very imperfectly—and often remain unknown and must become the object of educated guesses. Biblical truth is not questionable only on philological grounds, but also on account of our imperfect and limited knowledge of tradition. Hence, conversely, the necessity of the traditio-historical approach, or of whatever approach capable of reconstructing the relevant situations of the Old Testament text. These efforts, when successful, build up tradition; they heighten the degree of commonality that extends between our times and those of the Bible.

Secondly, biblical inspiration cannot be limited to scribes who held the pen at a particular moment and in a particular place, thereby to write the original texts of the Holy Scriptures. Such scribes never existed. For works which were orally transmitted, an original text is also a false conception. As long as these compositions exist freely, to be constantly renewed on the occasion of each performance, they have no normative form and they do not emanate from any particular author. Even written texts cannot claim their redactor as their author and integral cause, in view of the fact that texts are made possible thanks to the active influence of an intertextual setup. In brief, a Bible borne by tradition cannot be the fruit of individual inspiration. The inspiration that existed was shared by all those—and they were legion—who contributed something, even if only their intelligent listening, to the final written composition of the Old Testament.

Thirdly and finally, Yahweh, the God of the Old Testament, is historical in the sense that his word is uttered in the midst of

human situations, meaningful then and true in connection with
the concreteness of the said circumstances. He is consequently
a traditional God. Not a dead God, though. Except in the
sense that written texts are made to be read after the author's
death. Texts, says J. Derrida, are testaments.[29]

29. "*Tout graphème est d'essence testamentaire*" (Derrida, *De la grammatologie*, p. 100).

Chapter 7

Revelation through Tradition

Douglas A. Knight

The period since the Enlightenment has seen perhaps more changes to our understanding of revelation than to any other dogmatic concept or doctrine. This is surely true in the area of systematic theology, for in comparison with their medieval counterparts modern theologians have learned the nature and limits of discourse about God. This hardly means that revelation is no longer a topic of concern for theologians or laity; the discussion continues with full vigor, although the parties involved are more or less aware that they cannot speak facilely of divine disclosure as a self-evident, unproblematic phenomenon. Nonetheless, biblical scholars are often chagrined to see that the results of a century of biblical research are all too seldom brought seriously and directly into play by modern systematic theologians.[1] This need is as pressing with respect to the question of revelation as it is in other areas. If we no longer can speak of the whole Bible uniformly as the revealed word of God, to what extent is revelation still a meaningful concept to be used with reference to the literature in the Old and New Testaments, and how can such use accord with wider dogmatic discussions?

This question gains focus if we consider only traditio-historical work on the Old Testament. Since the early part of this century an ever-increasing number of investigators has as-

---

1. For discussion of this whole question of the relation between the biblical and theological disciplines, cf. D. H. Kelsey, *The Uses of Scripture in Recent Theology* (Philadelphia: Fortress, 1975).

sumed the presence in ancient Israel of a tradition process that yielded at its end the bulk of our present Hebrew Bible. Consensus on the exact extent and manner in which this occurred is, and probably always will be, elusive. But even the postulated process itself is of consequence for our understanding of revelation. Tradition, in all of its multiplicity, is *ex hypothesi* produced by the people, the community and its subgroups, engaged in the multiplicity of life. The process involves the people in an active rather than a passive way, for while the tradition preserves the memory of the past it is also subject to growth and change at the hands of new generations who face new situations that require a reconsideration of their heritage. To us the process may seem haphazard in that it is subject to the vagaries of history, yet what is striking is that the past constitutes the matrix for the people to deal with their present and their future. The actual form of each new stance may be unpredictable in advance, but in retrospect we can detect a certain constancy or cumulative intention at least in this manner of addressing the present needs.

Previous discussions in this book have dealt with constitutive situations of this Israelite tradition. There were impulses from the life and faith of the Israelites as also from their neighbors in the ancient Orient. There were historical incidents which the people understood to have a deeper meaning for them, and from generation to generation they continued to relate to these incidents and to probe their implications for them. There were spokesmen who saw the clear danger of relying on the past as a guarantor of the future, and they used these same traditions in a radically different way in order to jar the people back to the reality of their dependence, vulnerability, and obligations. There were centers of worship where often diverse traditions and theologies could converge and become submitted to the demands of religious practice.

In all of this it is possible, at one level, to explain this process of tradition growth solely in terms of human activity. In what respect is Yahweh, the subject of so much of this tradition, *directly* involved in this process? Where is revelation to be seen here? Confessionally, the question can be—and often is—given a simple answer: it is God who acts in the specific events of history, or who reveals himself indirectly in the cumulative course of Israel's history, or who speaks directly through his chosen spokesmen, or who guides the process whereby the tradition and the literature are developed. Actually, it is as easy to discount any of these answers as it is to give them; witness the scholarly debate on each point during recent years. The best example, to which we shall return later, is the question of God's revelation in history: quite aside from the fact that an affirmation about God's involvement in an historical event can in no way submit to scientific testing, it is commonly noted that such an act would be meaningless without interpretation; and if this interpretation itself emerged among the people over a shorter or longer period of time, in what sense can we still apply to this whole network of event and interpretation the concept of God's purposeful self-disclosure? This problem has been the object of much discussion, and it will not receive primary attention here. It is also not our aim in the present study to make a comprehensive analysis of revelation in the Old Testament. Rather, we will limit ourselves here to analyzing certain implications of traditio-historical research at the point of the interrelationship between tradition and revelation.[2] We might anticipate somewhat by stating that our results will be quite different from previous ones simply because, like most practitioners of this ana-

2. This restricted scope of the present study must not be forgotten. To be sure, we will be dealing also with matters which touch on the Old Testament view of revelation, and for this we are presupposing the numerous studies on this subject which have appeared in recent years. However, the primary questions which we are posing here emerge only indirectly from the Old Testament. They stem immediately from our common assumptions about and reconstructions of the Israelite tradition process, and thus also from the investigative method of modern tradition historians (and neither of these is by any means a uniform phenomenon!). There is only one other, very brief study that has dealt with part of this problem about the implications of a postulated tradition for the concept of revelation, and that is G. Gloege, *Offenbarung und Überlieferung: Ein dogmatischer Entwurf*, ThF 6 (Hamburg-Volksdorf: Reich, 1954).

lytical and historical method, we will be most attentive to the
human sphere where the tradition is formed and transmitted.
It remains to be seen whether at this level one should think
more in terms of human passive *reception* of revelation or
human active *participation* in the revelatory experience.

Some initial comments about the Old Testament understanding of revelation would be in order.   Recent investigations
have demonstrated that there is no technical terminology reserved for revelation in this literature.[3]   Verbal forms which
are used to refer to the frequent occasions when God manifests
himself, his will, or his power all occur in secular usage as well:
glh, "uncover, disclose"; *r'h*, "see" and "be seen"; niphal and
hiphil of *yd'*, "make oneself known," "make known"; hiphil of
ngd, "make known, tell."   In addition there is the expression
kĕbôd YHWH, "the glory of Yahweh," and the important
formula of divine self-presentation, *'ănî YHWH*, "I am Yahweh."[4]   Yet with the frequency with which these and similar
terms occur, it would surely be impossible to find a uniform
concept of revelation behind all of the occasions of divine involvement throughout the Old Testament.   Moreover, it is
methodologically incorrect for us to restrict Old Testament
revelation only to those passages where these terms are found.
This is all the more obvious if we consider the diverse modes by
which Yahweh works and can make his will known or through
which persons can recognize his presence and power: the sacred
lot, divination, dreams, natural occurrences and even nature
itself, the spoken or written word of his messengers, historical

3. Cf. especially H. Haag, " 'Offenbarung' in der hebräischen Bibel," *ThZ* 16
(1960), 251–58; R. Rendtorff, "Die Offenbarungsvorstellungen im Alten Israel," in
Offenbarung als Geschichte, ed. W. Pannenberg, 3d ed. (Göttingen: Vandenhoeck & Ruprecht, 1965), 21–41 = "The Concept of Revelation in Ancient Israel,"
in *Revelation as History*, ed. W. Pannenberg (New York: Macmillan, 1968), 23–
53; and R. Knierim, "Offenbarung im Alten Testament," in *Probleme biblischer
Theologie*, Festschrift G. von Rad, ed. H. W. Wolff (München: Chr. Kaiser,
1971), 206–35.   The reader is referred to these for detailed discussions on the
basis of numerous examples.
4. On the latter, cf. W. Zimmerli, "Ich bin Jahwe" (1953), *Gottes Offenbarung:
Gesammelte Aufsätze zum Alten Testament*, ThB 19 (München: Chr. Kaiser,
1963), 11–40.

acts, his name itself, his covenant, his promises, his faithfulness, his law, diverse cultic institutions, and others.[5] In light of such diversity it seems quite appropriate to argue[6] that in ancient Israel, as elsewhere in the ancient Near East (or even today in the Western world), revelation was not only a theological matter but also an ontological, epistemological, and cosmological one. What conditioned the people's ready tendency to recognize God's presence in so many phenomena was quite simply their fundamental view of reality and thus their capacity to apprehend it. This preconditioning is itself one facet of the tradition process, as we shall see below.

Quite correctly, James Barr[7] has discerned the basic reason why a clear concept of revelation was not developed in the Old Testament as it has been in modern theology: its function then was not like its function now. Whereas today the concept of revelation serves to oppose current denials of God's existence and also to distinguish divine knowledge from information gained through science, the ancient Israelites did not face such situations to any significant degree. There was virtually no disbelief in God or the gods, nor was there doubt that the deity would relate to the people.[8] There was no rationalism or positivistic historicism to present the problem of how one could know or say anything about God and divine matters. Revelation is not a leading, mandatory concept in the Old Testament in the same way as are, for example, the distinctive nature of

5. On several of these, cf. H. H. Rowley, *The Faith of Israel* (Philadelphia: Westminster, 1956), pp. 23–47; and various publications by H. W. Robinson, such as his *Redemption and Revelation in the Actuality of History* (New York and London: Harper & Brothers, 1942), pp. 95ff.

6. As Knierim has done, in *Probleme biblischer Theologie*, pp. 208ff.

7. J. Barr, *Old and New in Interpretation* (London: SCM, 1966), pp. 82ff., especially pp. 88–90; cf. also W. Joest, *Fundamentaltheologie*, ThW 11 (Stuttgart: Kohlhammer, 1974), p. 29.

8. The "only" problem which could face them was the absence, hiddenness, or inactivity of God—or stated from the other direction: the inability of humans to elicit response from God at will. This dilemma, which was shared with others in the ancient Near East, is a fundamental human problem with far-reaching theological consequences. Cf. K. H. Miskotte, *When the Gods Are Silent* (New York and Evanston: Harper & Row, 1967); L. Perlitt, "Die Verborgenheit Gottes," in *Probleme biblischer Theologie* (see note 3 above), 367–82; and on the resultant "crisis of revelation," also Knierim, in *Probleme biblischer Theologie*, pp. 230–35.

Yahweh, the meaning of "people," the understanding of covenant. It was not some doctrine of revelation but rather the import of the tradition that functioned in polemics and self-appraisal—to turn the people away from false gods and destructive ways and to help them recognize that the true God was in their midst. And this very process, like the historical situations themselves, was always in motion. Thus, rather than there being a static depositum which defined once and for all the entire terms of the true religion in Israel, "what matters is the question of what more will be added to that which is known; or, whether that which is known has already been falsified by the use and interpretation which men have made of it; or, in what ways and under what conditions this knowledge is to be spread abroad to those hitherto outside of the tradition; or, in what way elements within that which was known are now to be replaced or rejuvenated through new relations."[9]

This, then, thrusts us into a different situation. Instead of being guided primarily by our own philosophical and confessional preferences as we attempt to understand revelation in Israel, we should be more attuned to the Israelites' own structures. Two currently popular theological schemes based on distinct models of revelation—one virtually equating revelation with history and the other defining revelation strictly in Christocentric terms as the self-revelation of God—are notably inadequate to deal fairly with the entirety of the Old Testament literature.[10] If revelation was not a topic of conscious concern for the Isrealites, we can hope to do them justice only if our approach is oriented toward that with which they were directly engaged: the immediate situation with its human and divine claims. There is a distinct traditio-historical dimension to this because of the role played by tradition in this situation—that is,

9. Barr, *Old and New in Interpretation*, pp. 89–90.
10. The former is the program of W. Pannenberg and R. Rendtorff, although there are similarities here also with the "Albright School" of American scholars. The latter is most prominently represented by K. Barth. The extensive literature presenting and criticizing these approaches need not be listed here.

because the people were remembering, actualizing, reinterpreting, reversing, replenishing their heritage from the past. Inasmuch as this tradition is both the witness to revelation and also the scene for further revelation, this process may present us with implications that have not been sufficiently considered by biblical theologians or dogmaticians. For we are approaching revelation along lines of human activity, and not solely in terms of divine initiative. However, a word of caution is in order now, and it will deserve to be emphasized again later: Just as historical sciences are totally inadequate to verify revelation simply by describing the entirety of reality or the specific historical events in which God purportedly worked (this as a deserving criticism of the "revelation as history" idea), in like manner traditio-historical research should not presume that it can pinpoint revelation simply by decribing the tradition process. Revelation can be equated no more with tradition than it can be with history. As directly as the Israelites spoke of God and experienced his presence in their midst, the factor of his ultimate mysteriousness and his resistance to manipulation was never lost to them for long.

TRADITION AS WITNESS TO REVELATION

Since the Old Testament (as also the New Testament) ceased to be identified in its entirety as the revelation of God, it has become customary in many circles to consider this literature as a *testimony* to divine revelation. This represents a perceptible shift in the understanding of the nature of the traditions that yielded the scripture: the words preserved here do not point immediately and absolutely to God, as if he revealed himself directly in them and remains in some manner incorporated in them. Rather, God is a step removed "behind" the scripture, and the traditions throughout their development and in their final canonical form serve an important function for faith by testifying to his presence and revelation in the past experiences of the people. Thus by "testimony" it is meant that those

verbal accounts which speak of the experienced presence or
nature of God intend thereby to constitute a record of (what is
perceived to be) God's revelation and its meaning for the
people. So understood, these testimonies can be as religiously
significant for us as they were for the Israelites—to the extent
that we can identify existentially and perhaps historico-
genetically with that ancient people.

Closer analysis shows that this phrase, "testimony to divine
revelation," has been used in two distinctly different ways. On
the one hand, the emphasis falls on the first element, the process of testimony among the people. The classical traditio-
historical work by Martin Noth and Gerhard von Rad and also
much of the work that followed in their wake[11] seem to be
oriented toward the growing tradition and the development of
Israel's consciousness of being the people of God. Whatever
might have stood at the origin of each tradition—and historically it might be quite minimal in comparison with the later
description of it—primary attention is directed to the description itself, that is, its development and function among the
people. Accordingly, stress is laid on the kerygmatic objective
or intention of texts, the ongoing need to address given cultural
and historical challenges.[12] On the other hand and often in
direct opposition to this, for others the emphasis falls on the
second element, the revelation to which the tradition testifies.
Interested especially in recovering the historical events in which
Yahweh acted, such scholars as W. F. Albright and G. E.
Wright, and from a different angle also F. Hesse and S. Herrmann, find traditio-historical work of value insofar as it does not
detract seriously from the original act of revelation.[13] Some-

11. Cf. the discussion of relevant literature in D. A. Knight, *Rediscovering the Traditions of Israel*, rev. ed., SBLDS 9 (Missoula: Society of Biblical Literature, 1975), 71ff.
12. Cf., e.g., the various studies gathered together in W. Brueggemann and H. W. Wolff, *The Vitality of Old Testament Traditions* (Atlanta: John Knox, 1975).
13. Cf. Knight, *Rediscovering the Traditions of Israel*, pp. 131–32, 194–221. A sound, if not devastating, criticism of the Albright and Wright approach can now be found in T. L. Thompson, *The Historicity of the Patriarchal Narratives*, BZAW 133 (Berlin: de Gruyter, 1974).

what schematically, we may say that in the former instance tradition (testimony) is understood as an interpreting, actualizing process, whereas for the latter it is considered as a process of remembering and preserving the revelatory essentials.

Surprisingly, this touches on a basic difference in the understanding not only of the traditio-historical method but also of revelation itself. To what does tradition witness, and how important is it that we recover this initial point, the primal divine datum at the onset of a given tradition? Indeed, need there be such a revelatory origin for each or any tradition? The best approach to this problem may be to ask about the *content* of revelation in the Old Testament. Clearly, we do not find here a definitive, total, ontological disclosure of Yahweh's essence or being, nor is he ever experienced directly and fully. Instead, it seems as though the content that is revealed is Yahweh's *will*.[14] This cannot be found in its entirety at one single place but is given usually in limited, situation-bound form, with the overriding will emerging (at best) from the full series. The concrete forms taken by this divine will are act (ordering, delivering, punishing) and word (usually referring to an act, either antecedently as promise or warning or subsequently as interpretation). There is good reason for us to consider the divine name itself, Yahweh, as the quintessence of this revelation in the sense that it is disclosed that the God who is here involved is Yahweh and not some other deity.[15] In the usual Hebraic sense, the name is not a mere label but signifies the full reality of the one bearing that name. Yet at the same time this name of Yahweh cannot be reduced to a tangible, exploitable object with exhaustive content. With Zimmerli, we should recognize

---

14. Cf. G. von Rad, *Theologie des Alten Testaments*, 5th ed., vols. 1 and 2 (München: Chr. Kaiser, 1966 and 1968), passim = *Old Testament Theoolgy*, vols. 1 and 2 (New York and Evanston: Harper & Row, 1962 and 1965), passim.
15. For more discussion and literature on this, cf. W. Zimmerli, *Grundriss der alttestamentlichen Theologie*, ThW 3 (Stuttgart: Kohlhammer, 1972), 12–15; H.-J. Kraus, *Reich Gottes: Reich der Freiheit* (Neukirchen-Vluyn: Neukirchener Verlag, 1975), pp. 101ff.; Knierim, in *Probleme biblischer Theologie*, pp. 216ff.; and somewhat critically, R. Rendtorff, "Geschichte und Wort im Alten Testament" (1962), in *Gesammelte Studien zum Alten Testament*, ThB 57 (München: Chr. Kaiser, 1975), especially pp. 66–68.

Exod. 3:14 not as an absolute definition of Yahweh but as an underscoring of his identity and a statement of his freedom to act as he chooses in order to cause people to recognize his presence and power.

Thus the content of the revelation must be something complex and probably nonpropositional in character. The fact that it is usually anchored or at least perceived in some specific historical situation leads us to the important question of its *purpose*, and this is something which is implied already in the concept of Yahweh's *will*. Gloege[16] considers revelation historical in three senses: (a) the revelation has the character of *personal event* in which God with his will approaches humanity; (b) it confronts persons with the necessity of making a *decision*; and (c) it happens on *the plane of real history* and can affect institutions and ordinances of the community. Thus understood, this "structure" of revelation in the Old Testament has both a personal (a and b) and a concrete (c) side. By not restricting revelation to a simple unilateral act of God, Gloege has perceived the essential character of the Old Testament phenomenon: the purpose of revelation necessitates that the "recipients" play an important role.[17] And this is also a process: the implications of revelation need to be drawn out, and new generations can be confronted with a decision so long as the tradition is present to witness to the past and, through interpretation, to put the demands before the people anew.

In light of this, it appears that the question of an absolute, primal revelatory datum in the ideal sense of something to which later tradition "simply" witnesses (= recollects, remembers, preserves in memory) yields a contorted picture of Old

16. Gloege, *Offenbarung und Überlieferung*, pp. 23–25. It should be noted, however, that the Old Testament understanding of God's revelation in all of creation would have to be strained considerably to fit Gloege's pattern.

17. In the second section below, we will argue that Gloege has not carried this principle far enough—at least not if we consider the implications of traditiohistorical work. Cf. also W. McKane, "Tradition as a Theological Concept," in *God, Secularization, and History: Essays in Memory of Ronald Gregor Smith*, ed. E. T. Long (Columbia: University of South Carolina Press, 1974), pp. 44–59.

Testament revelation. To state it schematically again, a given act of revelation is not a punctiliar event limited to the original historical situation in which it occurred, but ideally it is a durative confrontation—sometimes with, but often without an identifiable, retrievable origin. Yahweh did not act in the exodus only for the benefit of that generation, and the Israelites were constantly enjoined not to forget those benefits and claims on them (Exod. 12:26–27; 13:14–16; Deut. 6:20–25; Ps. 78:1–8). As long as the tradition remained a vibrant, growing witness, the revelation continued and Yahweh's will and identity would be known.

Examples from several levels may elucidate this testimonial character of tradition and thus also the inadequacy of the concept of a primal revelatory depositum.

The first has to do with the Decalogue, considered by many (especially outside of the Old Testament discipline) as the prime example of God's revelation to Israel. What has traditiohistorical (and form-critical) work uncovered here? For one thing, the Decalogue's relation to the Sinai tradition and thus to the whole exodus/Sinai/wilderness/conquest complex is questionable, at least on the basis of internal, literary criteria. However we choose to understand the Sinai tradition and the revelation there, the pericope with these ten commandments stands out as an obvious insertion into the narrative. Analyses of the Decalogue itself have thrown serious doubt on its antiquity in its present form.[18] Although we need not think in terms of a form-critically uniform "primitive Decalogue," most of the commandments experienced an intricate history in which elements were added and deleted in different periods. Most have close parallels in other ancient Near Eastern collections. Even their apodictic form is not unique to the Israelite cult, for the latter six commandments clearly spring from a common

---

18. Cf. the literature discussed in Knight, *Rediscovering the Traditions of Israel*, pp. 357–66; also W. H. Schmidt, "Überlieferungsgeschichtliche Erwägungen zur Komposition des Dekalogs," VTS 22 (1972), 201–20.

clan-ethos. We can find shorter and longer lists other than this, and we must conclude that this collection of ten is itself a result of a long process of selection. The primary distinctive characteristics of the Israelite Decalogue thus appear to be: the religious motivation expressed in the opening commandments, and the concise, trim nature of this short compilation of central prohibitions, suitable in this form for recital in the cult. What do all these analytical results suggest about any revelatory depositum, a primary datum given at some point by God and remembered in the tradition? To say that "Israel was placed under the exclusive claim of the divine Lord of the Covenant" or that "the Decalogue was the charter of freedom which Yahweh had presented to his people delivered from Egypt," flies in the face of these analytical results—unless we understand these statements as referring to a long process in which the revelation became realized.[19] Externally, the text witnesses to a divine revelation and the unilateral bestowal of law. Traditio-historically, the text betrays a long developmental process with uncertain and not necessarily revelatory origins (at least not in the sense described in the text), and it testifies not to a single datum in antiquity but to the people's ongoing sense of urgency to face the religious and ethical obligations resulting from their covenant with Yahweh.

The problem of how tradition relates to revelation becomes especially obvious when we consider the self-manifestations of God, the theophanies. Since from all signs the texts in these cases intend to describe—be it in ever so poetic language—acts of divine self-revelation, we need to survey the nature of these traditions in somewhat more detail. Yahweh, either himself or through his angel (*mal'āk*), appears to the patriarchs, to Moses, to leaders, to his prophets, or in the form of his glory (*kābôd*)

19. The statements are from J. J. Stamm and M. E. Andrew, *The Ten Commandments in Recent Research*, SBT 2/2 (London: SCM, 1967), 113–14. That they perhaps also are thinking of testimony in this interpretive sense seems clear in their final sentence (p. 114): the Decalogue's "significance was, above all, in the position which, from the earliest times on, it came to occupy in the life of ancient Israel."

to those present in the cult. There can be little doubt about
the central importance of theophanies in the Israelite faith
(probably more so in the earlier period when they found more
frequent entry into the literature), as numerous recent studies
have demonstrated.[20] Again here the described phenomena
themselves are not open to verification,[21] but we can ascertain
through literary analysis some of their effect upon the recipients. Thus rather than asking how God actually revealed himself in these cases (as if these were objective phenomena capable
of empirical demonstration), we are better advised to frame the
questions in this way: how did the Israelites perceive and describe God's direct presence among them, and what are the
dynamics through which these perceptions emerged and were
incorporated in human tradition? With an eye to such factors
figuring into the tradition process, considerable analysis of these
testimonies to divine appearances is possible: (a) Certain
formal constancies can be discovered, at least in imagery and
perhaps also in genre. Jeremias finds a genre with two main
elements in it: Yahweh's coming and the accompanying tumult
of nature. While the latter element seems to have been taken
from Israel's neighbors, Jeremias considers (though mistak-
enly[22]) the former to be distinctly Israelite in origin, under the
influence of the Sinai tradition though without a direct literary
impress from it. The *"Sitz im Leben"* of this genre was originally the victory songs of the premonarchical period; the proto-

20. For discussions of texts and references to further literature, cf. especially
J. Jeremias, *Theophanie: Die Geschichte einer alttestamentlichen Gattung*,
WMANT 10 (Neukirchen-Vluyn: Neukirchener Verlag, 1965); J. K. Kuntz, *The
Self-Revelation of God* (Philadelphia: Westminster, 1967); and F. M. Cross,
Canaanite Myth and Hebrew Epic (Cambridge: Harvard University Press, 1973).

21. Indeed, it seems safe to say that most scholars today would not be willing to
affirm that God appeared and acted exactly in the forms described in these
theophanic texts. These descriptions can be studied at face-value in terms of
form, motifs, function, and their history, but in all such analysis historical
criticism is operating, at best, at the third level of symbolism (Ricoeur's
gnosis) in trying to express differently the experiences stated at the primary or
secondary symbolic levels by the ancient Israelites. (These categories are adapted
from the suggestive structure of Paul Ricoeur; cf. especially his *The Symbolism
of Evil* [Boston: Beacon, 1969].)

22. Cf. F. Schnutenhaus, "Das Kommen und Erscheinen Gottes im Alten Testament," *ZAW* 76 (1964), 1–21.

type is found in Judg. 5:4–5.[23]   Even after this genre was
removed from this cultic matrix, it continued for centuries to
have an effect on theophanic descriptions in Israel—in psalms
and hymns, in prophetic utterances, in narratives, and in apocalyptic visions.   (b) Certain affinities with *extra-Israelite theophanic descriptions* can also be determined, for it was not only
in Israel that a deity sought contact with humans, that is, that
humans felt contacted by a god.   Besides the above-mentioned
divine approach and the tumult of nature, there are numerous
other motifs that Israel shared with her neighbors, for example,
storm and thunder, images of warfare, chaos, fire, royal images.
Thus in the wider sphere as also in Israel there was a definite
interest in such divine manifestations, and much of the imagery
employed was not of Israel's own making.   (c) Besides the form
and motifs, certain *theological beliefs* seem to guide these theophanic descriptions in the Old Testament.   Among these are: it
is Yahweh who initiates the theophany (although persons can
cultically appeal for a revelation); Yahweh's self-manifestation
is always only partial and allusive; it is so tremendous that it
induces fear and dread in the recipient or observer;[24] divine
disclosures are not arbitrary or capricious, but for specific purposes and usually to special persons; theophanic holiness is
frequently juxtaposed with human sin and atonement; the use
of anthropomorphisms in the theophanies is deemed appropriate because of the Israelite belief in Yahweh as a personal and
living God, not because they conceived of him as having essentially a human form;[25] throughout Israel's history it is not an
unknown god who discloses himself, who comes as if from a

23. Somewhat differently, Cross (*Canaanite Myth and Hebrew Epic*, especially pp. 147ff.) finds two theophanic genres in Canaanite and early Hebrew poetry: the march of the Divine Warrior to battle, and the return of the Divine Warrior to assume kingship.   The mythic pattern behind them was replaced in early Israel by an epic pattern, and the battles fought by Yahweh the Divine Warrior were particularized temporally and spatially as the battles of the exodus and the conquest.   Cross associates the revelation at Sinai with the second genre.
24. These first three matters are discussed in Kuntz, *The Self-Revelation of God*, pp. 28–45.
25. Cf. J. Barr, "Theophany and Anthropomorphism in the Old Testament," VTS 7 (1960), 31–38; and Barr, *Old and New in Interpretation*, p. 22.

distance and without a distinct identity, but rather it is the same Yahweh who has been known and worshiped in Israel since early times. (d) The immediate and lasting *effect* of the theophany can be traced—whether on clans,[26] tribes, leaders, prophets,[27] those in the cult,[28] or whomever. Also the recognition-formula, "that you may know that I am Yahweh," can figure into this.[29] In sum, what do these theophanies contribute to our understanding of Old Testament revelation? Indeed they are generally presented as unilateral divine acts, and yet there is a distinctly human dimension to their expression in tradition. Biblical scholarship has focused as much on the latter dynamic as on the former, and quite appropriately so because of the important role played here by the people's ontological pre-understandings (*Vorverständnis*) and because of the function and history of the traditions themselves. From this we must conclude that the theophanic descriptions are not objective or reportorial accounts but testimonies to what the people perceived or experienced as divine encounters. While it may be inevitable that we say this because of our historicism and rationalism, we must also be clear that we are thereby perhaps departing from the form and spirit of the literature itself.[30]

26. Note especially the considerable discussion on this subject since A. Alt's pioneering thesis about the cult-founding revelations to the various patriarchs; "Der Gott der Väter" (1929) = "The God of the Fathers," in *Essays on Old Testament History and Religion* (Oxford: Blackwell, 1966), 1–77.

27. Perhaps the best example is Jeremiah who, without doubting that he had been called or that Yahweh continued to put his word in him, nevertheless struggled mightily with the consequences which this had for him. Cf. also discussions in I. P. Seierstad, *Die Offenbarungserlebnisse der Propheten Amos, Jesaja und Jeremia*, 2d ed. (Oslo: Universitetsforlaget, 1965).

28. Here the priestly *kābôd* concept is important, as also the priestly oracle. This whole subject about divine manifestations in the cult is vital for understanding the Israelites' concept of revelation, but it will not be treated further here. Cf. instead, e.g., the recent articles (with references to further literature) on *kābôd* (glory) and *pānim* (face) in *Theologisches Handwörterbuch zum Alten Testament*, ed. E. Jenni and C. Westermann, vols. 1 and 2 (München: Chr. Kaiser; Zürich: Theologischer Verlag, 1971 and 1976), s.v.

29. W. Zimmerli, "Erkenntnis Gottes nach dem Buche Ezechiel" (1954), in his *Gottes Offenbarung*, 41–119; and "Das Wort des göttlichen Selbsterweises (Erweiswort), eine prophetische Gattung" (1957), in ibid., 120–32.

30. That a certain skepticism among the Israelites themselves about specific instances of divine appearances and revelations was also possible can be seen most clearly in the problem of false prophecy. Cf. the instructive discussion by J. L. Crenshaw, *Prophetic Conflict*, BZAW 124 (Berlin: de Gruyter, 1971).

Yet on the other hand this testimonial characterization seems to accord well with the way theophanies function in the Old Testament itself—in confessionals, in praises and in acts of legit-imation (e.g., of a cultic place).

But revelation for the Israelites was much more extensive and fundamental than only this, and the Old Testament literature describes God's involvement in human affairs also in other ways than just what can be form-critically classified as theophanies. Such literary types as myths, legends, folktales,[31] historical narra-tives, parenesis, even psalms and instructions often intend to incorporate, either directly or indirectly, something of divine revelation.

A good example is the myth. Paul Ricoeur has done biblical scholarship a great service with his phenomenological analysis of the symbolic nature of myth, his case in point being the myths about the origin and nature of evil.[32] Stated briefly, his thesis is that myth is a symbol developed in narrative form, and as such it constitutes the secondary level after the primary at-tempt to express the experienced human phenomenon with elementary verbal symbols. Thus myth is disclosure (may we add "testified"?) in that it explicates, directly but not "ration-ally," the connection between the human and what is con-sidered divine. In its three functions of expressing concrete universality, temporal direction, and ontological exploration, myth has its own mode of revelation which resists facile transfer to another clear language by means of allegorical interpreta-tion. Yet for us who live and think in an age when myth and history are no longer bound together, it is finally possible through "demythologization" (not "demythization") to under-stand myth as myth, that is, to comprehend its symbolic nature and its disclosing power as a stage beyond the primal symbols. Thus, discovering the experiential sphere which the myth ex-

31. For an intriguing example of the testimonial potential of folktales, cf. E. Hal-ler, "Märchen und Zeugnis: Auslegung der Erzählung 2 Könige 4,1–7," in *Prob-leme biblischer Theologie* (see note 3 above), pp. 108–15.
32. Ricoeur, *The Symbolism of Evil*; cf. also discussions in *Die Eröffnung des Zugangs zum Mythos*, ed. K. Kerényi, WF 20 (Darmstadt: Wissenschaftliche Buchgesellschaft, 1967).

poses can constitute for us an existential verification of the testified experience and thereby bring us to the third level of
symbolism, that of *gnosis*, of speculation and recognition in
categories of understanding devoid of the etiological element in
myth. Ricoeur's analysis of the biblical "Adamic myth," under
this phenomenological perspective, yields unexpected insights.
While his approach is not clearly exegetical, it depends heavily
on the results of form-critical and traditio-historical scholarship
since Gunkel. Had biblical exegetes not stressed and traced the
communal, vital matrix from which the myths emerged, it can
be doubted that his thesis about the symbolic function and testimonial nature of myth among the people could have been
applied as effectively to the Israelite situation. Yet at the same
time, by demonstrating our access to the disclosing power of
myth, he has legitimated the modern effort to grasp ancient
phenomena (such as tradition) through framing our questions
at a level other than those of the ancients.

It is not only myth that can give witness to an experienced
disclosure of God or to the divinely ordered essence of life.
Other set forms also intend this, although they are not necessarily symbols in the same sense as are myths. Even psalms and
wisdom literature, which von Rad considers as Israel's answer to
Yahweh's revelation in history, nature, and individual lives,[33]
are thus based on the people's belief in God's presence. We do
not usually find revelation here in the direct sense of Yahweh's
self-manifestation as we see in the theophanies, although theophanic imagery occurs at numerous places throughout. The
psalms presuppose prior revelation and thus give witness to it
indirectly, through praises and thanksgivings for past divine involvement, appeals for new intercession, ruminations on the
divinely ordered nature of things.[34] Something similar could

33. Von Rad, *Theologie des Alten Testaments*, vol. 1, pp. 366ff. = *Old Testament Theology*, vol. 1, pp. 355ff.
34. Von Rad, *Theologie des Alten Testaments*, vol. 1, p. 376 = *Old Testament
Theology*, vol. 1, p. 364: "Israel's artistic *charisma* lay in the realm of narrative
and poetry. . . . In the art of making Jahweh and the splendour of his mani-
festation and his working visible in poetry, Israel was more daring than any
other people."

be said for much of wisdom literature, although there is a different thrust to the type of testimony appearing here.[35] Even in a broader sense it may be appropriate for us (although the Israelites may not have seen it like this[36]) to regard the majority of the whole Old Testament as Israel's response to Yahweh, for it was in the development of its tradition that Israel sought to state its beliefs and work out the implications that revelation had for it.

There is one final area that needs our attention—the complex of history, tradition, and revelation.[37] There can be no doubt today that Israel believed that Yahweh acted in its history and that it confessed this in its literature. However, this simple statement can raise numerous questions, and these have stimulated much debate in recent years. How did the Israelites come to this belief—both generally (that Yahweh is a god who acts in history) and specifically (that his presence or intervention is to be seen especially in one event or another)? Was there any development to this belief, such that an interpretation of history in general or of certain individual events in specific emerged in the course of time, rather than that this interpretation accompanied the events themselves and was preserved thereafter? In our own theological and historical work are we to distinguish carefully between Israel's confessional picture of history and the historico-critical reconstruction of what "really happened"—and not be bothered greatly by any discrepancy between these two? Where might revelation be found here—only in the interpretation, only in the events themselves, or indirectly in some careful correlation between the two (thus in history in a broad sense)? What is the relationship between word and deed? Can we determine whether it was the historical

---

35. See below, Chapter 10 by J. L. Crenshaw.

36. Chr. Barth ("Die Antwort Israels," in *Probleme biblischer Theologie* [see note 3 above], pp. 44–56) has, through semantic and exegetical analysis, sought to restrict the applicability of this term, "Israel's answer," to the Deuteronomic demand for decision. This has good biblical justification yet diminishes the equally valid thrust of von Rad's observations.

37. For more discussion and numerous literature references, cf. Knight, *Rediscovering the Traditions of Israel*, pp. 127–36.

act *or* the interpretative testimony that was more constitutive of Israel? These questions will not occupy our attention at this point, although we will take up some of them later.[38] Here it is sufficient merely to note that much of the Old Testament literature testifies to Yahweh's direct engagement in Israel's history—in calling and guiding the patriarchs, in leading the oppressed people out of Egypt, in guiding them through the wilderness, in giving them the law, in conquering the land, in coming to Zion and founding the Davidic dynasty, in working through other powers to bring doom to Israel and Judah, in releasing them from exile and giving them the land a second time. While modern scholars may question whether such "historical" acts can be classified as revelation in the sense of divine self-disclosure, the Israelites themselves were not concerned with fitting these deeds into some scheme of revelation as we are often inclined to do. For them God's engagement was self-evident (for "all flesh" to recognize, Ezek. 21:10 [21:5]; Isa. 49:26), and they could perceive in it Yahweh's will for his chosen people.

To conclude this section we need to look again at what we mean when we say that tradition is a witness to revelation and why this concept is important. Examples of different order have been given above, and our argument can be restated and expanded in the following summarizing points:

(1) The Old Testament describes many occasions of revelation (both as word and event), but traditio-historical work has taught us the intense difficulty of recovering those occasions. Thus only in an ideal sense can we speak of revelatory *deposita* at the base of the traditions, for the traditions themselves often experienced such a long and intensive development that precise reconstruction of their origins eludes us in most cases—and in some cases may even be drastically different from the present description in the Old Testament. Thus one service rendered by tradition history is to replace our fascination for absolute

38. Cf. also the discussion by R. Smend, above, Chapter 3.

origins with a need to understand the ensuing process of reflection and existential struggle.

(2) Statements about revelation—both those by the ancient Israelites as well as those by us—are essentially confessional in nature. Consequently, even when (or if) we can recover the revelatory occasion (e.g., the exodus, the prophet's call), the divine dimension is not subject to historico-critical verification —or to disproval. We need to remain clear about this, even though such a consideration would have been foreign to the Israelites. For after all, as we have noted above, revelation did not function as a doctrine for the Israelites in the same way that it does for us since the Enlightenment.

(3) The striking feature about Israelite tradition is its power of growth. With good reason this power can often be attributed to what happened at the origin of a given tradition, the perhaps revelatory experience which it may describe. This, however, is not to discount later formative impulses (with which we will deal in the next section). It is rather to ask why a testimonial, a tradition, arose in the first place and what gave it its tenacity.

(4) Our access to Old Testament revelation is through the tradition and the tradition process. In light of the above points, our research should focus on this tradition—the formation and function of this testimony. Thereby we are not denying the existence of a history of revelation but are recognizing that our immediate task is to understand the history of the *testimonies* to that revelation. This is especially important because it was in the tradition process that the community was engaged in, among other things, the task of identifying revelation. To describe the dynamics through which this occurred and through which that experienced as revelation was incorporated and retained by tradition, we need to deal with categories of history, society, religion, the demands of life, kerygma, existential choice, and the human relation to what is considered revelation.

(5) A further question concerns the potential and the limi-

tations of tradition to pass on to later generations the revelatory content experienced in previous times. On the one hand, tradition can lend itself to actualization, to formation of solidarity with the past, to apologetics, to confrontation and accusation, to promotion of new efforts to face present and future needs. Yet on the other hand, tradition can be a place of refuge and comfortable security, can be an excuse for institutional conservatism and personal callousness, can stifle rather than promote life.

(6) When the problem is formulated in this way, we are thrust finally upon the ultimate question not of *what* God reveals (whether himself, or truth, or insight, or moral priorities, or whatever), nor of *how* he reveals (whether through word, or action, or all of history)—but of *why* he reveals. In light of the diverse, unconscious witness of the Old Testament to the former two questions, a clear answer to these seems elusive, and there will be differences of opinion among scholars as long as these problems are addressed as if they are of primary importance. But the Old Testament shows more clarity on the third matter, the purpose of God's acts of salvation, of his words of promise and warning, of his acts of punishment, of his disclosure of his identity. These occur so that the people might recognize Yahweh's lordship, and thereby also human responsibility to him and to fellow humans. The phenomenon of tradition is all-important here because in it the claims are developed and placed before each new generation. By means of vibrant tradition and responsible reinterpretation of it the purpose of divine revelation can be fulfilled.

(7) Through our own engagement with the Old Testament tradition it is possible for the purpose of that revelation to which it witnesses to find fulfillment for us as well. This however does not mean that this engagement need take the form of uncritical, pious acceptance of the prima facie affirmations found in the Old Testament. On the contrary. Just as the vitality of the Israelite tradition depended on its promoters' remaining responsive to the changing situations of life and just as that process consequently saw the unceasing emergence of

new ideas, implications, and applications of past insights, so also today our task is to interpret the ancient traditions in light of the historical criticism and the existential needs of our age. The above discussion on the modern approach to myth provides one example of this critical, yet creative analysis that can bring to consciousness truths which for millennia have resisted explicit expression. The task of exegetical interpretation and also of biblical theology is not to restate the meaning of the Old Testament texts in ways which would be appropriate and meaningful to the ancient Israelites—but to us. As did the Israelites, we can find that the greatest service rendered by tradition is not its retention of answers to old questions—but its inadequacy to provide us with simple solutions to our own new problems. Precisely this challenge, coming at the nexus where the past and the future meet the present, is the locus of revelation.

TRADITION AS LOCUS OF REVELATION

The above section has, without intending to probe all aspects of the phenomenon of revelation in the Old Testament, sought to determine certain implications of traditio-historical research for our understanding of that revelation. In essence, it has drawn attention away from the revelation itself and has directed it instead to the history and the (often testimonial) nature of the traditions. This same shift, we might note, appears to be effected—perhaps unintentionally—by most traditio-historical investigations themselves. In the present section we will want to refine the above discussion on the relationship between tradition and revelation, especially at two points: the potential of tradition to promote *and* to hinder revelation.

In identifying tradition as a "locus" of revelation we are purposely avoiding the terms "mode" and "depositum." The latter would suggest that revelation is a static quantum which can be reduced to words, contained in tradition, and then apprehended by others (either then or now) who become familiar with these traditions. The Old Testament would stand in direct opposition to such a notion, for Yahweh is not bound by what people tell about him but is ever free to break common expectations and to appear in new and radical ways. Similarly, tradition cannot be considered a "mode" of revelation in the strict, direct sense of the "how" of revelation, that is, a form which Yahweh can use to channel the new communication of his will to the people (as with visions, angels, the sacred lot, the oracle). Both of these notions run aground on the essentially backward orientation of the *traditum*, the transmitted material with its testimonial character. The term "locus" is more appropriate because the tradition, both in *traditum* and *traditio*, constitutes the context of revelation. It does this in two respects: it provides the categories for apprehending and understanding revelation, and it is the springboard for new revelatory occasions.

In the first instance, *tradition constitutes the pre-understanding (Vorverständnis) and precondition for revelation*, and this is the case not simply because it precurses temporally a given revelatory occasion. Tradition delivers the framework—intellectual, historical, religious, hermeneutical—needed for a new event or word to be meaningful. It incorporates ethos and ontological structures, thus the predilections, priorities, pre-understandings, and linguistic patterns of a whole people or a subgroup within it (the latter of which usually will have a clear profile distinct from other groups—e.g., Rechabites, Levites, and priests in Israel).[39] This fundamental role of tradition in providing for each generation both the categories of understanding and the ground for personal meaning is underscored by modern philosophy.[40] It can easily be seen to be the case in the Israelite situation, especially with respect to how the presence of tradition bolstered the people's apprehension of revelation.

---

39. Cf. also the discussion by O. H. Steck, below, Chapter 8.
40. Cf., e.g., H.-G. Gadamer, *Wahrheit und Methode: Grundzüge einer philosophischen Hermeneutik*, 2d ed. (Tübingen: Mohr, 1965), especially pp. 250ff.; A. Schutz, *The Phenomenology of the Social World* (Evanston: Northwestern University Press, 1967); and Schutz and T. Luckmann, *The Structures of the Life-World* (Evanston: Northwestern University Press, 1973).

On the plane of historical events, for example, the exodus would have been a simple case of slaves' making a fortuitous escape—if there had been no belief in a god who intervenes benevolently in human affairs; the settlement of the land would have appeared as a not uncommon shift of semi-nomads to sedentary life—if there had been no notion of a god who promises land to the tribes; David's establishment of Jerusalem as the capital of his empire would have been merely a political and strategic choice—if the city had known no cult tradition which could combine effectively with its new political significance and other elements to form a powerful image of Zion as the dwelling place of Yahweh; the prophets' message would at many points have been incomprehensible—if the people had not recognized the allusions to past events and the often radical reinterpretation of them; the fall of Jerusalem and the deportation of the people would have had the finality of innumerable other such events in the history of the world—if the exiles had not recognized that it was the deserved punishment about which the prophets had spoken. On the plane of tradition, the literary context in which a narrative, a law, a prophetic utterance, a wisdom maxim is remembered affects the sense of it. Even the introduction of the divine name Yahweh (Exod. 3:15; 6:3) is effected through reference to the people's prior experience and knowledge. Similarly, ideas, notions, problems—as radically new and different as they may seem—do not enter the human sphere as if into a vacuum, but always find structures present which enable the people to comprehend them and relate to them. And at the foundation, as we have noted earlier, the very ontological and epistemological views which allowed the Israelites to perceive revelation as they did were elements of the heritage they shared with the ancient Near East. Thus it can be seen that tradition, by forming the framework in which revelation can be recognized as revelation and appropriated as a meaningful occurrence, participates in that revelatory occasion as a necessary precondition.

Secondly, *tradition is a locus of revelation insofar as it serves as the occasion or springboard for such revelation.* For all the importance of tradition in passing down structures of under-standing and meaning, its recipients did not always, perhaps not even usually, appropriate its content uncritically or unreflec-tively. To a great extent they remained in dialogue with the antecedent tradition—and at the same time in dialogue with their own times.[41] In this respect we can see a tension between the tradition and the given new situation. The new age could raise problems for which the tradition had no ready answer, and the tradition could force perspectives and demands on the new epoch which strictly speaking do not emerge from this new situ-ation alone. Of course, it was the given generation or group or individual that was caught here in the middle and that had to address this tension. This gave rise to interpretation—whether creative or conservative, responsible or irresponsible in light of the pressing human and divine claims. It was often, but not always, coupled with a kerygmatic intention. What was inter-preted was not only the tradition about Yahweh's great deeds in Israel's past—but anything (laws, instructions, promises, narra-tives, prophetic utterances) that was included in their heritage and that had or could be made to have a direct meaning for the present. It is the mere presence of the tradition that stimulates this engagement, that occasions the need to do more than merely acquiesce unthinkingly to one's situation. The out-come of each such instance of tension between tradition and the present can (though of course may not) in turn be incorpo-rated in the tradition for later generations. This is the vibrant process which yielded the Old Testament, a multiplex and intricate record of many persons' strugglings with the demands

---

41. For example, the essence of *"Vergegenwärtigung"* (actualization, re-presenta-tion; cf. Knight, *Rediscovering the Traditions of Israel*, pp. 5–6) is not that the past acts of God are re-told or re-presented (usually in the cult but also else-where, as in the family) merely for antiquarian purposes, as if simply to secure agreement that they had happened in the past. The purpose is rather to create a situation in which the people of a new generation can feel affected by the past events, can realize the implications for their own lives, can open themselves to the continued impact of previous revelation. But for this to be effected, inter-pretation geared to the new situation was mandatory, and through accumulation of such interpretations the tradition itself grew.

of life, old and new, human and divine. That we find here
failures as well as successes attests to this process—and to the
irreplaceable worth of the Old Testament. It was on this stage
that revelation (in Gloege's sense of God's personal and concrete confrontation with humanity) had to occur—in the
human struggle of facing present needs, informed by the past
and concerned for the future.

The implication of this whole picture is clear. We need to
claim for humanity a more significant, active role in the revelatory process than is commonly done.[42]   In this, however, the
human struggle, seen formally as the reception and reinterpretation of tradition, is not being equated in its entirety with
revelational discernment. For one thing there are too many
examples of human insensitivity and apostasy throughout this
process, and secondly the Old Testament tends to picture God
as the initiator of his revelation. Furthermore, the tradition
process, even in its best moments, cannot elicit or procure revelation in a formal sense (although we might assume that the
Israelites, like us, would be interested in gaining as much information as possible about the nature and will of God). Yet to
the extent that there is revelation in the Old Testament literature, the occasion for it must have been the tradition process
which produced this literature, in the circle of that human community. In a real sense the quest for the terms of the just life
in communion with Yahweh was no mean enterprise. The nature and responsibility of humanity (Gen. 1:26–27) had to be
pursued by all people and in all situations anew. This was
especially the case in times when radical discontinuity, triggered

---

42. It is a significant deficit of Gloege's outline on the relation between revelation and tradition that he did not consider more of the implications of this
formative creative process. Our thesis raises, of course, fundamental questions
about the definition of revelation. Perhaps it is wisest first to admit the ultimate
mysteriousness of divine disclosure, of God's communication with humans. Then
one cannot a priori restrict the definition to the *self*-revelation of God. To the
extent that God is engaged in life in this world, revelation will aim to serve the
purposes which he sets for this life, and thus the revealed content may not
always be identifiable with the personhood of God—except perhaps in a rather
extended or indirect sense.

by historical reversals or social change, yielded a need for reassessment and redirection.[43]   Revelation could enter into the process of legitimate quest—just as God could also break unexpectedly upon the scene of apostasy and injustice.

A series of brief examples will help to elucidate these two points, viz., that the tradition carries structures of meaning and that the tradition process creates new meaning.

The first example is the one with which we concluded the previous section: the complex of history, tradition, and revelation.   As is well known, von Rad has argued forcefully, supported also by the work of Noth, that the concept of a "linear historical span," embracing numerous events in which Yahweh intervened, emerged in Israel during a long process of interpreting those events through tradition formation, fusion, and arrangement.[44]   This linear course of salvific events came to constitute the Pentateuch (von Rad: Hexateuch), just as the later picture of God's continued activity despite Israel's failures was developed into the Deuteronomistic History and the Chronicler's History.   Whatever happened in the "real" course of history and however God may have acted in those events, for von Rad and Noth these "pictures of history" were the result of processes of human awareness and interpretation of divine activity.   It does not do to dismiss these kerygmatic interpretations as "unhistorical" figments of the imagination; they spring out of the people's experience of history and constitute a world of meaning which as such was also an historical reality, even if we often tend to consider its nature different from that of an incident or "event."[45]   The pictures serve an essential function

43. Cf. especially the discussion of P. R. Ackroyd, below, Chapter 9; and Knierim's comments on the "crisis of revelation," in *Probleme biblischer Theologie*, pp. 230ff.

44. Von Rad, *Theologie des Alten Testaments*, vol. 2, pp. 108ff. = *Old Testament Theology*, vol. 2, pp. 99ff.

45. Actually, it is misleading to contrast the event and the interpretation too sharply; cf. R. Smend's discussion on the complex relationship between tradition and history, above, Chapter 3. J. Barr's most recent statement, "Story and History in Biblical Theology," *JR* 56 (1976), 1–17, suggests that we should substitute the concept of story for that of history if we wish to grasp the essential theological thrust of the Old Testament or at least of its narrative corpus.   Barr has

for faith, and without them the events would be disconnected incidents of divine engagement, with no larger purpose stretching beyond the accomplishment of the isolated acts.   Israel's release from Egypt would be on the same plane as that of the Philistines from Caphtor and of the Arameans from Kir.[46] But the point is that divine revelation which took the form of historical events would, in order to be comprehensible, also have to find its complementary expression in human language and become a part of human tradition.   And traditio-historical research would suggest that such expression usually occurred not all at once close to the time of the events, but in the whole process in which the tradition emerged.

The creation traditions in Gen. 1–2 can be seen to be a locus of revelation in several respects.   Even if a fully developed theology of creation appeared only later in Israel's history, wonder and speculation about the origin of the world and of humanity were such common features in the ancient Near East (as in most cultures) that we can suspect that they contributed to the framework of understanding the events experienced in Egypt, in the wilderness, and in the newly settled land.   The traditions themselves about creation do not obviously have their origin in a word of God, and they can hardly be traced back to the event itself.[47]   Their origins lie in an impenetrable past, and we can do little more than observe similar motifs in other literature and attempt to draw whatever lines of connection we can.   The significant aspect that can account for the rise of these traditions is human grappling with the existential condi-

---

certainly touched an important point here, especially with respect to the final form of the narrative, and he can muster much support from modern discussions on the theology of story and storytelling.   Yet it is not entirely clear how this characterization of the literature is to do justice to the long history of the traditions, nor how the term "story" can be applied meaningfully to the non-narrative materials of the Old Testament.

46. Amos' relativizing utterance in 9:7 can be seen as a needed rebuke of the tendency in Israel to assume, because of their picture of history, that they could claim special privilege in Yahweh's eyes.

47. Despite the views of Calvin, Chemnitz, Pascal, and Astruc; cf. Knight, *Rediscovering the Traditions of Israel*, pp. 41–42.

tions and mysteries of life.[48]   Any revelation which we see in these chapters will seemingly need to be amenable to this base point.

The formation of the Israelite concept of her deity demonstrates also this important process of tradition growth.   Since the people in all periods presumably believed in a god and probably gave no thought to any developments in their concept of him,[49] they included in their literature no single definitive description of how they originally came to know him (as if it could be located at a specific point, with no antecedent or preparatory basis).   The description in Gen. 12:1–3 at the outset of the people's burgeoning self-consciousness—quite aside from the fact that it is commonly attributed to the later Yahwist as an ad hoc literary construction—does not serve this purpose. Similarly, the various divine self-presentations (e.g., Gen. 17:1; Exod. 3:6) do not constitute some initial introduction of a concept into a situation in which there was absolutely no belief in gods or in which a totally contrary view of deity existed.[50] Consequently, scholars have sought elsewhere for ways to account for the Israelite concept.   From all indications it appears that it is a conflation of numerous elements from the surrounding regions, each providing distinctive traits and the language to express them.   Cross has recently argued that the main features can be detected in Canaanite and early Hebrew poetry; the conflation was of 'Ēl (the god of the fathers, the

48. Cf. Ricoeur, *The Symbolism of Evil*; and C. Westermann, *Genesis*, vol. 1 (chs. 1–11), BK 1/1 (Neukirchen-Vluyn: Neukirchener Verlag, [1966] 1974), pp. 91–92.

49. Until perhaps the syncretism had been carried dangerously far, as, e.g., Elijah perceived.

50. Knierim's characterization of the self-presentation formula, *'ănî YHWH*, as a "revelation *sui generis*" (in *Probleme biblischer Theologie*, pp. 222ff.) is misleading.   As Zimmerli (in *Gottes Offenbarung*, pp. 26ff.) and Rendtorff (in *Offenbarung als Geschichte*, pp. 32–33) have discussed, both Gunkel and Gressmann found that this formula actually originated in polytheism where a god, in appearing to someone, would often identify himself so that he would not be mistaken for another god.   It thus cannot be considered a revelation unique *to* Israel, although it might be uniquely *Yahweh* who uses it in Israel.   Quite another question is whether this formula played a role in the formation of Israel's *concept* of God.

warrior leading his covenant-people, the creator-progenitor)
and Ba'al (the storm god, the dragon killer, the creator-cosmic
ruler).[51]   However we are to picture this conflation, it seems
certain that the Israelite view of God was something that
emerged in the course of time, bore imprints from diverse
sources, gradually separated itself consciously from its oriental
environment, and with time exerted an increasingly significant
influence on the Israelite traditions.   What does this do to the
concept of revelation?   If the Israelites grew to know their God
in this way, it would mean either that revelation had to occur in
small installments at several different times—or that it was based
in the human questing and reflecting process itself as the people
moved through history.   It would be a mistake to consider this
any more accidental or haphazard than is history itself.   Rather,
it was a vital, cumulative, and probably conscious process of
seeking to determine the contours of revelation.   The impact
which this emerging concept of their God Yahweh had for the
Israelites certainly played a, indeed *the* fundamental role in the
formation of their tradition.   And the people's search for full
understanding of the nature of their God had not stopped even
by the time their biblical history reached an end.

To dramatize this thesis about human tradition as a locus of
revelation we will allude briefly to two other cases.   In the book
of Ruth we do not find a god who acts terrifyingly in historical
events.   Yahweh here is a hidden God working through the
human sphere to fulfill his purposes (2:12, 20; 4:13–14).
From all signs it is the humans who do the struggling and thus
bring about their own salvation.   Yet God is nonetheless
present and active at all points.   This is one of numerous examples[52] of certain narrators' moving away from the portrayal

---

51. Cross, *Canaanite Myth and Hebrew Epic*, passim.   An earlier study by W. H.
Schmidt deals with many of the issues related to the development of Israel's
concept of God: *Alttestamentlicher Glaube und seine Umwelt: Zur Geschichte
des alttestamentlichen Gottesverständnisses* (Neukirchen-Vluyn: Neukirchener Verlag, 1968).
52. Cf. von Rad, *Theologie des Alten Testaments*, vol. 1, pp. 62–70 = *Old Testament Theology*, vol. 1, pp. 48–56, for other such cases.   See also P. Trible, "Two
Women in a Man's World: A Reading of the Book of Ruth," *Soundings* 59 (1976),
251–79.

of sacral events as the primary plane of God's actions. This occasional but decided preference for the least visible form of divine intervention may also give us grounds to suggest that, at all other periods as well, God's action (and thus also his revelation) might have occurred in the context of human struggles with the conditions of life—and that means also in the vital process of tradition reception and formation.

The final example may appear to be an unlikely one: the wisdom tradition as a locus of revelation. It is common for studies of Old Testament revelation to omit completely any consideration of wisdom.[53] In large measure this is due to the tendency today to define revelation solely in terms of divine *self-revelation* and to see history as the main sphere of God's activity. Thus, Wright is led to a highly problematic, even tendentious conclusion: "Wisdom literature is not the center of the scriptural canon; it is peripheral to it."[54] The problem is not so simple as this, neither literarily, theologically, or historically —as recent studies on the influence of wisdom in diverse parts of the Old Testament have shown. To be sure, the sage's word is not obviously revelatory. It is not oracular but is continuous with the world. The primary motivation evidently is to determine and to teach the structuredness of the world and the art of living. Instructions ranged over all facets of human existence: ways to deal with other people (the wise and the foolish, the disadvantaged, strangers, women), the managing of money, table manners, right speech and right silence, behavior at the royal court, and many more. It is not at all apparent that this could have anything to do with revelation—until we consider the sage's point of departure: "the fear of Yahweh is the begin-

---

53. This includes also the above-mentioned studies by Rendtorff, Zimmerli, Gloege, and (for all practical purposes) Kuntz and Knierim. Cf. however J. C. Rylaarsdam, *Revelation in Jewish Wisdom Literature* (Chicago: University of Chicago Press, 1946); several passages in von Rad, *Theologie des Alten Testaments*, vol. 1, pp. 382ff. = *Old Testament Theology*, vol. 1, pp. 370ff.; and also Barr, *Old and New in Interpretation*, pp. 72–74.

54. G. E. Wright, "Historical Knowledge and Revelation," in *Translating and Understanding the Old Testament*, Festschrift H. G. May, ed. H. T. Frank and W. L. Reed (Nashville: Abingdon, 1970), p. 291.

ning of wisdom" (Prov. 9:10; 1:7; 15:33; Ps. 111:10). Wisdom generally presupposes membership in the covenant community and reverent obedience to the divine will. From this base point the sage could seek to determine the rational ordering of the world, the limits set on humanity by God, and the most propitious means of conducting the daily affairs of life. The last enterprise had little to do with revelation expressly; it was a process of reason, common sense, and experience. Yet there was a clear notion that Yahweh stood behind wisdom per se (cf. *ḥokmat 'ĕlōhîm* in 1 Kgs. 3:28; also 5:9 [4:29]; Exod. 28:3 and 31:3; and even Gen. 41:16, 38–39). Precisely at the connection between world order (or creation) and Yahweh's will the sapiential circles related—indeed identified—cosmic wisdom with divine revelation (e.g., Ps. 104:24; Prov. 3:19–20; cf. Jer. 10:12). As von Rad states, "the word which calls man to life and salvation is the same word as that which as wisdom already encompassed all creatures at Creation. It is the same word which God himself made use of as a plan at his creation of the world."[55] Knowledge of order and of the world is indeed limited (cf. Job 38ff.; Eccl.), although it is the sage who with his reason can make the most of what we do know of this—and thus also of Yahweh's power and will. We can consequently see that revelation is by no means irrelevant for the wisdom tradition and is not merely limited to the plane of historical events. What is striking for our purposes here is that the means of apprehension were the human processes of reason and immediate observation.

One more aspect to our understanding of tradition as a locus of revelation needs to be faced directly, and this is a negative one: *tradition as a hindrance to revelation*. By no means must we esteem all tradition and all stages in the process of tradition formation so highly that we fail to see that, at many points in Israel's history, it was precisely the misuse and misinterpretation of past tradition that caused severe problems for the

---

55. Von Rad, *Theologie des Alten Testaments*, vol. 1, pp. 464–65 = *Old Testament Theology*, vol. 1, p. 450.

people. Much of prophetic preaching was directed precisely at this point.[56] Not all Old Testament tradition can be said to be based on revelation or to promote its apprehension by later generations. The same, in fact, could be asserted for religion itself—a problem which the prophets also perceived. Tradition has power simply because it is antecedent to us and implies experiential truths, and this makes its potential for constraint as great or greater than its potential for vitalization.[57]

It is not easy for us to find criteria for discerning legitimate witnesses to revelation and legitimate occasions of new revelatory insight, but two negative conditions stand out. Although these are formulated in our terms, it can be argued that they accord with the intent of the Old Testament itself with respect to the role of past tradition: (a) *An interpretation should not tend to petrify earlier revelation or its interpretation, absolutizing it into a convention that stifles rather than promotes life.* This would pervert revelation by thwarting its original purpose. A few examples of this problem and the way it was overcome:[58] In the face of barbaric and excessive principles of punishment for purposes of social control among other primitive peoples, the *lex talionis* (Exod. 21:23–25; Lev. 24:17ff.; Deut. 19:21) arose in order to limit measureless vengeance to no more than equal recompense; yet this in turn needed to be softened further in other later laws (and explicitly also in Matt. 5:38ff.). The concept of inter-generational punishment (e.g., Exod. 34:7), underscoring the absolute importance of obedience to Yahweh and forming a basis of the Deuteronomistic theology of history, became so oppressive to the people in exile

---

56. Numerous examples of this are given in the discussion by W. Zimmerli, above, Chapter 4, and need not be repeated here.

57. Cf., e.g., Barr, *Old and New in Interpretation*, pp. 190–91, and also p. 32: "But it is within the tradition, where man uses that which is God-given to form structures of disobedience to God, that the most deceptive and dangerous forms of sin have to be looked for."

58. Post-exilic treatment of the law cannot simply be classified as an example of such absolutizing a tradition into a convention, for its intent under Ezra was not to stifle life but to preserve both it and the community's national and religious identity in the face of foreign influences, religious syncretism, and a decline in morale.

(Lam. 5:7) that a word liberating them from their cynicism was needed (Jer. 31:29–30; Ezek. 18). Trust in the presence of Yahweh in the cult and also the conventions of worship there that demanded no moral counterpart in daily life elicited from Jeremiah a strong condemnation and a reordering of priorities (7:1–15). Observant of discrepancies between Yahwistic "orthodoxy" and the realities of life, Job and Qoheleth sought explanations or means whereby they themselves would be able to continue. (b) The second negative condition is that *an interpretation should not give false hopes to persons and thereby diminish the urgency of their coming to terms with their specific situation.* The best example of this is seen in the false prophets, those who in the name of Yahweh and through reference to Israelite traditions sought to fill the people with "false hopes" (Jer. 23:16) by calming them with the anesthetizing words *"šālôm šālôm"* when there was no *šālôm* (6:14 = 8:11). Similarly, the people in the eighth century could look with such satisfaction to the covenantal promise to Abraham and the guarantee of the Davidic dynasty that they neglected the obligations associated with the Sinaitic covenant. Yet the greatest danger possible under both of the above negative conditions was that of perverting the presence of Yahweh into a convention and domesticizing it for manipulative use whenever convenient. The repeated witness of the Old Testament is that such misuse of revelation, of tradition, elicited a severe reprisal from Yahweh. Yet it is striking that even this divine response is often presented as something which the people should have known, that is, if they had had the correct interpretation of tradition and had acted accordingly.

Our understanding of tradition as a locus of revelation elevates the process of tradition formation and transmission to a position of potentially high theological importance. This active participation of humans in the revelatory process affects directly our understanding of revelation in several ways:

(1) Narrow and exclusivistic definitions of what constitutes revelation and how it occurs usually grant only an insignificant,

passive role to human recipients, and this no doubt finds some (though not total) support in the biblical witness itself. Yet by our assuming the growth of tradition in Israel we tacitly shift considerable responsibility onto the people themselves, and it seems that we are best advised to face this squarely and to broaden our definitions as needed, especially in terms of God's involvement in the processes of this world.

(2) Revelatory inspiration becomes "democratized." It is not restricted to a very few chosen individuals, as if it were their private possession or special privilege. All members of the covenant community who participate in the slightest way in the formation of the tradition can be contributing to potentially revelatory occasions. This can be seen especially clearly in the case of the prophets' disciples. In contrast to previous tendencies to classify prophetic utterances as either "genuine" (from the prophet master) or "nongenuine" (from his anonymous disciples), scholars now avoid such prejudicial language since later additions and reworkings can be as theologically and historically important in their own right as the earlier ones. The point is that "traditioning" is a function of the community, and it is not for us to set up a scale of values with clear preferences for one stage or another.

(3) Important features that emerge in the tradition and that then give special thrust to the ongoing process can often be related to revelation. Examples may be the formation of their view of God, the notions of election, of covenant, of historical deliverance, of righteousness, of divine wrath, of apostasy, the essence of faith, the prohibition against idolatry, the importance of social ethics. Such central features, several of which are distinctively Israelite, gave special impetus to the tradition process —not as impulses that in finished form suddenly entered the stream, but as concepts which emerged slowly in the sense that the traditionists continually endeavored to probe their meaning and implications. These have revelatory impact insofar as they indicate the nature of the God to whom the people are to relate. Furthermore, it might be noted, because of this and because

of their importance in the development of the tradition they may deserve more of our attention than does some artificial quest for the "center" of the Old Testament.

(4) Just because the tradition develops we must be very careful not to connect this with the older idea of "progressive revelation."[59] Tradition understood as a locus of revelation suggests in no way that there may have been an evolutionary development of revealed religion from an early stage of primitiveness on to later, more advanced and enlightened stages. Our discussions above have instead put the emphasis on each individual stage in the history of the people, not on some overriding progression. Each generation, group, and individual face a distinctive situation to which they, informed by their tradition and yet interpreting it anew for themselves, must respond. This very struggle can constitute for them an occasion of revelation. To be sure, there is a forward thrust and cumulative power to tradition, but this only means that the person later in time simply has more historical and reflective data at his disposal and contributing to his decision than did the earlier person.

(5) It becomes clear, then, that we can speak of a "history of revelation" only in a limited, nonevolutionary sense. The points along the way which we can set in chronological order are the individual acts of revelation, whether on the plane of history or on that of tradition. But in neither sphere is it such that we can add together the individual points as if producing a mathematical sum. An element of continuity can be seen in the growing understanding of God, but the ultimate purpose of all revelation, viz., the appropriate relation of humanity to God and of human to human, puts the individual situation in priority over the whole historical sweep. This is a lesson to be learned not only from the postulated tradition process but also from the Old Testament witness itself.

59. Cf., e.g., C. H. Dodd, *The Authority of the Bible* (London: Nisbet & Co., 1928, revised 1938), especially pp. 245–85.

CONCLUSION

The choice of preposition in our title, "Revelation through Tradition," proves to be important. Revelation is not understood "as" tradition in the sense that the latter may be its mode or even its identity, nor is revelation contained "in" tradition like some ready commodity. It distorts the picture even to assert that revelation is "prior to" tradition—either in the temporal sense of preceding it as an initial, retrievable datum, or in the hierarchal sense of superiority (and thus without considering the purpose of revelation). The relationship between revelation and tradition is too complex to be reduced to any of these formulas. It can even be questioned, as we have seen, whether we today are correct in looking so hard for a clear concept of revelation in the Old Testament, for certain things that were assumed and perceived then do not submit easily to "revelation" (as we are accustomed to structure it) and yet were fundamental to their view of God. Nevertheless, insofar as we believe that God did in revelation approach the Israelites, this occurred to a great extent "through" tradition. The multiple sense of this term is intentional: First, tradition delivers the structures of understanding that are prerequisite to apprehending revelation as revelation. Second, revelation could come by reason of the process in which the Israelites engaged the dilemmas of life and fashioned their faith in covenant with Yahweh—a process which was fundamental also to the formation of the tradition and which was often carried out on the stage of tradition. Third, once revelation had "occurred" it could be channeled to later generations only through the *traditum*, which would then function as witness to the prior revelatory occasion and could confront later persons with its implications as well. In all of this we see the people themselves acting, and we have no basis for supposing that God was somehow guiding or steering this total process *despite* human participation.

This intricate relationship between revelation and tradition clearly does not exhaust all categories of revelation, which in its ultimate mysteriousness resists simplification to convenient propositions. For this reason also theology must not be equated with the history of tradition; since the latter is marked all too often by cases of injustice and apostasy, tradition can constitute only one, albeit a very important contribution to our understanding of theology. The strength of tradition, like that of revelation, is its direct relation to concrete human situations. Its pluralism and multiplicity signify its authentic tie with life. Similarly, revelation cannot be abstract, timeless, absolutistic, impervious to the varied fabric of the community itself. Yahweh's revelation occurs in his continuous involvement with the people's strugglings for survival and meaning. The relationship between revelation and tradition is consequently parallel to the relationship between Yahweh's commitment and Israel's creativity. There is a reciprocity and mutuality here which yield a dynamic of high theological significance. This perspective, usually neglected in biblical-theological and systematic-theological treatises on revelation, is a significant consequence of the traditio-historical postulate about the anchorage of Old Testament literature in the situations of life.

Part III

CONTINUITY AND DIVERSITY

Chapter 8

Theological Streams of Tradition[*]

Odil Hannes Steck

METHODS DEALING WITH ANTECEDENT
MATERIALS IN A TEXT

When historico-critical analysis considers the shaping, formulation, and meaning of a given Old Testament text, in innumerable instances it is not a completely unexpected *novum* that is observed, but rather an entity that has ties with antecedent materials appropriated from the past. Such prior materials within the text, thus older than the text itself, confront the exegete in diverse forms.

For one thing, this older substance may be recognizable as a *clearly defined textual unit* which has found entry into the present textual context. In comparison with the final form of the text which the exegete has before him, this unit can be more or less demarcated and its original extent ascertained.

If textual factors should indicate that this older unit which was incorporated into the text existed earlier as a firmly formulated, *written* entity, then the literary-critical method has the task of analytically separating older and younger textual components from each other and identifying each entity—whether as individual unit or as component within a more extensive source or redactional network—according to its historical peculiarities. Synthetic redaction-critical analysis complements this then by seeking to illumine how these literary layers, recovered through literary-critical analysis, developed at the written level

[*] Translated by Douglas A. Knight.

183

into the present form of the textual passage.   These circumstances are well known, and we need not supply examples here
or give any further description of the method.[1]

However, older textual antecedents introduced into a literary
section need not be only in written form.   All Old Testament
exegetes are familiar with textual data which require the assumption that certain clearly defined components, in more or
less fixed form, have been taken from an *oral* tradition and been
incorporated into the written form of a text, whether this latter
be literarily homogeneous or complex.   For examples of this we
could point to narratives from the historical books of the Old
Testament prior to their inclusion in written collections and
source documents; similarly, legal maxims, sapiential proverbs,
cultic texts, prophetic logia were all at home in oral speech
before they were committed to written collections and literary
redactions.   For identifying and reconstructing the prior oral
form of such components in any given text, there is another
method currently in use that is basically related to the literary-
critical search for earlier literary stages of a text.   This method
derives its distinctiveness, though, from the fact that it deals
with the special process of oral transmission, and for this reason
it must be differentiated from the literary-critical approach.
The problem of which name to give to this method is of secondary importance; we call it the traditio-historical *("überlieferungsgeschichtliche")* method, dealing with the phase of oral
tradition prior to the written composition.   This *überlieferungsgeschichtliche* investigation is, on the one hand, engaged in
analysis insofar as it isolates the piece of oral tradition within a
passage, reconstructs it, and identifies it historically.   On the
other hand, it involves synthesis in that it traces the history of

---

1. For more details, cf. H. Barth and O. H. Steck, *Exegese des Alten Testaments: Leitfaden der Methodik,* 5th ed. (Neukirchen-Vluyn: Neukirchener Verlag, 1974), § 4 (literary criticism) and § 6 (redaction criticism).   This handbook
contains presentations of the exegetical methods.   Our discussion in the present
essay will not repeat those materials but will presuppose that the reader is familiar
with them.

this oral tradition down to the point where it was recorded in writing.[2]

Regardless of the size of a text under analysis, the literary-critical and redaction-critical as well as the *überlieferungs-geschichtliche* methods aim to determine which older—written or oral—clearly defined segments were incorporated into the present literary form of the text. This approach accords with the indisputable fact that the form of the Old Testament as we now have it must be regarded largely as the final stage of a "tradition history" (*"Überlieferungsgeschichte"*), in the wide sense of the term. During this process texts lived independently and were subjected to transforming processes while being transmitted in oral tradition and in initially smaller bodies of written tradition, later attaining their place in the great literary complexes of the Old Testament where we now find them.

Without a doubt, antecedent elements in an Old Testament text are limited not only to the text's own earlier stages, that is, not only to its prior form as an oral or written tradition, identifiable now as an older component in an available text. Let us consider the oldest attainable phase in the formation of a text within oral or written tradition, the point where there was probably no anterior stage of the text; or similarly, consider passages—oral or, above all, written—that represent the productive reception of an older text and that by definition do not incorporate this older text but adapt it creatively. Also in such cases as these we do not meet with totally free and unconditioned creativity, but rather with the reworking of pre-given material—with the one distinct difference that what is antecedent is not some prior stage of the text under analysis, not some clearly defined segment incorporated into the text and thus fair game for literary-critical and *überlieferungsgeschichtliche* study. Actually there are quite diverse antecedent elements

2. On this, cf. Barth and Steck, *Exegese des Alten Testaments*, § 5.

that cannot be retrieved by literary criticism or *Überlieferungs-geschichte* and that must in principle be considered for every phase of growth during the development of a text. Such elements confronting the exegete are similar in type only inasmuch as they do not appear in the form of an older text inserted into a larger context, but rather constitute indicators of some different circumstances—self-evident, yet all too seldom considered methodologically. We are referring to the fact that texts, accordingly also those in the Old Testament, do not use only older textual elements but also the intellectual world* of the individual or group that shapes and transmits the given text. This applies no less to the initial formation of the text than to all elements throughout its later stages of production. Of course, literary-critical and *überlieferungsgeschichtliche* investigations yield positive results that point to the contents of this intellectual world: even older textual segments incorporated into the given text belong to this world. But these are of little interest for our present discussion since the phenomenon of the intellectual world embraces much more. Besides any such integrated textual segments, pre-given elements from the intellectual world (in addition to historical and socio-cultural conditions) that have left tangible marks in the text include: language itself with its rules, its meanings, and its limits; idioms and formulas; genres (*Gattungen*) with their typical elements (*"Topik"*), forms which fashion the text at its different developmental stages; knowledge of the most diverse type, of which distinctive materials (*"geprägte Stoffe"*) as well as linguistically characteristic notions and literary allusions (though without inclusion of a portion of another text) are the most easily identifiable; clearly defined thought-patterns and appropriation-patterns; and also experiences that come from as-

---

* *Geistige Welt.* Recurring frequently in this discussion, the expression covers a wider range than does its English equivalent, which is usually limited to the sphere of sober, rational thinking. Lacking a better term, however, we will use "intellectual world" and urge the reader to understand it in this broader sense.— TRANS.

similating occurrences in the context of a distinctive intellectual world. While at present there is little chance for some analytical method to lay hold of many of these aspects in the antecedent intellectual world which affected the formation of a given text, the situation is somewhat more favorable in two areas. One area is the way a textual passage—often at its various stages of development—bears the imprint of genre. The form-critical approach is directed toward this area:[3] in a given text it identifies formative patterns which existed as such in other texts prior to the composition of the text under analysis. It is not these other texts but the genres, the controlling patterns, which are appropriated, and therefore literary-critical and *überlieferungsgeschichtliche* analyses cannot uncover them. The second rather clearly understood area in which the antecedent intellectual world affects the formation of a specific text is the area of prior materials (*"Stoffe"*) and, above all, prior notions (*"Vorstellungen"*). We will give special attention to such notions in our study of streams of theological tradition; the phenomenon of received materials and individual motifs is more difficult to localize and will not be treated in the present discussion.

When Old Testament texts—whether independent oral or written traditions or editorial additions—were formed for the first time, they certainly assimilated notions[4] current in that period. This is no less true in the instances that interest us most here—where we cannot explain this appropriation solely in terms of familiarity with some oral or written tradition which we can still find in the Old Testament. A pregnant concept, a characteristic circumstance, the mode of formulation, the distinctive thrust or development of a statement (*"Aussagegefälle"*)—comparative work with a concordance of the Old Testament or in the area of pertinent ancient Near Eastern materials can determine whether any of these may have been taken from some

---

3. On this, cf. Barth and Steck, *Exegese des Alten Testaments*, § 7.
4. The term "motif" means something different and should not be used in this connection. On the problem of a *motivgeschichtliche* approach, cf. Barth and Steck, *Exegese des Alten Testaments*, pp. 75–76.

sphere which was their earlier, or perhaps even their original and natural home. In such cases we find this occurring in the context of an initial, independent fashioning of a text. Thus, this appropriation is similar to the impact of form on such texts, for in neither case does it simply happen together with assimilating an earlier stage of this text. Consequently, from the standpoint of the exegete it is absolutely necessary to separate this *"traditionsgeschichtliche"* analysis[5] of a text not only from the literary-critical and redaction-critical steps but also from the *überlieferungsgeschichtliche* phase of the investigation. This is needed even though both the *überlieferungsgeschichtliche* approach and the *traditionsgeschichtliche* approach deal with questions about which oral traditional materials preceded a text and were assimilated into it.[6]

Perhaps several concrete examples of *traditionsgeschichtliche* instances may serve to clarify what we have been saying.

It is commonly held that the prologue to the flood narrative in Gen. 6:5–8 was formulated by the Yahwist and that no older textual prototype, oral or written, was incorporated in it. Nonetheless, the pregnant concept *maḥšĕbōt* ("thoughts, inclinations") in 6:5 is evidence that, as is often the case in his primeval history,[7] J composes with reference to the ancient Israelite world of sapiential thoughts and notions. Several studies of the Joseph story and of the Davidic succession narrative have shown that they bear numerous imprints from the

---

5. On this, cf. Barth and Steck, *Exegese des Alten Testaments*, § 8.

6. The *"überlieferungsgeschichtliche"* approach and the *"traditionsgeschichtliche"* approach represent two different exegetical steps. The dissertation by the editor of this volume correctly underscores this distinction and observes the resultant terminological dilemma; cf. D. A. Knight, *Rediscovering the Traditions of Israel*, rev. ed., SBLDS 9 (Missoula: Society of Biblical Literature, 1975), 21ff., 26ff., 187ff. Knight suggests (p. 29) dividing *"traditionsgeschichtliche"* analysis into its parts: the history of a notion, of a motif, of a theme, of a concept, of a tradition stream, of the ideological background. This has the disadvantage, though, of methodologically separating elements which belong together in substance. Although the terminological designation is of little consequence to me, the lack of any other single embracing term forces me to continue using *"Traditionsgeschichte,"* thus distinguished from *"Überlieferungsgeschichte."* The reader is requested to understand these terms in the sense in which I am using them.

7. Cf. O. H. Steck, *Die Paradieserzählung*, BSt 60 (Neukirchen-Vluyn: Neukirchener Verlag, 1970), 64.

thought-world and characteristic notions of wisdom, without themselves being wisdom texts and without the wisdom influence taking the form of integrated sapiential textual portions.[8] It is common knowledge that statements in the psalms are frequently based on Canaanite notions or on ancient oriental notions mediated through Canaan;[9] yet again these relations do not in most cases appear to have resulted by directly incorporating extra-Israelite cultic texts into the Israelite psalms. Examples of *Traditionsgeschichte* in prophetic texts are legion;[10] for instance, Isaiah: as can be proven from characteristic formulations, he makes use of notions from diverse origins, for example, in 1:2–3 from wisdom, in 1:21, 26 from Jerusalem's traditional qualifications, in 6:1–4 from the Jerusalem cult, in 7:9b from the kingship of the Davidides, in 28:15, 17 and 30:2–3 suggestive predications of Yahweh on Zion. These examples in Isaiah are, without exception, found in texts which constitute new prophetic creations and which have no prior history as textual portions antecedent to the prophet. Isaiah's allusions do not even come into view in the course of *überlieferungsgeschicht-*

---

8. Cf., e.g., G. von Rad, "Josephsgeschichte und ältere Chokma" (1953), in *Gesammelte Studien zum Alten Testament*, ThB 8, 4th ed. (München: Chr. Kaiser, 1971), 272–80 = "The Joseph Narrative and Ancient Wisdom," in *The Problem of the Hexateuch, and Other Essays* (Edinburgh and London: Oliver & Boyd, 1966), 292–300; H.-J. Hermisson, "Weisheit und Geschichte," in *Probleme biblischer Theologie*, Festschrift G. von Rad, ed. H. W. Wolff (München: Chr. Kaiser, 1971), 136–54. On the question of the wisdom tradition, cf. now the critical study by R. N. Whybray, *The Intellectual Tradition in the Old Testament*, BZAW 135 (Berlin: de Gruyter, 1974).

9. Cf., e.g., W. H. Schmidt, *Königtum Gottes in Ugarit und Israel*, BZAW 80, 2d ed. (Berlin: de Gruyter, 1966); F. Stolz, *Strukturen und Figuren im Kult von Jerusalem*, BZAW 118 (Berlin: de Gruyter, 1970); and also the discussion by A. S. Kapelrud, above, Chapter 5.

10. Cf., e.g., E. Rohland, "Die Bedeutung der Erwählungstraditionen Israels für die Eschatologie der alttestamentlichen Propheten" (dissertation in theology Heidelberg, 1956); G. von Rad, *Theologie des Alten Testaments*, vol. 2, 5th ed. (München: Chr. Kaiser, 1968) = *Old Testament Theology*, vol. 2 (New York: Harper & Row, 1965); G. Wanke, *Die Zionstheologie der Korachiten in ihrem traditionsgeschichtlichen Zusammenhang*, BZAW 97 (Berlin: de Gruyter, 1966); H.-M. Lutz, *Jahwe, Jerusalem und die Völker*, WMANT 27 (Neukirchen-Vluyn: Neukirchener Verlag, 1968); as well as W. Zimmerli, *Ezechiel*, BK 13 (Neukirchen-Vluyn: Neukirchener Verlag, 1969) = *Ezekiel*, Hermeneia, vol. 1 (Philadelphia: Fortress, 1977); H. W. Wolff, *Hosea*, BK 14/1, 2d ed. (Neukirchen-Vluyn: Neukirchener Verlag, 1965) = *Hosea*, Hermeneia (Philadelphia: Fortress, 1974); and Wolff, *Joel/Amos*, BK 14/2 (Neukirchen-Vluyn: Neukirchener Verlag, 1969) = *Joel/Amos*, Hermeneia (Philadelphia: Fortress, 1976).

liche analysis and literary analysis.   Neither can the form-
critical approach alone catch sight of these data, for it deals only
with the appropriation of existing genres and associated genre-
topoi. The above-mentioned references—as in innumerable
other instances of *traditionsgeschichtliche* connections—do not
fall under the category of *topoi* which appear simply because of
the chosen genre.   How is one analytically to lay hold of this
type of reference to antecedent material if one does not allow
for a special approach alongside the *überlieferungsgeschichtliche* and the literary-critical/redaction-critical methods—
namely, the *traditionsgeschichtliche* approach?

It may be helpful to summarize this preliminary result since
it forms the starting-point for investigating streams of theological tradition. If with respect to a specific Old Testament text
the question is raised about which intellectual ingredients were
at hand during its formation and thus exerted influence on this
text, two analytical paths are available for the exegete.   First, it
must be determined whether the text per se already has a prehistory in the form of older, clearly defined textual segments
that have been incorporated into it.   This is the literary-
critical/redaction-critical and the *überlieferungsgeschichtliche*
investigation, and according to the circumstances we may reach
a positive or—with an entirely homogeneous text—a negative
result.   Second, it must be determined which elements from the
text's antecedent intellectual world affected its composition—
yet without these elements' being component parts of some existing, integrated text.   This is the linguistic, form-critical, *Stoff*-
critical, and especially the *traditionsgeschichtliche* investigation, and it is to be executed on both homogeneous and
nonhomogeneous texts at every stage of their growth.   In every
instance this investigation will reach a positive result since it is
impossible for a text to originate fully detached from its background in an antecedent intellectual world.   Both of these
analytical procedures correspond to historical evidence, namely,
that Old Testament exegesis confronts, on the one hand, texts

and textual strata which pass on and reaccentuate earlier stages of the textual tradition and, on the other hand, other texts which are formulated indeed freely and independently from an earlier prototype and yet in the context of an existing, formative intellectual world.

While from the standpoint of method and steps in the exegete's analysis it is necessary to separate these two stages of the investigation, nevertheless we cannot dispute that they can also be viewed together at a later and higher level of reflecting on what preceded the origin of texts. For, the antecedents from the intellectual world where the text originated include of course, as we have stated above, also any integrated, earlier, oral or written stages of the text, that is, the positive findings of the *überlieferungsgeschichtliche* and literary-critical analyses. Similarly, on the other hand, the genres, notions, and thought-patterns undoubtedly present themselves to the author of a new text in the form of concrete textual units. This is true even if these textual units are not known to us and were not incorporated in that form into the new text but exerted their influence on the new composition through the mediation of the intellectual world and as elements of its makeup. Consequently, at the higher level of reflection this question about the intellectual world of a text's origin proves to be the overarching one. For it embraces the literary-critical, *überlieferungsgeschichtliche, traditionsgeschichtliche,* and form-critical methods, treats them as aspects of a single exegetical endeavor, and shows that each of them independently has only relative value.[11]

DETECTING STREAMS OF TRADITION

But let us turn now to the phenomenon of theological streams of tradition. If we hope to make progress here, we need to reflect further on the method of *"traditionsgeschichtliche"* analysis. Such analysis can be executed on a more or less exten-

11. Cf. Barth and Steck, *Exegese des Alten Testaments,* pp. 102–103.

sive series of individual cases where the texts were not formulated freely but had appropriated prior notions and thought-patterns, either directly or in a form modified by the text's own new thrusts. These antecedent notions and thought-patterns included at the composition of the text are, of course, not formless and rootless particles. The author knows them in the shape of fixed, characteristically formulated sentences—even if these sentences have not been transmitted directly down to us. In his new text the author alludes to such sentences without integrating them into his own composition as intact textual segments, that is, in the tradition form familiar to him. This very fact brings into view the important mediating role played by the author's own intellectual world: here such sentences appear as elements of his knowledge, separate themselves from their original structured contexts in familiar texts, break up into individual items, and then through his own intellectual processes can be combined anew and introduced into his new literary creation.[12] This consideration is essential if we are to comprehend the historical nature of the process by which, for example, the Yahwist, the Joseph story, the succession narrative, or Isaiah could work with wisdom notions—without themselves becoming wisdom texts or without integrating such texts even partially into their own literary creations. To be sure, such recoverable elements in the knowledge of someone authoring a unified text stratum are frequently of the most diverse types; just consider the Yahwist, the Joseph story, or the words of Isaiah in this regard. Even the more specialized application of the *traditionsgeschichtliche* method often brings to light very diverse influences in this context. Nevertheless, we can see very clearly that, in comparison with expressions of modern people who are flooded with information and much less settled intellectually,

---

12. For methodological considerations of this problem, cf. Steck, *Paradieserzählung*, pp. 56ff.; and Steck, *Der Schöpfungsbericht der Priesterschrift*, FRLANT 115 (Göttingen: Vandenhoeck & Ruprecht, 1975), 28–29. We must also note that such ties to older materials can indeed be deceptive in implying true continuity, as P. R. Ackroyd shows below, especially pp. 223ff.

the notions of the Israelite *traditionsgeschichtliche* sphere do not constitute simply a multitude of disconnected, independent particles of knowledge. Rather, they are parts of a larger whole, indeed not expressed as such, yet still known to the author and his listener/reader. This whole often confronts us in more comprehensive form in other sections of the Old Testament. By way of example, when Isaiah characterizes Yahweh as a refuge, a hiding place, a fortress, and a help, we can by means of *traditionsgeschichtliche* analysis determine that they are *elements* of a notion and that they belong to the more comprehensive *notion* of Yahweh on Zion; this in turn is one of a number of notions that comprise the Zion-*tradition*, which itself belongs to the comprehensive *conceptual design* ("*Konzeption*") of the Jerusalem cult tradition.[13] Thus when we recover by *traditionsgeschichtliche* means such notional elements in a text or in an author, they frequently point to much more extensive intellectual spheres. This fact is usually underscored also by converging results from analyzing other parts of the same homogeneous textual complex: Isaiah's and especially Deutero-Isaiah's allusions to the conceptional design of the Jerusalem cult tradition are by no means limited to a single notional element; the Yahwist, the Joseph story, and the succession narrative refer not infrequently to the wisdom tradition; the situation is similar with respect to Ezekiel's relation to the priestly tradition. If one surveys the entire stock of notional elements used in a single homogeneous text complex and if one relates them to the larger intellectual spheres to which they belong and from which they derive, then the question arises about which spheres were actually the most determinative for the text complex at hand and which spheres played a comparatively minor role. For example, Isaiah had contact also with the sphere of priestly tradition and, as already mentioned,

---

13. Cf. O. H. Steck, *Friedensvorstellungen im alten Jerusalem*, ThSt 111 (Zürich: Theologischer Verlag, 1972), pp. 56–57, nn. 153–54, and pp. 9ff. on the general conceptional design of the Jerusalem cult tradition.

with the sphere of wisdom tradition; however, the actual formation of his message was determined primarily by the spheres of the Jerusalem cult tradition and of the prophetic tradition with which he was undoubtedly also connected. On the whole, such an approach that organizes the stock of notions within homogeneous textual complexes in the Old Testament brings a varied picture into focus, for we can then perceive that ideas and guiding features in the intellectual world behind such texts are indeed very diverse. They are distinguishable in terms of time, location, and socio-cultural matrix. For instance, in the premonarchical age they are different from those in the period after the formation of the state, and again different from those in the exilic period and the post-exilic phases; the area of the Northern kingdom has notions distinct from those in the South, and Jerusalem's intellectual world varies from that in the country of Judah. When analyzed from this point of view the utterances of the literary prophets produce a striking picture.

What can be determined about these *extensive intellectual spheres* with which an Old Testament text complex, as evidenced in the provenance of its notional elements, is associated via its intellectual world? One important clue is the fact that, through *traditionsgeschichtliche* analysis, we can discern this connection precisely in persistent formulations of specific subject matter by means of pregnant concepts, semantic fields, structures of expression, thrust of an affirmation ("*Aussagegefälle*"), and distinctive movement of thought. This indicates that these spheres are each identified by its own peculiar, characteristic linguistic world. For such a linguistic world to originate and endure presupposes processes of reflection and teaching. This was possible basically only after the formation of the Israelite state; the processes reflect continuous needs associated with established institutions (e.g., cult, royal court, education, and judicial court). Corresponding to these are the main spheres to be mentioned: the Jerusalem cult traditions of the temple-singers, the wisdom tradition probably connected

primarily with the Jerusalem court, the specific priestly tradition, the legal tradition—all of these certainly attached to sites
and institutions which produced texts on the basis of learned
reflection. And the least tangible as an historical process is the
prophetic tradition, the themes and especially the genres of
which were certainly familiar to prophets as early as Amos and
Isaiah. With respect to their characteristic stock of notions and
movements of thought, these more extensive intellectual
spheres, or *spheres of tradition*, are marked not only by their
own respective, characteristic linguistic world. Nor do they
possess only peculiar themes, materials, and experiences.
Above all, they have their own special genres in order to express
their message in appropriate form. Only a differentiated picture of these spheres of tradition, which can interrelate with
each other in diverse ways, helps us to perceive the vibrant
intellectual life in Israel. For it found expression not only in
the collections of genuine texts stemming from the respective
sphere of tradition (e.g., the Old Testament collections for cult,
law, and wisdom); in addition, this intellectual life in Israel left
its stamp also on those textual complexes which cannot be regarded as genuine self-expressions of a sphere of tradition but
which make use of this intellectual world in new literary creations (e.g., the literary prophets or the narratives about Joseph
or about the succession to the throne).

The phenomenon of *streams of tradition* comes into view
now when we consider these Israelite spheres of tradition in
terms of their temporal prolongation. We can see both long-
term growth of their genuine traditions and also frequently
occurring references to these spheres without literary mediation through older texts already in written form. Both of these
show that such spheres of tradition can maintain surprising constancy in the form of lively intellectual movements—despite the
considerable developments, expansions, differentiations, and
changes to which they are submitted. Apparently this is due to
the stability of the sites where they are preserved, the groups

that transmit them, and the needs which they meet.   References, for example, to the Jerusalem cult tradition and to wisdom can be detected far into the post-exilic, late-Israelite period, yet for the most part they are not explainable as derivatives from literary models but only because of contacts with an intact, still living sphere of tradition.   Thus we encounter here the phenomenon of streams of tradition.   How are we to recognize this phenomenon, and how should it be defined?

The concept of a stream of tradition emerges as a synthetic inference from analytic-exegetical findings.   Constitutive for forming this concept are the results of *traditionsgeschichtliche* examination of Old Testament texts over a longer period of time, such that we encounter individual notions and thought-patterns repeatedly appropriated from a more extensive intellectual sphere, that is, a sphere of tradition—whereby their appearances cannot be explained simply on the basis of literary use of older sources.   As we have already mentioned, such is the case for the Jerusalem cult tradition and the wisdom tradition from the period of Israel's early monarchy until the inter-testamental age.   From this analytical evidence we must infer by historical synthetic means that the sphere of tradition in question remained alive over a long stretch of time, that it affected the intellectual life of Israel during this period, and that it left its mark on the intellectual world of authors composing texts at the time.   Such a sphere of tradition that remains intact and alive for a long time is what we call a stream of tradition, and with this we attempt through historical synthesis to interpret analytical evidence as a phenomenon in the history of theology.[14]   Such a sphere of tradition, still only inferred, is of course historically subject to certain conditions for it to be possible.   With respect to its identity, consistency, and recognizability it is necessary that it be a movement with an intel-

---

14. Cf. O. H. Steck, "Das Problem theologischer Strömungen in nachexilischer Zeit," *EvTh* 28 (1968), 445–58; and Barth and Steck, *Exegese des Alten Testaments*, pp. 73 and 78.

lectually extensive reach and with a comprehensive conceptional design that is discernible in the distinct features of its starting-points, its contents, and its goals. It is not closed to other tradition streams and influences, yet it must lend itself to delimitation and differentiation from them and also be able to preserve its identity in the face of internal processes of development. Only those phenomena with intellectual expanse and conceptional design should, in view of their continued vitality, be considered streams of tradition; the continual appearance of individual notions or even of individual traditions is not enough to constitute a tradition stream, although it does point to such streams in whose current they can remain alive. The wisdom tradition and the Jerusalem cult tradition are such streams of tradition, and both these examples show also how the intellectual sphere of such a stream is structured. The nucleus of its identity is a peculiar, distinctive conceptional design of how to deal with experiences, and this is presented concretely in an arsenal of characteristic usage of language, genres, leading notions, and movements of thought. As an intellectual movement bearing such marks, a stream of tradition can extend to new experiences, new materials, oral and written traditions of different origin, and thus it can expand itself and undergo change. It will retain its identity and its existence as a tradition stream as long as the homogeneous development of its own conceptional design maintains control of the way in which new impulses are assimilated. This process could be demonstrated in detail with respect to the course and development of the wisdom tradition all the way down to Sirach, Baruch, the legends of Daniel, and the later apocalyptic collections. The persistence of such streams of tradition is furthermore dependent on certain historical circumstances. Distinctive, long-lasting, intellectual movements of this kind are not borne by individuals but only by groups in which the tradition streams are kept in flux through transmission, learned discussions, and development of new witnesses to the tradition. For carrying out their activities and training their successors these groups need fixed meeting places and durable, more or less established institutions which can meet long-term needs in a society with a structured division of labor, as existed in Israel after the formation of the state. In Israel the continuity of such groups, their teachings, and thus also the survival of certain tradition streams was made possible because even the collapse of the political and social structures at the end of the monarchical period did not extinguish homogeneous intellectual groups. This collapse lasted only a relatively short time until it was again possible and necessary for continuous intellectual life to exist in the Babylonian exile and also in Judah. We can discover such groups that keep streams of tradition alive for centuries: for example, "the wise" for the wisdom tradition and the temple-singers for the Jerusalem cult tradition.

DOMINANT THEOLOGICAL STREAMS
DURING ISRAEL'S HISTORY

With respect to *Traditionsgeschichte,* Old Testament research still tends to devote itself primarily to analytical work on individual texts, and the synthetic-historical problems are generally left untreated.[15] For this reason we are not presently in a position to offer a precise and fairly reliable *description of the main streams in the course of Israelite history.* What follows is no more than an attempt at a rough sketch; without intending to present final results, it aims to concretize the task and stimulate further work. Even this much is difficult because one cannot limit oneself to the homogeneous streams of the wisdom tradition and the Jerusalem cult tradition but must also include other streams of theological tradition which present a much more complex picture.

---

15. Cf. however—though using "parties" in a different sense than our "streams" —M. Smith, *Palestinian Parties and Politics that Shaped the Old Testament* (New York and London: Columbia University Press, 1971); cf. R. A. Hall, "Post-Exilic Theological Streams and the Book of Daniel" (Ph.D. dissertation, Yale University, 1974), pp. 80ff.

In Israel's *premonarchical period,* socio-cultural conditions are such as to counsel us against reckoning with the formation of streams of theological tradition in the narrow sense of the term. Nonetheless, we have text materials going back to that age and stemming from the diverse, formerly nomadic groups of settlers who later became Israel, and these testimonies betray early marks of what later emerged in the theological streams. The nomadic manner of experiencing and appropriating was characteristically preserved in Israel.[16] Regarding the substance, important marks are the monolatrous worship of the God Yahweh, the constitutive experience of his guidance in contingent events involving the group of people associated with him, and the critical appropriation of the religious and legal culture already present in the land. In areas where the old traditional materials thrived from the patriarchal period until Saul, these marks appear to constitute a rather uniformly distinctive, religious existence. This was localized in the territories of the ten Northern tribes, the groups that strove ethnically, politically, and in their religious traditions to form an entity of "all Israel," into which the tribes worshiping Yahweh in the South were also drawn, together with their own specific traditions.

In the above sense in which we defined streams of theological tradition, their real point of departure in Israel is found in the following period, in *the time of David and Solomon,* when radical changes especially in the historical and also the literary areas occur. Probably picking up on traditions cultivated at certain sites, transmitted by certain groups, and having certain developed needs in Canaanite Jerusalem, the Israelite wisdom tradition and the Israelite cult tradition in Jerusalem are consolidated in the City of David with a manner of critical appropriation that is to have momentous consequences. Here are the starting-points for two theological streams which remain alive

---

16. Cf. V. Maag, "Malkût JHWH," VTS 7 (1960), 129–53.

in Israel for a whole millennium. Their radiating power is initially to be seen primarily in this city itself where they affect the intellectual life, experience, and thinking in areas even beyond the guild of temple-singers and the "wisdom school." Literature influenced by wisdom in this period, the succession narrative and the Joseph narrative, gives evidence of this effect on the intellectual world of authors who, in narrative style and (in the case of the Joseph story) also in materials, maintain continuity with subject matter and capabilities of pre-state and early-monarchical Israel. This is all the more noticeable in the Yahwistic History: it demonstrates impressively how the intellectual world prevalent in the agricultural countryside of Judah and committed to the ten Northern tribes could maintain control, receive impulses from the Jerusalem streams (wisdom, world horizon, materials on primeval history), and combine into a singular, grandiose determination of Israel's identity in view of the Davidic empire. We cannot determine whether in the land of Judah, with its religious distinctiveness guiding him and with its—as it were—theological-geographical difference from Jerusalem,[17] the Yahwist served as a starting-point for a theological stream. For the land of Judah as also for the region of the Northern tribes we have to reckon with a continuous religious imprint from premonarchical traditions and from their notion of the constitutive relation Yahweh-Israel; they differed above all in their estimation of David and his dynasty. It is especially noteworthy that apparently neither Jerusalem stream had any recognizable effect on the large region of the ten tribes, with its border only a short distance to the north. As long as that territory remained in Israelite hands, wisdom and the universal scope of the Jerusalem cultic conceptional design found no acceptance there. To have such effect even the Davidic kingdom was too inorganically imposed upon the old

---

17. Cf. O. H. Steck, "Genesis 12,1–3 und die Urgeschichte des Jahwisten," in *Probleme biblischer Theologie* (see note 8 above), 525–54, especially pp. 552–53, n. 73.

tribes, and developments in the tribal territories were too widely separated from those in the city of Jerusalem.

In the following *period of the divided kingdoms until the fall of the Northern kingdom*,[18] Judah and Jerusalem presumably continued peacefully to develop and cultivate the heritage from the time of David and Solomon. This finds expression in texts from the Jerusalem cult tradition and from the wisdom tradition and in expansions of the Yahwist; it is also seen in the character of the prophets Amos and Micah from the Judean countryside and also in the work of Isaiah, who was affected especially by the Jerusalem streams. For our purposes we can disregard the legal tradition, which certainly enjoyed a continuous existence in the North and the South since early times; because of its specific function it hardly has the character of a theological stream with conceptional design. Moreover, the Jerusalem priestly tradition is not to be included here since any conceptional breadth that it possibly had does not come to the fore until Ezekiel. By the end of this period, then, there is only one, albeit a significant sector, where we can observe the onset of a new theological stream joining the two Jerusalem streams in the South: the tradition of the literary prophets. Amos, Isaiah, and Micah constitute its inception as a theological stream; the Hosea-tradition from the North enters it at a later point. To be sure, the roots of this stream remain in the dark, and we do not know whence Amos, Isaiah, and Micah received the themes and genres of prophetic expression. Furthermore, this is not a stream as homogeneously constant in language and themes as are the Jerusalem streams, and regular internal references within the tradition stream are missing altogether. What makes this rising tradition of literary prophets qualify as a theological stream, nurtured steadily by the new appearance of similar prophets, is the broad current of reception, collection, and productive actualization of prophetic utterances, a current

18. The division of the kingdom certainly posed serious questions about which region represented the true succession; cf. Ackroyd's discussion, below, p. 233.

that continues to flow until late in the post-exilic period. This movement is based on a constitutive, substantive conception: it is no longer in the *heilsgeschichtliche* or the Jerusalem traditions that Yahweh is immediately present, but only in the words coming forth from the prophet's mouth; prophetic utterances thus provide the only basis for apprehending Yahweh in the present and in the future; the contents of tradition are past phenomena, necessary only for special understanding of the new. Clearly, this stream remains in contact with antecedent intellectual-religious life and also, on occasion, with the two Jerusalem streams—especially with wisdom in the new manner of transmitting series of individual prophetic utterances. Yet these influences are no longer controlling. So far we do not have a concrete historical picture of these centers of prophetic traditon.

In the Northern kingdom some circles remain tied to the old traditional Israelite perceptions dating from the pre-state and early-monarchical period and thus viewing the territory of the kingdom from the standpoint of Yahweh's traditional significance for the tribal territories. Religious life within these circles intensifies as a result of the conflict with Canaanite religiosity. This process is observable in the appearance of prophets, especially Elijah and Elisha, and in the reception which their work found. It is also seen in the further development of traditions from the pre-state and early-monarchical period on to the Elohistic collection, as well as in Hosea. This process as such does not yet lead to the formation of a theological stream, but the situation changes with the appearance of the Deuteronomic tradition founded on this intellectual life and its traditions. The Deuteronomic movement probably emerges in the Northern kingdom in the eighth century and bears all of the marks of a theological stream: a breadth in substance and conceptional design, characteristic thought-patterns, leading views, and not least of all a distinctive, stereotyped language which exerts a uniform influence for centuries. Levites with their

preaching activities at first among the population of the North-
ern kingdom are the historical bearers of this rising stream.
Somewhat later it makes a broad appearance in the land of
Judah.

In the *period between the fall of the Northern kingdom and
the end of the kingdom of Judah*, lively intellectual life can be
seen only in Judah and Jerusalem. We can reckon with the
steady current of the wisdom stream, and there are indications
that the cultic stream in Jerusalem sought through means inherent to its tradition to master the contemporary situations of
national distress.[19] Yet these cult-prophetic actualizations held
tenaciously to the positive, immediate qualifications of the
status quo, and precisely at this point they are opposed by the
stream of prophetic tradition which perceives the approach of
unavoidable, comprehensive judgment; Zephaniah and especially Jeremiah are new exponents of this latter tradition.
Only for a short period and under the impact of the rapid
collapse of Assyrian dominance in the land during Josiah's
reign, this prophetic tradition found its way back—though with
due modifications—to the legitimacy of the conceptional design
of the Jerusalem cult; this can be observed in a distinct redactional stratum of the Isaianic tradition.[20] Of special consequence for Israel's theological life is, as already mentioned, the
emergence of a fourth vigorous theological stream, and indeed
now in the land of Judah: the Deuteronomic-Deuteronomistic
stream. An occurrence with great significance for the history
of literature accounts for this. After 722 B.C. the oral and written texts from the Northern kingdom, together with their traditionists, entered the land of Judah, were accepted there, and
apparently set in motion a process which reinforced a specifi-

19. Cf. Jörg Jeremias, *Kultprophetie und Gerichtsverkündigung in der späten
Königszeit Israels*, WMANT 35 (Neukirchen-Vluyn: Neukirchener Verlag, 1970),
111ff., 128ff., 183ff.; and Steck, *Friedensvorstellungen*, pp. 46ff.
20. Cf. H. Barth, *Die Jesaja-Worte in der Josiazeit: Israel und Assur als Thema
einer produktiven Neuinterpretation der Jesajaüberlieferung* (forthcoming in
WMANT, Neukirchen-Vluyn: Neukirchener Verlag).

cally Iraelite consciousness of being the people of Israel, a consciousness which found its assurance in the historical traditions of the early period. This awareness is to prove very significant for Israel's identity in the following period as every political self-representation of Israel crumbles and the immediate universal qualifications of the Jerusalem cult tradition are questioned to the point of totally negating their basis in reality. The reception of the prophetic traditions (including Hosea's) from the Northern kingdom, the appropriation of the traditions about the judges, Samuel, and Saul, and especially the incorporation of the Elohistic narrative into the Yahwist (the latter having arisen and survived in the countryside of Judah) are the significant components in this Judean process of activating Israel's early historical traditions and the Israelite self-understanding connected with these traditions. Together with the positive assessment of the Davidic dynasty in the land of Judah, they make up the fundamental, theological-historical constellation essential for understanding the Josianic period and its hopes and for comprehending as well the intellectual world of Jeremiah. The traditionists who brought the Deuteronomic stream to Judah are the controlling theological curators of these texts, and their productivity now is directed to a Judean revision of the core of Deuteronomy (inclusion of notions from the Judean countryside stemming from the Jerusalem cult stream) and to a first draft of the Deuteronomistic History (reflection on the reasons for the fall of the Northern kingdom). To express itself publicly, this theological stream may have continued the Deuteronomic preaching activity in the land of Judah, the goal being to warn the Israelites there about the imminent judgment and to lead them to the Deuteronomic law. In this effort, the goal of this stream may coincide now with that of the contemporary Jerusalem streams of wisdom and the cultic tradition, although each has a completely different stock of notions, conceptional design, and thought-pattern. Yet at the same time this goal makes it distinct from the stream of prophetic tradition.

By the end of the pre-exilic period at least four theological streams can therefore be distinguished in Judah and Jerusalem. Despite more or less close interconnections—as is only to be expected for the intellectual life in a single country—these streams nonetheless have and maintain their respective characteristics: both the cult tradition and the wisdom tradition being concentrated in Jerusalem, the very diverse prophetic tradition, and the Deuteronomic-Deuteronomistic tradition dominating in the land of Judah. From each of these streams separately we have homogeneous textual traditions. But beyond these it is also possible for texts of other derivation to be integrated into the stream, as can be seen in the Deuteronomic-Deuteronomistic stream with its traditional materials from the Northern kingdom. Here as in the prophetic stream, living tradition is united with its own written heritage, to which actualizing interpretations are directed. The literary prophets are especially distinctive: on the strength of the prophetic inspiration to innovate, their work evinces both reference to and contingent separation from ruling traditions. Furthermore, when they step forth to speak, their appearance cannot be viewed as public proclamations that represent the prophetic stream and are homogeneous with it—which is the case with the productive transmitters of prophetic texts. In the literary prophets we observe how the spontaneously inspired separation from the usual streams leads, in the course of collecting prophetic utterances, to the inception of a new and different stream, namely, the prophetic stream of the eighth century. To conclude our discussion on this period, we can note that the dominance of the different streams alternates decidedly. Apart from the wisdom stream which led a separate existence due to its special character, the vitality of the Jerusalem cult tradition probably continued in the country of Judah especially in the peaceful times

until the middle of the eighth century, and it remains alive
even after that in Jerusalem. Beginning at that point, however, the prophetic and the Deuteronomic-Deuteronomistic
streams step more into the foreground, at least in terms of
substance, in order to deal with the new, momentous events
that occur.

This theological-historical profile characterizes above all the
following *exilic period*,[21] during which Israel's intellectual life
extends to two geographical areas: the deportees' settlement in
Mesopotamia and the remnant of the population left in the
land of Judah. Among *the exiles*, the prophetic stream receives
new nourishment and a new substantive direction as it predicts
that Israel, now so obviously struck in judgment, will find its
fate turned into salvation. Ezekiel and his disciples activate
prophetically the Jerusalem priestly tradition. Deutero-Isaiah,
probably a deported temple-singer, effects a grandiose prophetic
assimilation of the universal elements of the Jerusalem cult
stream, combined with influences from the wisdom stream, and
he forms their affirmations about the present into his message
about the coming, imminent salvation. Both of these, Ezekiel
and Deutero-Isaiah, alter tradition in characteristic ways in
order to account for current experiences of guilt and judgment.
Zechariah is also to be mentioned in this regard. Besides the
prophetic activating of priestly concepts from Jerusalem, the
priestly tradition among the exiles also finds expression in the
basic draft of the Priestly History. This tradition stems perhaps from the land of Judah and is acquainted with Israel's old
historical heritage preserved there. The Priestly History intends to serve the purpose of forming a new Israelite identity,

---

21. For the following discussion of this period, cf. P. R. Ackroyd, *Exile and
Restoration: A Study of Hebrew Thought of the Sixth Century BC* (London:
SCM, 1968); Ackroyd, *Israel under Babylon and Persia*, New Clarendon Bible
(London: Oxford University Press, 1970); Ackroyd, *The Age of the Chronicler*,
The Selwyn Lectures, Supplement to *Colloquium* (Auckland: Commercial Press,
1970); and O. H. Steck, *Israel und das gewaltsame Geschick der Propheten:
Untersuchungen zur Überlieferung des deuteronomistischen Geschichtsbildes im
Alten Testament, Spätjudentum und Urchristentum*, WMANT 23 (Neukirchen-
Vluyn: Neukirchener Verlag, 1967), 110–218, especially pp. 196ff.

although it replaces a national-eschatological expectation with a narrower view of Yahweh's cultically clean community gathered around the sanctuary. This position, although not a start of a continuous stream, will exert considerable influence in religious politics. All of these expressions of theological life in the Babylonian exile must also be understood—at least in part—as oppositional stands against the views dominating at that time in *the land of Judah*. There it is the Deuteronomistic stream that prevails. Its position develops in order to master their situation theologically, and it makes its appearance in a characteristically didactic and stereotyped phraseology and, in terms of content, in a distinct picture of history. The latter view considers the present situation as a result of Israel's history of sin, teaches that the present is the prolongation of guilt and judgment, and finally discloses that conversion and obedience to the Deuteronomic law are the path for Israel to follow until God again acts to bless them. The public activity of this stream takes the form of penitential prayer and preaching. Their intellectual conviction is expressed in their developing their own textual tradition (the Deuteronomistic History) and in their productively appropriating existent texts (Jeremiah, Amos, perhaps also JE).[22] The influence of this position can be seen in its effect on the transmitters of the Jerusalem cult tradition in the country. These latter take up the Deuteronomistic view, in the course of this become interested in the people of Israel, and create the genre of "communal lament"; important examples of this are Pss. 79 and 105/106 as well as the book of Lamentations.[23]

With the onset of the *post-exilic period*, groups of the redeemed people return to their homeland and manage to rebuild the temple. This results in new theological-historical constellations—indeed confrontations—ignited by the question of how the current Palestinian situation, in all of its ambiguity, is

22. Cf. Steck, *Israel*, pp. 110ff., 137ff., 184ff., 196ff.
23. Cf. Steck, *Friedensvorstellungen*, pp. 48ff.

to be interpreted theologically. Is it the realization of the new salvation which was expected in the exilic period and which Haggai and Zechariah explicitly claim for the present? Or in spite of everything, does the absence of essential signs of salvation indicate that judgment is still continuing into the present and that the new salvation is yet to come? Perhaps even Haggai finds himself in this controversy.[24] Strong differences of opinion on this fundamental question persist until late in the post-exilic period. The streams of active theological tradition certainly continue as such in this age, despite an increase in their written texts.[25] At multiple points of connection and development they now become attached to the two alternative positions which O. Plöger has termed the "theocratic" and the "eschatological."[26]

The "theocratic" position understands the post-exilic temple and its cult as the fulfillment of God's ordinance of salvation, as the exilic prophets had proclaimed it. It is championed by the priests at the temple of Zerubbabel, and in the Persian period it probably became the dominant position due to the political measures in religious and administrative affairs taken by Ezra and Nehemiah, in accord with Persian efforts. The lawbook which Ezra brought back to Jerusalem, that is, the Priestly History which was expanded with sacral-legal materials and the Holiness Code, gains great importance under these circumstances. The Nehemiah Memoirs and the redaction of Haggai as a chronicle of the building of the temple also belong in this context. The stream of the Jerusalem cult tradition, borne by

---

24. Cf. O. H. Steck, "Zu Haggai 1, 2–11", *ZAW* 83 (1971), 355–79.

25. Cf. Steck, "Das Problem theologischer Strömungen in nachexilischer Zeit," *EvTh* 28 (1968), pp. 449–50; and critically proceeding further, D. L. Petersen, "Israelite Prophecy and Prophetic Traditions in the Exilic and Post-Exilic Periods" (Ph.D. disseration, Yale University, 1972), forthcoming in revised form in the SBL Monograph Series as *Late Israelite Prophecy*; and Hall, "Post-Exilic Theological Streams and the Book of Daniel."

26. O. Plöger, *Theokratie und Eschatologie*, WMANT 2, 3d ed. (Neukirchen-Vluyn: Neukirchener Verlag, 1968), pp. 129ff. = *Theocracy and Eschatology* (Richmond: John Knox, 1968), pp. 106ff.; Plöger's investigation is a first attempt and needs further differentiation. Cf. now also P. D. Hanson, *The Dawn of Apocalyptic* (Philadelphia: Fortress, 1975).

the temple-singers, reassumes its former location where, in immediate and salvific terms, it can underscore the legitimacy of the temple, though now the post-exilic temple. And because of the need for education in this established Persian province, the wisdom stream can play an important role in intellectual proximity to the temple and its theology. Here as also in the circle of temple-singers[27] there is a conspicuous effort to reflect seriously on the existential experiences of the individual person (the dialogues of Job).

Alongside of this, the "eschatological" position also thrives in Judah. Its exponents are theologically more reserved with respect to the current situation, and they expect the new salvation to come yet in the future. Their ranks include the Deuteronomistic stream, which presumably continued to be active after the exilic period. Despite interconnections and occasional theocratic adaptations (late strata in Proto-Isaiah and Zephaniah), the stream of prophetic tradition also belongs on this side. It makes itself heard in its productive appropriation of prior prophetic texts, but it grows also in the form of new prophecies (Trito-Isaiah, Joel, Malachi).

In the situation after Nehemiah the dominating theocratic circles apparently become engaged in trying to unify the population of the Judean province, including the divergent theological streams. At any rate, this must have touched the significant texts of each stream. This is evidenced in the theocratic reworking of the textual traditions about Israel's history, which had been transmitted in the Deuteronomistic stream; these traditions are joined with the Priestly document and supplemented by priestly elements to form the massive literary work stretching from Gen. 1 to 2 Kgs. 25. It is evidenced furthermore in the positioning of the Pentateuch, designated by Ezra's lawbook (including Deuteronomy!), to be the controlling

27. Cf. G. von Rad, " 'Gerechtigkeit' und 'Leben' in der Kultsprache der Psalmen" (1950), in *Gesammelte Studien* (see note 8 above), 225–47 = " 'Righteousness' and 'Life' in the Cultic Language of the Psalms," in *The Problem of the Hexateuch, and Other Essays*, 243–66.

foundation. The integrating efforts are also evidenced in the Chronicler's History, almost a classical presentation of the theocratic position despite the use made of the Deuteronomistic History. This position's concrete relations with the world are possibly represented in the legends of Daniel, in the book of Jonah, and in the book of Esther. It is uncertain whether material from the prophetic tradition was also appropriated; if so, it had to occur in the form of historicization.

Political instability at the end of the Persian period and during the Ptolemaic period evokes new crises, and these lend renewed importance to the prophetic stream as it attempts to deal with the concrete problems of the times. Building on its own inherent elements from the Jerusalem cult tradition as well as on that cult stream itself, the prophetic stream flings open on a universal scale the future horizon of a new world epoch (Isa. 24–27; Joel 4; Deutero- and Trito-Zechariah). Above all, the powerful influx of administrative, economic, and cultural forces from early Hellenism and its life-style causes new fronts to be formed within the Israelite population of Judah. The only direct traces of this controversy found in the Old Testament are in Qoheleth. However, in this period productive transmission of older texts comes to an end, and this itself as well as the effort to consolidate the literature of what later becomes the Old Testament can probably be regarded as a process of securing oneself in the face of Hellenism. Similarly, we can assume that the new Hellenistic front relativized old differences among positions and streams, in order to achieve anti-Hellenistic unity. This pressure elicited a movement and grouping which is theologically complex and yet united in its opposition to Hellenism. This can be detected in Sirach: the wisdom stream moves beyond its earlier connection with the theocratic temple-position and becomes open also to the prophetic streams; the expectation of Israel's restoration enters wisdom, and the interpretation of prophetic predictions becomes an essential task of the wisdom teacher. Only connections with the Deuteronomistic stream do not appear explicitly.

We need to emphasize, though, that the theocratic stream (priests, temple-singers, wisdom teachers) and the eschatological stream (prophetic tradition, Deuteronomistic tradition) certainly continued to exist in this period. Their traditions, movements of thought, and notional elements remained alive notwithstanding their being committed to writing; they were vibrant in respective circles of transmitters and represented a still progressing intellectual life. As we can conclude from Sirach and later writings, the wisdom stream was the locus where the anti-Hellenistic coalition carried out its controversy with the knowledge and spirit of the times, the result of this being an actualized Israelite position in thought and deed that was faithful to tradition. In this context oppositional forces were also mustered from other streams. For the wisdom school was the place where the entire body of knowledge current then in Palestine was gathered and could be mastered. This potential becomes visible and the reservoir bursts as the anti-Hellenistic controversy comes to a peak shortly after Palestine's inclusion in the Seleucid empire. In the movement of the Ḥasidim a greater conflux of the diverse streams establishes itself in order to present a common front. The picture of history in the Deuteronomistic stream had continued to be handed down and in the meantime had been modified toward an inner-Israelite, eschatological separation, and now this view of history becomes the conceptional framework embracing the various standard traditions of the streams. In this confluence the wisdom stream increasingly takes the intellectual lead, whereas the diverse characteristics of the respective streams still express themselves in each of the individual themes, notions, and traditions.[28] This development prior to the outbreak of persecution is recorded in such literature as Tobit, the core of Jubilees,

28. Cf. Steck, *Israel*, pp. 205ff.

and the Testaments of the Twelve Patriarchs as well as in the Apocalypse of Weeks (1 Enoch 93:1–10; 91:12–17). From the period of persecution it is expressed in the Deuteronomistically flavored penitential prayers of Dan. 9; Bar. 1:15ff.; and the Prayer of Azariah; also in 4QDibHam and in the book of Daniel, the book of Jubilees, the book of Baruch, as well as in the apocalypse of animal symbols (the second Dream-Vision, in 1 Enoch 85–90) and in the parenetic sections of 1 Enoch.

The further path taken by the theological streams in Palestine, after the Ḥasidic movement fell apart, leads us out of the Old Testament. For reasons of space in the present study we will not follow it further; more details are provided elsewhere.[29]

THEOLOGICAL IMPLICATIONS

To conclude this discussion, we need to consider what this quest for streams of theological tradition can yield. We have sought to determine how the active intellectual life behind the Old Testament texts produced continuous, theological-historical connections, despite all of the developments and changes. In the light of our findings, we might suggest three implications of this:

(1) By determining the basic currents in the history of theology as they relate to the context and the conditions of the history of ancient Israel, we can succeed for the first time in gaining an overall, living perception—not only one which compares transmitted texts with reconstructable political situations, but also a perception which understands Old Testament discourse about God in terms of the reciprocal relationship between historical experiences and the functioning of dominant traditions and effective theological streams to interpret and master these experiences. Only by viewing Old Testament affirmations in connection with a picture of Israel's history—and

29. Cf. Steck, *Israel*, pp. 209ff. See also M. Fishbane's discussion on patterns of Jewish interpretation, below, Chapter 12.

that includes the movements of intellectual life as well—are we able to recognize that these affirmations are living, dynamic occurrences in a specific time under specific conditions. Such a perception is essential if in preaching from the Old Testament we wish to respect the lasting index, the authentic intention, and the situational boundaries of a text.

(2) Connections of content between the Old Testament and primitive Christianity or early Judaism are by no means limited merely to citations from codified scripture. Well into the early centuries of this era, the Old Testament writings remained in close association with the diverse theological life of late Israel, a life which unfolds and endures independently in the respective traditions of Christianity, Judaism, and Islam. This diverse theological life of late Israel establishes the connection with primitive Christianity, in both ties and tensions. When we endeavor to develop a biblical theology with a descriptive and historical base, such knowledge of theological streams connecting late Israel and primitive Christianity is of great significance.

(3) And finally, an Old Testament text needs to be examined in connection with the traditions, streams, and specific movements of thought which shaped it, for only then will the exegete, having analyzed it also form-critically, be able to comprehend this text as a living intellectual occurrence instead of as a detached product of the mind. Furthermore, it will be possible for him to bring his own exegetical models of understanding under control with respect to the thought-patterns and association-fields peculiar to the text. With this perspective the exegete will see the extent to which a text is indebted to its antecedent intellectual world for its ideational point of contact, its thrust, and its frame of thought, and to what extent the text receives and shares in tradition which is held in common with its hearers or readers. And this analysis will give the exegete reasons and scholarly evidence for perceiving the points at which the text creatively exceeds its own prior intellectual world and steps forth with a special, new assertion which at

times may even reverse tradition or impose critical limitations. For tradition and innovation are the factors which mold most texts.

Our discussion has dealt with traditions and streams as the provenance of texts; the next two chapters will address the problem of continuity and discontinuity as well as the phenomenon of innovations, of the creative transcendence of tradition.

Chapter 9

Continuity and Discontinuity: Rehabilitation and Authentication

Peter R. Ackroyd

The existence of major strands of thought, traceable over long periods of the life of ancient Israel, is witness to the degree to which, in spite of all the political hazards, particular lines of belief and particular styles of expression continue to be effective in the community's life. The previous chapter has clarified some of these strands of tradition, presenting them as the contexts within which particular elements in the literature may be understood. Such a presentation rightly stresses the continuity in tradition. But the element of discontinuity is a political reality, and the doubts which are raised by major or minor disruptions in life must affect the attitudes of those who experience them and in turn have repercussions upon the way in which they understand the traditions, and upon the way in which they express them.

The purpose of this chapter is to examine the nature of the breaks in continuity and the ways in which men seek to overcome them, and to suggest the effects that these processes have upon the formation of the literature and the modification of the thought. To a large extent men attempt to incorporate the discontinuity into coherent thinking, and to find means of authenticating the reestablished sense of continuity. It must, however, be evident that there will remain a measure of uncertainty, a question mark put against the validity of the tradition, which may in the end lead to more radical questioning of it.

That questioning is a theme which is taken up in the following chapter.

BREAKS AND BRIDGINGS

When Saul attempted to consult the deity after the battle in which Jonathan had infringed the oath the king had laid on the army, he was met with silence (1 Sam. 14:37). The contact between man and God, essential for the ordering of public as of private affairs, was broken. To reestablish contact was a matter of urgency, and necessitated the appropriate inquiry, the obviating of the offense by the appropriate mechanism. Then, and only then, the continuity of relationship could be assured. The example is but one of many; it concerns public policy, in this instance a matter of warfare and its successful pursuit. It illustrates a principle expressed in many areas of life, that of the need for a continuing relationship between man and God, and that of the danger to life which must follow from discontinuity. Continuity and discontinuity are correlative;[1] the need to maintain relationship is cut across by the mischances which introduce breaks into it. Such breaks may be at a relatively trivial level, although this will not be unimportant to the one who experiences it; it may derive from some temporary impurity which debars a man from full participation in religious life (so, e.g., Lev. 14, the law governing ṣāra'at[2]). It may be the result of a major calamity, a total political collapse, such as the Babylonian conquest and the exile of the sixth century B.C. In each case there must be found ways of overcoming the break in continuity, and it is evident that some of the situations will be more readily and simply met than others.

The two extreme examples just cited represent the two major subdivisions of discontinuity. The one may be termed *cultic*, not simply because it is clear that a problem immediately con-

---

1. Cf. my *Continuity: A Contribution to the Study of the Old Testament Religious Tradition* (Oxford: Blackwell, 1962), p. 28.
2. Not leprosy; see, e.g., E. V. Hulse, "The Nature of Biblical 'Leprosy,'" *PEQ* 107 (1975), 87–105.

nected with cultic observance is involved, but also because, while the particular instance will have an historical setting—the affliction will affect this man at that moment in time—this setting is less important than the provisions which govern cultic observance and continue to operate over a long period of time. So long as these particular provisions exist, there will be countless examples of infringement and of consequent break in relationship. The other may be termed *historical*, since it belongs to a particular moment of political change and adjustment. It will for that reason be unique in that the particular moment of time at which it happens is unrepeatable. But a closer examination of the examples shows that the distinction between them is less precise than this. We may, in relation to the first type, recognize that, while the origins of such practices and beliefs are so remote that we can hardly now hope to describe them, they are nevertheless rooted in precise experience; and when, as in Lev. 14, we get a long catalogue of instances, believed to be related because of a certain external similarity, we may detect something of the historical process by which a law applicable to one type of condition—say a skin condition in men—may be understood to be relevant also to other types of condition, which we would not, in our culture, associate at all, namely, the condition of mold in materials and mildew on building plaster. We cannot say just how the development of the legal descriptions proceeded; we may simply recognize a degree of ordering, of correlating and harmonizing, which serves not only to provide satisfying methods of diagnosis and action, but also, by the ordering together of apparently unrelated experiences, makes them more manageable, more comprehensible, and therefore more easily resolved and less a matter of anxiety. To classify, as sociological and anthropological studies have made clear, is in itself a procedure which aids security; it is the anomalous which appears dangerous because it does not fit into known categories.

Similarly, we may observe that while, in some instances at

least, we may see the precise historical context for a particular moment of break, a merely historical approach is less than adequate to understanding the way in which such experiences are regarded. There will, inevitably, be some degree of change in the points at which external military and political pressures bring disaster to a given community. To some extent we may perhaps be right to recognize, in the men and women (prophets or others) who forecast such moments of disaster, those who by that very forecasting assist the process of meeting the emergency when it comes.[3] To foretell an earthquake (and is this perhaps how Amos 1:1 "two years before the earthquake" was understood by whatever editor gave us the reference?) will not prevent it happening, but it may well serve to reduce the shattering effects which it must have on those whose understanding of seismology is limited to cosmological conceptions of insecurity and beliefs in divine anger which could, momentarily at least, allow the firm pillars of the earth to move. To speak of national disaster in terms of divine judgment provides a comment on the contemporary situation and invites reform; it also makes possible a handling of the disaster when it comes by those for whom the prophecy of it is accepted as genuine. Once this is accepted, even the unexpected, the unprophesied disaster, may be fitted into a known pattern, recognized for what it is, and thus become less terrifying; it ceases to be anomalous.[4]

What is true of the external disaster will be seen even more clearly in internal affairs. Changes which bring a break in continuity will acquire a pattern and therefore be both recognizable and manageable. When dynastic kingship is accepted as the system of government, as it was for roughly four centuries in Judah, the death of the king will be an unforeseen event; ill-

3. Thus "discontinuity is resolved in the discovery of a continuity within it" (Ackroyd, *Continuity*, p. 29).
4. The Moabite scribe who wrote, "Chemosh was angry with his land" (Moabite Stone, lines 5–6), may be seen to fit the experience of defeat at Israel's hands into an intelligible pattern. Restoration of relationship brings victory and the reestablished contact of people and deity.

ness, battle, old age have some measure of predictability but not absolute precision.[5]   But the event will also be anticipated in the sense that it is inevitable, and provision can be made for it by the designating of a successor (so 1 Kgs. 1) or by the appointment of a regent (so 2 Kgs. 15:5 where Jotham acts for Azariah/Uzziah).   Thus a dangerous break is handled.   There will be occasions, even in so orderly a dynastic system, when the process will be broken; Amon son of Manasseh was assassinated, for reasons not known to us, but whatever the assassins had in mind was presumably frustrated by the placing of Josiah on the throne by "the people of the land" (2 Kgs. 21:23–24).   We may readily see that such changes of ruler as normally take place within a dynasty will have a pattern, a form; there will be particular procedures to be carried through, although we may only project these from the information given us about the exceptions (e.g., the coronation of Joash in 2 Kgs. 11 after an interregnum).

The break involves the relation between deity and people; for whatever the precise religious status of the king is believed to be, there is no doubt of his functioning in religious matters. The recognition that there are psalms concerned with the king and his function (e.g., Ps. 72), and prophetic oracles equally so concerned (e.g., Isa. 11:1–9 [10]), carries with it the possibility of using such words in association with the transfer from one king to his successor of the status and functions which eventually may be seen to belong to the whole dynasty and be projected back into its origins (so in the final complex form of 2 Sam. 7).   Then the particular break at the death of a king becomes only one in a series.   It is not to be viewed casually, for we can see how, particularly in the Northern kingdom of Israel, the death of a ruler is on a number of occasions taken as an

---

5. Cf. 2 Kgs. 20:1–11 for the first—a literalist would suppose that death for Hezekiah then becomes certain at the fifteen-year term; 1 Kgs. 22 provides a prophesied example of the second; 1 Kgs. 1–2 a somewhat sorry picture of the third.

opportunity for breaking the dynastic principle;[6] indeed in terms of political overlordship, the death of an Assyrian ruler could be a moment for revolt and the regaining of independence. But there is, nevertheless, a subordinating of the particular instance to a known scheme. Only when, with 722 in the North and 587 in the South, kingship comes to an end, is the pattern irrevocably broken. We shall note subsequently some indications of attempts to recover it.

Just as these particular historical instances acquire something of a cultic dimension—although irregular, they are nevertheless susceptible to order—so too we may detect an interchange between the historical and the cultic in other circumstances too. The exposition of Ps. 74 by F. Willesen[7] relates this and other comparable psalms to a cultic background, illuminated by Babylonian and other examples, in which disaster to shrine and city, as the dwelling place of the deity, is depicted in military terms—siege, destruction, and the like—where it may be held in reality to concern a cultic situation, a moment of defilement, of loss of communication with the deity, which is, for the community, just as disastrous as the destructive event which appears to be described. It is probable that the matter is more complex; the imagery of disaster derives from experience or knowledge of actual destructions, and the interrelationship between event and cultic form is subtle. But the point that Willesen makes is valid insofar as he sees that what is described

---

6. The dynasties of Omri and Jehu are sufficiently extensive for it to be clear that the North did not reject the principle (as A. Alt argued: "Das Königtum in Israel und Juda," *VT* 1 [1951], 2–22 = *Kleine Schriften zur Geschichte des Volkes Israel*, vol. 2 [München: Beck, 1953], 116–34 = "The Monarchy in Israel and Judah," in *Essays on Old Testament History and Religion* [Oxford: Blackwell, 1966], 239–59; for cogent criticisms, see T. G. G. Thornton, "Charismatic Kingship in Israel and Judah," *JTS* 14 [1963], 1–11). One factor in the greater instability of the North must be the greater power attaching to military leaders, who were in most instances the new claimants to the throne (cf. also the interesting reaction of Joab as military commander to his position at the siege of Rabbath-Ammon in 2 Sam. 12:28; another than Joab might well have broken the kingdom, the dynasty, by making claims for himself). But such a claimant needs religious support if he is to establish some continuity with what has preceded, and hence the stress on prophetic revelation of the divine will in the change.

7. "The Cultic Situation of Psalm 74," *VT* 2 (1952), 289–306.

in such political language need not have that particular quality. So, even if Ps. 74 and others like it derive their present form in part at least from some particular historical moment— although commentators have never been able to agree absolutely which moment it is—their significance is not limited to such a moment, nor is it limited to a series of such moments; it has meaning for other situations, less outwardly drastic but nevertheless serious for the continuing religious life and well-being of the community.[8]

There is a clue here to the methods adopted by the community for the *overcoming of breaks* in continuity. The more commonly experienced internal emergencies provide a basis for the meeting of the more urgent but less frequent major crises. That this is so becomes important for the understanding of the overall, as distinct from the more particular, purposes of such compilations as the Holiness Code (Lev. 17–26) and the Priestly Work. Here we may observe how an endeavor is made at clarifying the nature of the community and the ways in which it is to be reestablished and preserved as the true and holy people, partly by the reinterpretation of older traditions and the giving of a wider and more coherent portrayal of the past as a normative period, from creation to the entry to the promised land, partly also by the stress upon purity and its maintenance, in the gathering into a coherent form of the great mass of legislation, now viewed as related to the overall purpose and not merely to the particular needs. For our discussion at this point, the relevance of the occasional internal breaks is that they provide indications of the mechanisms which are available, as well as providing a basis for their reapplication to wider con-

---

8. The same point must be made in regard to the poems of the book of Lamentations. If at certain points there appear to be clear references to 587 B.C.—and there are admittedly very few that really are clear—there is no adequate ground for supposing that the poems originated then, rather than being examples of a particular form which, like some in the Psalter, have been given greater precision. Equally they are seen to be applicable to other situations, both precise and historical (the fall of Jerusalem in A.D. 70, the crucifixion of Jesus), or less precise and personal, linked to the experiences, inward or outward, of the ordinary worshiper.

cerns.   Particular rituals, of which some are clearly know to us
in the various purificatory requirements laid down especially in
the books of Leviticus and Numbers, provide the means by
which the individual who is cut off for some specific reason from
full participation in the community's life may be restored and
recognized to be restored.   The two aspects are important; for
it is not simply a question of carrying through a specified
mechanism—the offering of particular sacrifices, the undertaking of particular recitals of formulas, the passage of a certain
fixed period of time—but also one of certification that the break
has been overcome, a reacceptance into the life of the community which is acknowledged.

   When this is considered in relation to the experiences of the
whole community in major moments of crisis, we may see how
the attempt is made at placing the particular event and experience in such a context of interpretation that it becomes meaningful and capable of resolution.   Thus, without specifying the
precise relationship between event and celebration in such an
instance as the defeat of Sisera, described in Judg. 4 and
hymned in Judg. 5,[9] we may observe that the presentation in
the poem of the moment of disaster overcome gives it a universal or a typical quality: "So may all your enemies perish,
Yahweh" (Judg. 5:31).   The break in religious continuity
which is presented in the poem (e.g., vss. 6–7) is seen to be
overcome by the direct delivering action of God, through the
agency of his faithful.   "But let those who love him be as the
sun when he rises in might" (vs. 31) underlines the reestab-
lishment of the relationship and the blessing which is the
appropriate concomitant of it.   The particular historical event,
now only partly discernible, becomes significant for other moments of disaster in that it provides the reassurance which
enables men to meet them.

   The point just made lays the stress on the one aspect of the

9. The relationship of the prose and poetry is, of course, more complex than
this.   For a particular attempt at handling the problem of the poem in relation
to its celebration of the event, cf. A. Weiser, "Das Deboralied," *ZAW* 71 (1959),
67–97.

overcoming of the break—that of the action, both divine and human, which is essential for it to be achieved. Both the laws and customs governing warfare and the provisions for purificatory rituals presuppose that both deity and people are involved in the restoration of order: the deity by his willingness to act, to restore relationship, as well as by his recognized responsibility for the laying down of the mechanisms which open up the way to restoration; the people by their response to the situation, their recognition of responsibility, or their fitting the experience into a context which points to the particular actions needed. There is, as we have seen, another aspect involved. Restoration is not simply a matter of experience; it is also a matter of *authentication*. In theory at least—and here we move into an area which touches on the whole problem of truth and falsity in religious interpretation—restoration, the apparent renewal of contact with the deity, could be an illusion. When the prophet Hananiah (Jer. 28) speaks of the speedy overthrow of Babylon and the restoration of exiled king and leaders, he is giving an assurance of the overcoming of the break which Jeremiah declares to be nongenuine. In another context, Jeremiah says: "They have healed the calamity (*šeber*) of my people lightly, saying 'All is well (*šālôm šālôm*); but there is no well-being (*šālôm*)'" (Jer. 6:14). The belief may exist in men's minds that all is well, when in fact all that has taken place is a restoration of outward security, apparent blessing from the deity. Authentication of the restoration requires the assurance that the break really has been overcome, that relationship really has been restored.

Now this, it is clear, is a point on which views may differ. With the collapse of the kingdom of Judah in 597 and 587, it is evident that there was not one single view of what would constitute restoration. There was even, so Jer. 44 relates, a segment of the people which claimed that the disaster was due to the neglect of the worship of the Queen of Heaven, and that restoration could only be possible with a due acknowledgment of her status and claims. For them, the break in religious continuity lay not in a loss of contact with Yahweh, but in a relatively long-standing loss of contact with another deity, perhaps understood as his consort. For them, the assurance of reestablished relationship would be made in terms of her renewed favor, her blessing, the bestowal of life and well-being deriving from her resumption of her proper place. For others— and their position is now largely obscured in our texts— rehabilitation lay with the appointment of Gedaliah as this is described in the longer texts of Jer. 40–41. The willingness of Jeremiah to stay with him and his unwillingness to go to Egypt argue for a positive evaluation of this particular political setup, although in fact it was doomed to failure. A vivid picture is drawn in Jer. 40:7–12 of a renewed community, a gathering of scattered Jews to join the remnant *(šĕ'ērît)* with Gedaliah. There is no precise information, and our sources are limited in scope, but we may legitimately suppose that there were those (and presumably including Jeremiah) who were prepared to authenticate this as the point of rehabilitation.[10] We have no means of determining the sequel. Our sources provide no direct information about what went on in Judah after the assassination of Gedaliah, beyond a possible inference in Jer. 52:30 that a further exiling of Jews in the twenty-third year of Nebuchadrezzar (583/2) could be one aspect of this. That there were many who remained in Judah—although how many must be quite uncertain—is clear enough. That they thought of themselves as the true and continuing community would seem very likely, but nothing that has survived indicates this clearly. That some of the problems of fifty years later derive from conflicting claims to true continuity is again probable, without our being able to specify just who made what claims. What we do observe is that eventually any claims that were made to continuity in Judah were overshadowed by those made for continuity through the exiled group in Babylonia. Both the Deuteronomistic writers and the Chronicler claim this; it is

10. Cf. my comments in "Aspects of the Jeremiah Tradition," *IJT* 20 (1971), 1–12, especially pp. 5–6.

less certain, but probable, that the same is true for the Priestly writers, though conceivable that some Palestinian material from this period may be incorporated in their work.

The problem of authentication becomes acute in the early Persian period. The purpose of this discussion is not to investigate the alternative views of different groups, although it is important to recognize the problems that are created by the existence of differing claims.[11] What we need to observe is the *processes* involved. At the moment when restoration is brought about, its validity is claimed on the basis of lines of succession to the past. The rebuilding of the temple and the rehabilitation of Jerusalem in themselves constitute endeavors to reactivate the past. When the rebuilding was initiated it is said that many of those "who had seen the first temple, when the foundation of this temple was laid before their eyes, wept with a loud voice, and many shouted aloud for joy" (Ezra 3:12). It is often assumed that the weeping was in distress at the comparison between the impoverished post-exilic temple and its earlier and richer form. The basis for such an interpretation is found in Hag. 2:3 ("Who among you is left who saw this temple in its former glory? and how do you see it now? is it not as nothing in your eyes?"). But this latter passage is making a different point: it is in reality contrasting the new temple, less rich than the old, with the glory that is about to break out (Hag. 2:4, 6–9). The passage in Ezra 3 shows a community weeping and rejoicing, responding in the forms of worship, to the reality of the rebuilding of the temple which brings back again the reality of the former temple.[12] It is the recognition that in this rebuilding the link is reestablished; continuity is recovered.

Closer examination of the Chronicler's presentation reveals

---

11. For renewed discussion of such problems, see P. D. Hanson, *The Dawn of Apocalyptic: The Historical and Sociological Roots of Jewish Apocalyptic Eschatology* (Philadelphia: Fortress, 1975).

12. On weeping and laughter as ritual forms, cf. F. F. Hvidberg, *Weeping and Laughter in the Old Testament: A Study of Canaanite-Israelite Religion* (Leiden: Brill, 1962), cf. especially pp. 144–45; Hvidberg does not mention this passage.

how this is elaborated.   The theme of the temple vessels provides a bridge.[13]   Priestly genealogies[14] provide another link,
and this is taken a stage further with the direct association of
Ezra with his immediate pre-exilic ancestor Seraiah (Ezra
7:1).[15]   This theme of priestly genealogy is in fact used a great
deal in the post-exilic period, and particular elements now to be
found in the Chronicler's work take us further in tracing the
differing claims to true continuity in priesthood with the past.
The Samaritan high priestly lists offer a comparable claim to
authority.[16]   In another area, appearing at the end of 2 Kings
and reflected subsequently in hopes centered on Zerubbabel,
there is raised the question of the revival and hence the continuity of the Davidic dynasty.   The claim at the end of 2 Kgs.
25 (vss. 27–30) is clear, but no consequences are drawn.
Deutero-Isaiah, whose reflections on the servant figure may have
some link with the royal line and perhaps more particularly
with the (recently) released Jehoiachin,[17] at one point expresses confidence in the "sure mercies (*ḥasdê*) of David" (Isa.
55:3).   It must remain uncertain how far such a reference is to
be understood in political terms, but it is clear that there is here
an expression of confidence that the restoration to which the
prophecies point involves a link back to the Davidic covenant,
just as so much of what Deutero-Isaiah envisages is expressed in
terms of a new exodus, and hence, by implication, a new entry
into the land.   (For this latter, see especially Isa. 35 and also
the further developments of the theme beyond Deutero-Isaiah
in such passages as Isa. 62:1–5.)   The subsequent repercussions

13. Cf. my "The Temple Vessels: A Continuity Theme," VTS 23 (1972), 166–81.

14. Cf. R. R. Wilson, "The Old Testament Genealogies in Recent Research,"
JBL 94 (1975), 169–89, and his forthcoming *Genealogy and History in the Biblical World* (New Haven: Yale University Press).

15. Cf. K. Koch, "Ezra and the Origins of Judaism," *JSS* 19 (1974), 173–97, see
p. 190.

16. Cf. R. J. Coggins, *Samaritans and Jews* (Atlanta: John Knox, 1975), pp. 143–
44.

17. Cf. references and discussion in my *Exile and Restoration: A Study of Hebrew
Thought of the Sixth Century B.C.*, OTL (Philadelphia: Westminster, 1968), pp.
124ff.; K. Baltzer, "Das Ende des Staates Juda und die Messias-Frage," in *Studien
zur Theologie der alttestamentlichen Überlieferungen*, Festschrift G. von Rad, ed.
R. Rendtorff and K. Koch (Neukirchen: Neukirchener Verlag, 1961), 33–43.

of hopes of a restored Davidic monarchy may be detected in passages in Jeremiah and Ezekiel which are probably later additions (e.g., Jer. 33:14–26 [not in LXX]; Ezek. 37:24–25). Attempts have been made to find the theme in Nehemiah, although this is very uncertain.[18] It is evident in later writings still, in the Testaments of the Twelve Patriarchs (especially Levi and Judah), the Psalms of Solomon (especially Pss. Sol. 17 and 18), the Qumran texts and the New Testament (cf., e.g., Matt. 1:1; 20:30–31; 21:9), and in some Rabbinic writings.[19]

These are some of the mechanisms used to bring out the claim for the reestablishing of continuity with the past. They may clearly be used in the interests of different groups, and it is characteristic of the post-exilic period that, after the extreme break of the exilic age, there should be indications of rival and conflicting groups, even though these do not become fully articulated until the second century B.C., in the various parties within Judaism and in the Samaritan community. But it is there again important to observe how, for example, such a theme as that of the true Zadokite line appears to be employed by more than one group in its endeavor to demonstrate itself to be the true succession. Rival claimants to status will perhaps most readily appear after a break. Thus it is no surprise to find that the break brought about in the period of Antiochus IV Epiphanes is followed not only by the restoration effected under Judas Maccabeus, but also by a gradually sharpening conflict between various claimants to be the true community. We may observe the same again in the first century A.D., not only in the various groups which appear within Judaism itself, including the Christian group, but also in the attempts at establishing the claims of Jewish and Christian communities, particularly in the period after the disaster of A.D. 70.

18. U. Kellermann, *Nehemia: Quellen, Überlieferung und Geschichte*, BZAW 102 (Berlin: Töpelmann, 1967), see 154–59; W. T. In der Smitten, "Erwägungen zu Nehemias Davidizität," *JSJ* 5 (1974), 41–48. For criticism of Kellermann, cf., e.g., S. Herrmann, *A History of Israel* (English translation, Philadelphia: Fortress, 1975), p. 319.
19. Cf. the summarized treatment under *chriō* in *TWNT* IX (1973), 482ff.; *TDNT* 9 (1974), 493ff.

IMPLICATIONS FOR LITERATURE AND THEOLOGY

What has been said so far has concentrated on the nature of
the breaks in continuity and the means which may be employed
to overcome them, with some comment also on the effects that
such breaks may have on the internal life of the community and
particularly on groups which may emerge within it. We must
now turn to another aspect of this and attempt to define more
closely the literary and theological handling of these breaks and
bridgings, asking how they may be reflected in the literature,
and what kinds of effects are produced in the thought by moments of crisis, major or minor. Again it will be clear that our
limited knowledge of the history means that we can only postulate certain of the effects, generalizing in some degree from the
moments in which a clearer picture of the literary and theological developments may be obtained.

It is not possible in such a survey as this to discuss more than
a few examples of the procedures and effects. They may serve
as pointers to the thorough discussion which is needed for a
more adequate assessment.

We may begin with a relatively simple example. The de-
bates of many years concerning the dating of the psalms have
eventually shown up the weakness of discussions which center
upon trying to pinpoint the moment of origin. Indeed, we
may properly suppose that the origins of Israel's cultic poetry
lie far back in her prehistory, and we may further consider it
likely that, together with sanctuaries and festivals and rituals
already existing in Canaan, Israel took over the concomitants of
religious worship such as psalms and prayers, making perhaps
only slight modifications to qualify them for inclusion in the
Yahweh cult (Ps. 29 is often held to be a good example of such a
takeover.)[20] So too we must recognize that from a very early
date such religious poetry was used and reused, and in the

---

20. See recently A. Fitzgerald, "A Note on Psalm 29," *BASOR* 215 (October 1974),
61–63, including some bibliography.

process came to be charged with new meanings corresponding to the current trends of thought and practice.[21]   It is a matter of debate how far such changing use produced modifications in wording; at some points, where precise allusions appear to be made, we may naturally suppose a particular adjustment. More often we may see the reuse itself providing a reinterpretation, not in itself necessitating change of wording, or requiring only such relatively small adjustments as might better fit contemporary usage.   Where this becomes clearest is, of course, in psalms which refer to the king.   It is no longer necessary for commentators, set on a post-exilic date for all psalmody, to argue for a late Maccabean, Hasmonean date for such royal psalms; but equally while a pre-exilic date may rightly be claimed, it must also be observed that use extends beyond the boundary imposed by the end of the monarchy.   Whatever adjustments of wording took place, the references to the king remained, and in one way or another were reinterpreted.   This process—and clearly it may be illustrated more broadly—has two effects relevant to our present discussion.   On the one hand, the retaining of older wording and of older references, here to an outmoded politico-religious institution, may serve to stress continuity where the realities of the situation point to discontinuity.   There is no longer any king; but the references to the king are not dropped, and their very preservation provides an automatic recall of the days of the past with which continuity needs to be preserved.[22]   On the other hand, it is clear that the use of the same wording in widely different periods—different not only in time, but in political order and religious organization and outlook—conceals the degree to which there has in fact been change.   The preservation of the older material may be deceptive in its suggestion of continuity; in actual fact, the

---

21. See the discussion by A. S. Kapelrud above, Chapter 5.

22. A comparison may here be made with some of the points made by B. O. Long, "The Social Setting for Prophetic Miracle Stories," *Semeia* 3 (1975), 46–63. Stories about the prophetic institution may serve to validate it in a period of stress and uncertainty.

difference between the point of earlier and more literal use and the point of later and reinterpreted understanding, may be so great that there is more of discontinuity than of continuity in thought. And when the community endeavors to articulate its beliefs in contemporary language, it will hardly be surprising if there are some for whom the evidence of change will appear to imply an abandonment of older belief. We may, in the light of contemporary discussions of doctrinal formulation in Christian circles, the better appreciate the problem. We may wonder how far the contemporaries of Hosea could accept the use of what appears to be "fertility cult" language for the restatement of Yahwistic faith, and we may the better understand the debate between "Hellenizers" and "traditionalists" in the second century B.C.

The moment of crisis which brings to an end certain familiar patterns of life and established institutions must by its very occurrence raise questions about the validity of received ideas. If certain central elements of religious thought turn on the existence and meaning of a temple, established as linked to the ruling dynasty and to the life of the kingdom, and expressive of the reality of the divine presence in the people—we need not here attempt to make more nearly precise the particular styles of interpretation here hinted at—then the destruction of the temple immediately puts a question mark against what has been held and done. Insofar as the very existence of the temple is held to guarantee the presence of the people's deity, the reality of this presence must at the very least be regarded as less than sure.[23] One way to meet this may be the simplest, that of rebuilding the destroyed shrine; the Jews of Elephantine, faced with such an emergency, sought both authorization and support in carrying through just such a rebuilding. But even this cannot fail to leave open the anxious thought: if this has happened

23. We may note the antagonism which is associated with Jeremiah's comparison of the destruction of the Shiloh shrine with that foretold for Jerusalem (Jer. 26). Such a reaction is expressive of the horror and fear felt at such a prospect. A similar horror may be seen in the reaction to Paul in Acts 21:27–29.

once, can it not happen again, and if so, what becomes of the assurance of divine presence and blessing? Another way, and here we may instance the reaction of Jews and Christians after A.D. 70, is to argue either that the particular significance which the temple had is maintained in another form (for Christians this could be associated with sayings about the destroying and rebuilding of the temple attributed to Jesus himself and understood of his own person, thus focusing on him sentiments otherwise directed to the temple); or alternatively (though not to the exclusion of the first) that the destroyed temple, though lost, points to a future and ultimate rehabilitation, a final temple, not susceptible to the chances which may destroy an earthly building. The last chapters of Ezekiel (40–48), in an earlier situation (though precisely what situation remains uncertain), and the "heavenly temple" ideas, found, for example, in the Revelation of John (cf. Rev. 21 for the heavenly city in which the presence of deity and Lamb constitutes the temple), illustrate such projection. In the interim, regret for the loss of the destroyed temple may be replaced, in part, by anticipation of the final temple; continuity of sentiment concerning the temple may find a different focus in piety, seeing such forms as prayer and almsgiving as substitutes for the sacrificial worship characteristic of temple practice.[24]

If, as has been argued, the writing down of traditions is particularly linked with general crises of confidence,[25] it may also be seen that the written product of such a process is not identical with the traditions which it replaces. It inevitably possesses a different character, and in particular a different kind of authority may come to be attached to it.[26]

24. Cf. J. Neusner, "Emergent Rabbinic Judaism in a Time of Crisis: Four Responses to the Destruction of the Second Temple," *JQR* 21 (1972), 313–27 = *Early Rabbinic Judaism: Historical Studies in Religion, Literature and Art*, SJLA 13 (Leiden: Brill, 1975), 34–49.

25. Cf. E. Nielsen, *Oral Tradition: A Modern Problem in Old Testament Introduction*, SBT 11 (London: SCM, 1954), 33, citing the views of I. Engnell and H. S. Nyberg (see my *Continuity*, p. 27 and n. 67).

26. Cf. the discussion in D. A. Knight, *Rediscovering the Traditions of Israel*, rev. ed., SBLDS 9 (Missoula: Society of Biblical Literature, 1975), 9–10, 390–91.

The natural sequel to this is to recognize in this process of fixation in writing an attempt at guaranteeing a continuity which might otherwise be lost.[27] But a further effect is that of showing more clearly inconsistencies within the tradition which may create difficulty and uncertainty. While we may observe how, in the transmission process itself, some inconsistencies will be smoothed out—differing versions of the same story will tend to be dovetailed, as if they were one—it is only when the texts appear in written form that the more detailed comparison can be made and the inconsistencies adjusted, either by an editorial process, with the texts emended to conform, or by an interpretative process, by which what are quite evidently nonequal elements are explained as being in reality in accord.[28] Insofar as it is at moments of break that the rethinking takes place and the gathering of the materials associated with the tradition is undertaken, we may recognize this harmonizing process, incorporated in the text or superimposed upon it, to be an aftereffect of discontinuity, and itself in part a literary and theological procedure by which a single, intelligible tradition is shown to be present, linked in the rehandling of the earlier materials with what is regarded as an earlier orthodoxy.

But such harmonization may conceal the more basic problem, that of knowing where the true tradition, the true theological interpretation, is to be found. Stress upon the different theologies within the Old Testament is an important aspect of its study; critical analysis has made this possible. But for centuries it was possible for both Jews and Christians to read the Old Testament as a coherent theological document, assuming or demonstrating the unity of its theological witness. The issue between the two religious communities must always be defined in part as being a difference of view in regard to what was the

---

27. Cf. my *Continuity*, p. 27.

28. Clear examples of this may be seen in the earlier materials incorporated in the Priestly Work, where the inconsistencies are resolved partly editorially but more frequently by the simpler device of requiring a given passage (e.g., Gen. 2) to be read in the context of another (Gen. 1) which then superimposes its meaning upon the earlier material.

correct understanding, and whether the discontinuity which appears in the major breaks of the last centuries of the pre-Christian era is to be regarded as bridged by the continuity claimed for Christian or for Jewish tradition.

At a much earlier stage we may see the same kind of problem posed, after the division of the kingdom, by the undoubted claims of both kingdoms to represent a true succession. The charge of apostasy leveled at the Northern kingdom cannot be satisfactorily substantiated; we are dealing with a polemical situation, in which the story of Jeroboam's setting up of golden calves is understood in terms of religious disaster from the viewpoint of a later Judean writer, but could undoubtedly be seen in terms of the upholding of the religious succession by those who saw in them the symbols of continuity with the God "who brought Israel out of Egypt" (1 Kgs. 12:28). It would appear probable that the story of the golden calf in Exod. 32, in which Aaron has a central place and which now points to religious failure even on his part, could have been differently related by those who would seek in the ancient traditions—and perhaps with propriety—a basis for current Northern practice.[29] What eventually became of the Northern religious tradition is a matter, in part at least, of hypothesis; the preservation in the South of prophetic traditions associated with Hosea and Amos, directed to the Northern community, shows that at some point endeavors were made at drawing together into one the broken elements of what was believed to have been one community, however much of separateness may be traceable even in the earlier stages. And the same is true of the significant Elijah and Elisha traditions with their emphasis on the preservation of true Yahwism in the North as well as their elements of critique directed against Northern apostasy.

If discontinuity must be the experience of any community,

---

29. Cf. B. S. Childs, *The Book of Exodus*, OTL (Philadelphia: Westminster, 1974), pp. 553–81 for a very full discussion, which does not, however, sufficiently examine the question of what attitudes may have been taken by Northerners to this theme. Cf. M. L. Newman, *The People of the Covenant: A Study of Israel from Moses to the Monarchy* (New York: Abingdon, 1962), p. 182.

political or religious, then the problem of what constitutes the true succession will always be present. Whatever changes, political or social, come, there must be some means for recognizing and authenticating the handing on of the true tradition, what is acknowledged to be the same faith.[30] But in this there is no simple shortcut. The very richness and diversity within the tradition, its pluriformity, mean that, however much particular groups may wish to claim a direct and clear link between their own position and what they, with some selectivity of outlook, regard as the true faith of the past, there will be other groups for whom that particular link is not valid. It is in such a context easier to see the unsatisfactory nature of claims for a simple succession than to define where true continuity lies. An adequate theological understanding must go beyond that to the recognition that the religious tradition is rich enough to allow of more than one development, and that in assessing the validity of particular aspects of that development, regard must be paid both to the richness of the tradition and to the degree to which particular political and social pressures lead to the stressing of this particular claim or that. If the ultimate reality underlying the religious tradition is to be described, it must be in terms which allow for the element of the unknown and the unknowable which must be present in any valid theological statement.[31]

30. Cf. my "The Theology of Tradition: An Approach to Old Testament Theological Problems," *BTF* 3 (1971), 49–64, see pp. 49–50.
31. Cf. ibid., pp. 63–64; and also W. McKane, "Tradition as a Theological Concept," in *God, Secularization, and History: Essays in Memory of Ronald Gregor Smith*, ed. E. T. Long (Columbia: University of South Carolina Press, 1974), pp. 44–59.

Chapter 10

The Human Dilemma and Literature of Dissent

James L. Crenshaw

THE BIBLE AS PROTEST LITERATURE

The Bible opens with vigorous protest. The Priestly author dissents from the prevailing understanding of creation and its cosmological implications. The birth of man and woman was purposive, not an afterthought. Their calling was noble response to the creator rather than bondage to religious ritual. Their destiny, open to vast potential and freedom, was not hedged in by bondage to the elements. Sun and moon, erstwhile deities, function as mere lamps. Warmed and guided by this light, man found his fulfillment in woman, before whom he neither bowed in worship nor cringed with fear. The created order received divine blessing as exceptionally good. Man and woman's future on the good earth depended upon divine grace, rather than upon royal representation and reiteration of heavenly procedure, priestly recital of sacred texts, or solemn marriage ritual. *This*, not *that*, the author contends, belongs to a proper understanding of creation![1]

Dissent[2] characterizes the Hebrew Scriptures from first to last. It moves freely on the horizontal and vertical planes, and

---

1. For the text of the Enuma eliš, see Pritchard, *ANET*, pp. 60–72, 501–503.
2. A phenomenon with a rich and varied meaning, dissent constitutes in this essay: (1) a literary motif; (2) a structural feature of social change; (3) an ongoing phenomenon in Israel's history; (4) conflict between contemporaries; (5) a disintegrative force in society; and (6) Promethean attack against heteronomy. Dissent in the latter sense, perhaps conceived by the others, provides the primary focus for the present discussion.

occasionally penetrates into the region occupied by introspection. Men raise their voices against other men, both in their own name and in God's name. Chosen people dissent from less favored nations. Their protest assumes many forms: militant aggression, assimilation, conversion, indoctrination. Within elect circles Judah separated herself from Ephraim, exiled people scorned society's "dregs" who remained in Judah, and the "people of the land" looked askance at a distinct group outside the favored circle. Select prophets thundered dissent from a way of life that ripped the social fabric apart, and protested against neglect of sacred tradition. Such dissent borders on the vertical, for prophets voiced celestial dissent against terrestrial inhabitants. Those attacked from above launched a counter-offensive; man went on the offensive against God. This bold venture took a stand upon the character of the one it accused, and relied to the very end upon God's much lauded long-suffering. In extreme cases, such protest went full circle, resulting in self-interrogation and critical reflection. God, too, mused over the disparity between his ways and man's, and perceived a chasm between his character and that of his creatures (Hos. 11:8–9).

Inasmuch as protest pervades Old Testament literature, traditio-historical work must take the phenomenon of dissent seriously. Considerable study has been devoted recently to the prehistory, both Israelite and extra-Israelite, of specific texts and ideological traditions within wisdom circles.[3] Arising largely from anomalies and discontinuities which life presents us,[4] the protest tradition is crucial in the present volume for two reasons. First, literature of dissent discloses reasons for protest and various ways of responding to such attacks. Second, the pathos of dissent cannot be silenced even when precedent for such stridency exists. Use of traditional protest genre and

---

3. For an overview, see Chapter 8 above by O. Steck; and for literature on wisdom, see the Prolegomenon and Bibliography in my anthology, *Studies in Ancient Israelite Wisdom* (New York: KTAV, 1976).
4. Cf. P. R. Ackroyd, Chapter 9 above.

language does not indicate any lack of personal sincerity.[5]   In short, *pathos* gives rise to voices of protest, and places a question mark over all tradition.

SOURCES OF DISSENT

The sources of Israel's dissent are multiple.   Three stand out above all the rest: (1) her institutional fabric; (2) the nature of man; and (3) life's ambiguities.

The Old Testament canon is tripartite, representing the sacred sedimentation of priest, prophet, and sage.   The aims of each division accord with the peculiar role and function of Israel's institutions.   Conflict of interest arose inevitably, for men differ in their understanding of human response to divine summons or social responsibility.   Priests, proud guardians of *ethos*, treasured sacred legal traditions in which the divine will for the community found expression.   Valued, too, were the dice by which diviners discovered the deity's will, and the educative task that endeavored to make the Lord known to infant and gray-haired one.   Prophets, proponents of *pathos*, gave expression to their participation in divine suffering.   Having shared God's agony over human perversion and his ecstasy over faithful reliance upon the divine word, these spokesmen for another surrendered to the power of the word and became instruments of the spirit.   Sages, powerful advocates of *logos*, used rational arguments grounded in experience for the purpose of persuading society to maintain the order established at creation and to recognize the limits of all knowledge.   Three institutions, each with its own center of gravity,[6] vied for human allegiance.   Collision could not be avoided.   The conversion

5. In this respect, von Rad's hesitancy vis-à-vis traditio-historical research of wisdom literature makes sense; cf. *Weisheit in Israel* (Neukirchen-Vluyn: Neukirchener Verlag, 1970), pp. 7–8 = *Wisdom in Israel* (Nashville and New York: Abingdon, 1972), p. ix.

6. Of course each group treasured the other two understandings of reality.   For instance, prophets championed their particular ethos and used their rational powers to clothe the divine word in persuasive garb.   But each had its *essential* perspective by which the other two stances were judged.

of a member of one group to the ranks of another produced rancor, both from the sense of loss and from the convert's articulation of reasons for the change. Inevitably a downgrading of the old way of life constituted partial justification for shifting allegiance. In short, dissent became for the convert a matter of integrity and a means to survival. Protest, it follows, is woven into ancient Israel's institutional fabric.[7]

In addition, protest arose within the ranks of priests, prophets, and sages. Abiathar and Zadok, Aaronide and Levite, jockeyed for power. In like manner prophets squared off against other prophets,[8] rejecting both their inspiration and integrity. The wise also gave birth to disssent within the ranks. Those whose experience cast a serious question mark on the claims of pious peddlers of tradition insisted upon equal time. Behind all of this stands an arc of tension between official and popular religion, old ways and new departures of the spirit.

Israel's institutions merely reflect human nature. Men (and women) differ from one another in experience and disposition. The pages of the Old Testament throb with human differences to fundamental needs. Encounters with boundary situations varied, even within the same person. Real men and women, not idealized figments of the imagination, walked the Judean hills, fought battles, made love, aspired to do the impossible, died. Dauntless heroes at one moment betrayed trusted friends and Sovereign alike at another moment. Confronted at every crossroad with life's uncertainties, ancient Israelites lifted their voices in protest because they were men and women. They knew the threat of annihilation, the sorrow of death, shame's disgrace. The doubting thought nestled within the thickets of their souls. Impregnated by alien beliefs and life styles, it conceived with regularity, giving birth to fools or tragic figures.

---

7. See, for example, W. McKane, *Prophets and Wise Men*, SBT 44 (London: SCM, 1965), for discussion of strife between two groups within ancient Israel.

8. J. L. Crenshaw, *Prophetic Conflict*, BZAW 124 (Berlin and New York: de Gruyter, 1971); and F. L. Hossfeld and I. Meyer, *Prophet gegen Prophet* (Fribourg: Verlag Schweizerisches Katholisches Bibelwerk, 1973).

The disparity between religious claims and actual experience worked differently upon various people. For some, tradition sufficed despite repeated contradictory evidence. Divine withdrawal and consequent inactivity sprang from human guilt; in due time God would act redemptively once again. Others found it impossible to confess the faith of their fathers and mothers. Reluctantly they hurled charges in God's face, daring to endure the heat of his wrath. Earlier solidarity gave way, eventuating in demands that placed the individual at the center of everything. The older tension between the one and the many now eases, and dissent multiplies one thousandfold. The course of Israel's history exacerbated the problem. Protest ascends to the heavens in behalf of an oppressed people. Surely, these dissenters contend, those who punish God's wayward people possess no special virtue other than expertise in using the sword. Like Tamar, a ravaged people tears her garments, dons mourning clothes, and lifts her voice in protest. "Such a thing ought not be done in Israel," she cries into the aching void.

INTEGRATIVE FORCES

Such dissent functioned toward fragmentization of a people already diverse in origin and divided in commitments. How did Israel manage to withstand the impact of divisive forces within her institutional fabric, as well as those arising from human fallibility and experienced ambiguities? What held Israelite society together and prevented it from jettisoning the tension created by alternative approaches to reality? Answers to these questions vary, but a common foe and a shared faith functioned as unifying factors of great consequence. A minority religion in the ancient world, Yahwism conceived its strongest threat to be the fertility principle lying at the heart of neighboring faiths. In a world view that bestowed pride of place upon male and female pairs, an "a-sexual" deity had to fight for survival. Small wonder Yahwism first drew back in

horror at Canaanite religion. Initial shock gave way to curiosity, experimentation, endorsement on the part of many.[9]
Recognizing genuine impoverishment within Yahwism's par-
ticularism and militant intolerance, these brave innovators
enriched Israel's beliefs greatly, particularly by using erotic
language and familial expressions. Nevertheless, Israel's faith
stood firmly against a view of history as spiral or cyclical, con-
tending for *telos*. Believing in sex as divine gift, Yahwism
protested loudly against orgiastic prophecy and obeisance before works of human hands. Its understanding of God led to
an aniconic demand: nothing in heaven above or on earth be-
neath adequately represents God. Human sacrifice, early
abandoned, surfaced only in dire calamity.[10] Even the *lex
talionis* placed rigid controls on revenge, functioning effectively
as a curb against wanton cruelty. Religious movements, too,
protested against fragmentization. The Deuteronomic reform,
promulgated with governmental sanction, strove for unity of
worship in one holy place. Israel's struggle for survival remained constant through the centuries. Though it lost ground
in the area of royal cult, Israel never lacked champions summoning it to withstand a common foe by relying completely
upon ancient traditions.

Herein resides a second clue to Israel's cohesiveness in the
face of disintegrative forces: the power of religious experience.
The faith of the fathers constantly beckoned, and those who
turned to the Lord with heart and soul found sufficient nurture
for their faith. Even when their own poverty of spirit pre-
vailed, like Job they remembered earlier brightly burning fires
of worship. Beyond nostalgic personal memory they knew, too,
that others still found adequate nourishment in the old faith.
By this means they shut the door to religious privatism and

9. G. W. Ahlström, *Aspects of Syncretism in Israelite Religion*, HS 5 (Lund:
Gleerup, 1963); and G. von Rad, *Theologie des Alten Testaments*, vol. 1, 5th ed.
(München: Chr. Kaiser, 1966) = *Old Testament Theology*, vol. 1 (New York:
Harper & Row, 1962), especially Part One.
10. See the author's discussion entitled "Journey into Oblivion: A Structural
Analysis of Gen. 22:1–19," *Soundings* 58 (1975), 243–56.

rejoiced that others could confess with believing hearts. A common foe and a shared faith—these two held Israel together despite dissonant voices.

LEVELS OF DISSENT

Job and Qoheleth mark the apex of dissent in the Old Testament. They stand in a rich tradition sprinkled throughout Israel's sacred memory. Refusal to rest content with a malevolent or inactive deity has its basis in a conviction that Yahweh, God of the fathers, took active interest in the well-being of his devotees. Compassion lay at the center of the relationship between the Lord and his people, whom he chose to be a peculiar people, holy as he is holy. To accomplish his purpose, Yahweh commissioned and empowered special persons: judges, Nazirites, prophets. Personal encounters with divine compassion produced a literary heritage as people told their story in a way that made it God's story. Recounted history evoked enthusiastic response and gave rise to further anticipation. When, like Abraham, faithful followers confronted a famine in the land of promise, they raised serious questions about the veracity of the stories passed on from generation to generation. Can God be trusted? Seldom expressed so bluntly, this question surfaced in copious forms.

Faced with prospects of dark wrath overwhelming the people whom Yahweh had redeemed from Egyptian bondage, Amos protests against divine fury. "O Lord God, please forgive. How can Jacob stand, for he is so little?" (7:2, 5). In this instance prayer rose to heaven in another's behalf. At other times self-interest tempers the petition. Evildoers prosper while virtuous God-fearers go hungry and naked. Complaint psalms thus wrestle with the paradox of an inoperative retribution scheme. The psalmists' self-vindication rides on the final verdict rendered. The inner struggle to make sense of reality's cruel blows carries the soul on a perilous odyssey (Ps. 73). At first tempted to adopt a skeptical stance fashioned by those who denied divine power and interest, the suffering psalmist perceived the bestial quality of such response in time to seek refuge in the holy sanctuary. There he glimpsed a new vision; in the end God will act decisively. On the strength of this insight he renews his faith in divine goodness and experiences divine presence like the gentle touch of a father's hand. Having resolved to his satisfaction the question of God's trustworthiness, with renewed conviction the psalmist now confesses that the Lord is good to the upright. In the process the psalmist has redefined goodness.[11]

Jeremiah's confessions raise the issue of divine integrity within the context of a *via dolorosa*.[12] Step by step the prophet moves toward an abyss devoid of basic trust in God. A faithful proclaimer of God's destructive word, the prophet from Anathoth felt betrayed by God as prosperity continued to reign. Angrily he branded God a rapist, for in God's presence he was powerless to resist. Habakkuk, too, confessed an inability to reconcile what he had heard about God with actual experience. His questions, like Jeremiah's, address God with stark reality. If your eyes look only upon pure things, why do you permit sin's ugliness? Oppression of innocent people runs rampant, and you sit idly by. In the end the prophet receives an answer that satisfies him: the just shall live by his faithfulness. Broaden your vision, God challenges him, and catch a glimpse of divine activity in another corner of the world. Comforted by this enlarged perspective and motivated by the appeal to faith, Habakkuk soars to remarkable heights. The book's hymnic

11. The literature on Ps. 73 is extensive. My interpretation of the text follows Martin Buber at many points (*On the Bible* [New York: Schocken, 1968], pp. 199–210).

12. Von Rad, *Theologie des Alten Testaments*, vol. 2, 5th ed. (München: Chr. Kaiser, 1968), p. 214 = *Old Testament Theology*, vol. 2 (New York: Harper & Row, 1965), p. 206, writes: "However, just as the confessions are confined to the development of the prophet's inner life, so the Baruch narrative is only concerned with describing the outward circumstances of this *via dolorosa*." For recent discussions of Jeremiah's laments, see J. Bright, "Jeremiah's Complaints— Liturgy or Expression of Personal Distress?" in *Proclamation and Presence*, ed. J. I. Durham and J. R. Porter (London: SCM, 1970), pp. 189–214; and Sheldon H. Blank, "The Prophet as Paradigm," in *Essays in Old Testament Ethics*, ed. J. L. Crenshaw and J. T. Willis (New York: KTAV, 1974), pp. 111–30.

confession of faith counts as naught all evidence that had earlier troubled the prophet. Henceforth the faithful one marches victoriously in God's cause.

Jonah's dissent produces no recorded transformation in his own attitude to God. This prophet's protest strikes a dissonant chord, in some ways reminiscent of Jeremiah's anxiety over his own reputation for accurate proclamation. Jonah's dissent from divine compassion evokes an object lesson aimed at correcting the prophet's self-centeredness and narrow understanding of God's compassion. The deity's long-suffering finds expression in the way God spares a sinful but repentant city and in the manner of his gentle rebuke aimed at a sulking prophet.

The author of the dialogue between Abraham and God over the fate of Sodom and Gomorrah used calamity to illustrate divine compassion. Abraham's poignant question "Shall not the judge of the whole earth do justice?" loses its sting when set alongside the Lord's eagerness to spare the cities. Given God's readiness to concede arguments voiced by one fully conscious of his finitude, the reader is tempted to fault Abraham for stopping short of asking whether one righteous person sufficed to spare the doomed cities. In the end the wrath of God fell upon the unfortunate victims of their own lewdness, and Abraham's question burned itself into healthy consciences. The story itself bears witness to this reality.

Divine fury evoked yet another vocal protest in the cycle of traditions about Moses. Distraught over the prospects of losing all who had ventured forth from Egyptian bondage and comforted little by the promise of a new following, this dauntless leader pleaded for divine compassion. He who knew the splendor of divine self-manifestation and who talked to God face to face and not in riddles threatened to give up that precious relationship if God refused to repent of his plans to destroy Israel. God's response to Moses' protest comes like a chilling blast. Picking up on Moses' powerful metaphor, God ignores its force and terminates the conversation with a decision to blot out of his book all who have sinned.

DISSENT IN EGYPT AND MESOPOTAMIA

In protesting against God's manner of ruling the universe, Israel's dissenters join hands with a significant dissident force outside its borders. Both structure and language link Israel's complaint psalms with kindred laments in Babylonian literature. A single note rises to heaven: *'ad mātay* "How long, O Lord?" Similarities exist also in another genre, dispute or discussion literature. In this instance affinities extend in two directions; both Egypt and Mesopotamia possess rich treasures of such dissent.

The collapse of Egypt's Old Kingdom brought on a serious religious crisis and gave birth to a significant body of protest literature.[13] The old way of life centered upon the pharaoh and the state. Magic characterized religious life, and optimism reigned. With the reversal of economic fortunes, doubt arose about the purpose of living. Skepticism followed close behind. Such doubt and skepticism surface in expostulation with the deity, and eventuate in a new world view. Two features characterize the new reality: cosmic focus and natural emphases. The state gives way to the universe, and magic bows before a strong appeal to nature. Arguments with a culpable deity abound. The critic laments, reasons, questions, even threatens, and the deity responds with enigmatic language. The substance of the human portion of the dialogues can be reduced to a single sentence: God has lost control of the universe which he created. In the light of such a reality, man admonishes others to make the most of the fleeting moment since a future life cannot be counted upon, or he counsels suicide. The other partner in the dialogue insists that he has control of the universe and that he is just. Recounting his abundant benevolent deeds, God informs the skeptic that he grants fertility, that evil is man's doing, and that the future lies before man as a closed

13. E. Otto, "Der Vorwurf an Gott," *Vorträge der Orientalist. Tagung in Marburg, 1950,* Fachgruppe: Ägyptologie, 3 (1951), 1–15; and H. H. Schmid, *Wesen und Geschichte der Weisheit,* BZAW 101 (Berlin: Töpelmann, 1966). The description below depends largely upon Otto.

book. Eventually faith conquers doubt, and divine compassion for lowly creatures stills the voice of dissent. Out of the crisis a new position of man in the universe emerged. Protest produced rich fruit.

Expostulation with the deity arose early in Mesopotamia.[14] A Sumerian "Job" points an accusing finger at the gods for inappropriate response to a life of devoted service. Later Akkadian texts develop considerably the theme of innocent suffering. Life's unpredictable character surfaces in these dialogues, together with recognition of limits imposed upon human knowledge. The qualitative difference between gods and human beings stands out. For themselves the gods reserved life, while bestowing lies upon creatures. Consequently, men do not know what pleases the gods, and cannot extrapolate from human experience what conduct guarantees well-being. The lack of any discernible order to reality prompts serious soul searching. The resulting ennui expresses itself in complete indecision. Neither one course of action nor its opposite promises any relief from a sickness unto death. Contemplation of suicide naturally follows. Occasionally these dissenters dare to threaten the gods by withholding sacrificial offerings. The opposite response also characterizes this literature, suggesting that the authors have not entirely abandoned a belief that the gods reward those who wear their yoke joyously. Accordingly, dissent dissolves in proper ritual as the devotee demonstrates loyal devotion worthy of reward.

YAHWISM AND WISDOM

Within Israel's canonical literature one body of texts stands out as an alien corpus.[15] Its unusual character prompts some

---

14. W. G. Lambert, *Babylonian Wisdom Literature* (Oxford: Clarendon, 1960), gives pertinent texts and translation.

15. H. Gese, *Lehre und Wirklichkeit in der alten Weisheit* (Tübingen: Mohr [Siebeck], 1958), p. 2, observes: "It is recognized that wisdom teaching represents a foreign body in the world of the Old Testament." The next step is highly problematic: that Yahwism functions as the norm by which wisdom must be evaluated. I prefer to emphasize the complementarity of the two approaches to reality, and to consider each appropriate.

interpreters to view wisdom as pagan in spirit and content.[16] Others defend the Yahwistic character of wisdom vigorously,[17] despite essential differences between wisdom literature and the rest of the Old Testament. Those differences give an impression of conscious decisions to remain silent about major traditions of Yahwism and to make use of ideas shared by the entire ancient Near East. If this is indeed the case, wisdom deserves the label "dissent."

Yahwism

At the heart of Yahwism lies the belief that Yahweh has chosen Israel for a special destiny and works toward that goal by active participation in the life of the elected people. Deriving from an old tradition about "the God of the Fathers,"[18] the conviction that God cares passionately for a favored nation and enters into a covenant with its representatives eventuates in legal codifications, sacred memory, and liturgical confession. Multiple traditions[19] tell about One who makes his will known to chosen persons, who function as divine spokesmen, warriors, and representatives. Undaunted by human rebellion, Yahweh performs redemptive acts from time to time. When sin abounds, he withdraws for a season: the *Deus revelatus* becomes *Deus absconditus*.[20] In time Yahwism interprets creation itself

16. Notably H. D. Preuss, "Erwägungen zum theologischen Ort alttestamentlicher Weisheitsliteratur," *EvTh* 30 (1970), 393–417; and "Das Gottesbild der älteren Weisheit Israels," *Studies in the Religion of Ancient Israel*, VTS 23 (1972), 117–45.

17. Most recently, von Rad, *Wisdom in Israel*; and R. E. Murphy, "Wisdom and Yahwism," *No Famine in the Land: Studies in Honor of John L. McKenzie*, ed. J. W. Flanagan and A. W. Robinson (Missoula, Montana: Scholars Press, 1975), 117–26. Murphy refuses to judge wisdom by standards derived from Israel's liturgical life. His distinction between confessional remembrance (the particularity of its faith) and literature of daily experience, though in need of qualification (liturgy is a part of experience too), contains much promise.

18. For considerable revision of Alt's thesis about the God of the Fathers, see F. M. Cross, *Canaanite Myth and Hebrew Epic* (Cambridge, Mass.: Harvard University Press, 1973), pp. 3–43.

19. Von Rad, *Old Testament Theology*, vols. 1 and 2.

20. K. H. Miskotte, *When the Gods Are Silent* (New York and Evanston: Harper & Row, 1967); and L. Perlitt, "Die Verborgenheit Gottes," *Probleme biblischer Theologie*, ed. H. W. Wolff (München: Chr. Kaiser Verlag, 1971), 367–82.

as a redemptive act: the created order becomes the stage on which a divine-human drama unfolds.[21] To sum up, Yahwism proclaims an active God who guides his chosen people to their special destiny. Grace characterizes Yahwism, and divine favor underlies the course of Israel's history. That steadfast love expresses itself in revelatory deed, and survives heinous offenses of the covenant bond. Wrath may break out, but beyond God's destructive act stands a door of hope.

Wisdom

Wisdom accords ill with such a description of Yahwism.[22] One enters an entirely different world of discourse when coming to wisdom literature. Although the sages believe that divine activity accounts for the universe, this creative act took place in primeval time and bestowed upon the cosmos rules for sustaining order in the face of impulses toward chaos. God acted, that is, in the remote past. Furthermore, that divine activity embraces the whole world, not some specifically favored group. Inasmuch as all peoples benefit from creation, the God responsible for it possesses no special name. Wisdom, therefore, employs traditions grounded in High God theology.[23]

Divine election plays no role in wisdom, and forgiveness is rarely mentioned. The wise do not speak of a chosen people or of special individuals through whom God makes his will known to the masses. No revelations shatter the barrier separating creature from creator. Knowledge comes from experience; it does not arise in a revelatory encounter with God.[24] The sole means of discovering truth rests in the human mind, and serious

---

21. For further elaboration of this point, see the author's *Hymnic Affirmation of Divine Justice*, SBLDS 24 (Missoula: Scholars Press, 1975); and *Studies in Ancient Israelite Wisdom*, Prolegomenon.

22. See my review of von Rad's *Wisdom in Israel* published in *RSR* 2, no. 2 (1976), 6–12.

23. On this terminology, see Cross, *Canaanite Myth and Hebrew Epic*.

24. The exception, of course, is Job, which describes the revelatory experience (4:12–17; cf. 33:15) and culminates in a theophany. Does this author consider wisdom's experiential base inadequate for life's mysteries?

limits to knowledge confront the one who wishes to know the mysteries of the universe.

Since God does not play favorites, no nation receives preferential treatment. Before God all creatures enjoy equality. Consequently, the individual surfaces in wisdom, his or her concerns, anxieties, aspirations. Distinctions among individuals apply. Some people belong to the ranks of fools; others share the fruits of wisdom. Such categorizations depend upon behavior rather than lineage.

Wisdom's rhetoric consists of proverbs, dialogue, instruction.[25] Sages seek to master things by observing reality. They study human nature, the habits of birds and animals, and nature itself. Discovered truth clothes itself in poetic dress, and accumulated tradition becomes a father and mother's testament to their children. The educative task stands at the center of wisdom's values. Sages give advice and admonish others to fruitful conduct. Behind the counsel lies the father's authority and the power of a learned tradition. In dialogue various viewpoints receive treatment. In this way different alternatives can be offered.

Such an approach to reality found it exceedingly difficult to survive over against Yahwism. Compromises crept into wisdom's teachings, particularly with regard to God's self-manifestation. In Job the powerful theophanic tradition of its literary prototype prevails. One can confidently say that the God who reveals himself in the whirlwind bears little similarity to Yahweh. Perhaps the most productive compromise arose in the tradition of personified Wisdom, itself a potential protest against Yahwism's "nonsexual" character. By this means God granted to his creatures a measure of contact with his will for their lives. Slowly Dame Wisdom assumes the functions of holy persons in Yahwism: she summons to life, she threatens, she

25. Treated at length by the author in John H. Hayes, ed., *Old Testament Form Criticism*, TUMSR 2 (San Antonio, Tex.: Trinity University Press, 1974), 225–64.

instills knowledge, she grants security.   Once such Yahwistic concepts enter wisdom, old ideas (for example, fear of the Lord) take on a wholly different meaning.

Such compromise comes to fruition in Sirach. Here Yahwism and wisdom join hands.   Not only does the sage take over Torah, but he also begins to utilize national traditions.   Israel's heroes now appear in a roll call of persons through whom God has been at work.   In Sirach the sage becomes a worshiper of Yahweh.

To recapitulate, wisdom differs sharply from Yahwism in regard to its view of God and his relationship with humans.   In time, however, the powerful forces of Yahwistic tradition make themselves felt even among the sages.

The relationship between Yahwism and wisdom can be expressed somewhat differently.   A fundamental presupposition of Yahwism was divine trustworthiness.   Above all an ethical deity, Yahweh demanded a high standard of morality.   He rewarded a pure life generously.   Besides longevity, Yahweh granted riches and honor to pious worshipers.   External circumstances reflected one's inner condition, and the supreme good could be summed up in one word—life. Its opposite, of course, was death.   Exceptions occurred, but various explanations for the disparity between inward life and external circumstances sufficed.   Death, even premature, could be endured so long as trust in God's goodness remained intact.   Slowly the doubting thought surfaced, brought on by occasional instances of divine caprice and serious reflection upon divine wrath. Exacerbated by the Deuteronomistic theology of retribution, the doubting thought produced a significant literature of dissent within Yahwism.   Precisely at this point differences between Yahwism and wisdom begin to break down.

DISSENT WITHIN WISDOM

Dissent within Israel's wisdom addresses both the sages and those outside their membership.   Attack upon nonwisdom circles assumes many forms. For instance, appropriation of prophetic language for wisdom's own ends occurs in Proverbs. Here Dame Wisdom speaks inspired utterances and goes remarkably beyond what any prophet dared. She invites sinners to come to her for life. The linguistic structure recalls Amos' words, with one single exception: the object of seeking. Whereas the prophet says, "Seek the Lord, and live" (5:6), Dame Wisdom ventures the following invitation: "Leave simpleness, and live" (Prov. 9:6). She warns in prophetic language (1:20–28) that a foolish people will call, but Wisdom will not answer, will "seek her diligently but will not find her" (Prov. 1:28). Similarly, the author of Job describes the moment of inspiration (!) in language highly reminiscent of that used in the oracles of Balaam (Job 4:12–17). Qoheleth adopts the same tactic, and develops it to perfection. One example graphically illustrates this practice. Whereas Gen. 1 spoke of creation as exceptionally good, Qoheleth concedes that God made everything appropriate for its moment, but goes on to place that judgment under a heavy cloud of divine neglect or mischief (Qoh. 3:11).[26] Conscious avoidance of the language in Gen. 1 signifies Qoheleth's caution in using Yahwistic tradition.

One could work through the entire book of Qoheleth searching for that skeptic's rejection of traditional values in Yahwism. For Deutero-Isaiah[27] the word of the Lord alone survives earth's wasting away; Qoheleth grants that lasting quality to the earth itself. Whereas Deutero-Isaiah admonished his hearers to forget former things in anticipation of the glorious work God will perform, Qoheleth claims that none will remember former things *or* things yet to come. Adam's judgment ("Dust thou art, and to dust thou shalt return") prompts Qoheleth to speculate about the vanity of breath's ultimate destiny (in God?). Ps. 8

26. See the author's essay entitled "The Eternal Gospel (Eccl. 3:11)," in *Essays in Old Testament Ethics*, 23–55.
27. S. Terrien, "Quelques remarques sur les affinités de Job avec le Deutéro-Esaïe," VTS 15 (1966), 295–310, has shown a remarkable kinship between certain aspects of Job and Deutero-Isaiah.

celebrates man's exalted place upon the earth by proclaiming the universe's majesty. Truly one must ask, "What is man?" in the context of eternity. But the psalmist considers man something special precisely because God visits him. Qoheleth, on the other hand, insists that man has no advantage over beasts. Job goes even further afield. His comments amount to a parody of Ps. 8.

> What is man, that thou dost make so much of him,
>   and that thou dost set thy mind upon him,
>   dost visit him every morning,
>   and test him every moment?
> How long wilt thou not look away from me,
>   nor let me alone till I swallow my spittle?
>   (Job 7:17–19 RSV)[28]

The troubled author of 2 Esdras breathes Job's spirit when asking, "But what is man, that thou art angry with him; or what is a corruptible race, that thou art so bitter against it?" (8:34 RSV).

A psalmist could speak of the Lord as one fully aware of the worshiper's troubles, and could expect God to collect all his tears just as he kept a book of life (56:8). Qoheleth beheld the tears of the oppressed and sighed because no comforter existed (4:1). The prophetic claim to special insight into the future finds an antagonist in Qoheleth, who insists that no one can predict what is yet to happen (8:7).

Sages also direct their polemic at others within the ranks of wisdom. Here dissent strives after the whole truth, for the wise recognize the ambiguity of experience. Qoheleth's rhetorical question "Who knows?" prefaces everything skeptical wisdom says. Over against it stand the dogmatic affirmations within Proverbs and upon the lips of Job's friends. Qoheleth gives

---

28. M. H. Pope, *Job*, AB 15 (Garden City, N.Y.: Doubleday & Company, 1972), p. 62, writes: "What in happier circumstances would be regarded as providential care (cf. Pss. viii, cxliv 3) is here ironically presented as overbearing inquisitiveness and unrelenting surveillance. . . . These two verses are often regarded as a bitter parody of Ps. viii."

voice to a wholly different understanding of knowledge and its benefits. Increased knowledge adds sorrow to one's life; wisdom cannot be located. He puts forth views at variance with received traditions: reward and punishment happen by chance rather than design; God tests man to show that he is no different from a beast; old age brings deterioration instead of honor; nothing has lasting value. Job agrees that wisdom does not restrict itself to the aged (32:9). While he thinks the struggle with God worth the effort, Qoheleth considers such odds overwhelming.

JOB AND QOHELETH ON DEATH

Such dissent from "school" traditions reaches its zenith in what Job and Qoheleth say about death. Positive wisdom concurred with Yahwism in affirming life as the highest good. Proverbs build upon a solid foundation that affirms life and its blessings. Instructions endeavor to equip the wise for life. Admonitions seek to enrich life, and warnings guard against action that would bring about premature death. The sole aim of wisdom can be summed up in Qoheleth's question: "What is good for man?"[29] Even religious obligation falls under such a judgment: one should be neither too religious nor too irreligious. The sole criterion for such a statement is man's well-being.

The supreme good loses its power for Job and Qoheleth. Herein lies the most astonishing cry of dissent in the Old Testament. In a word, Job continues to love life, although loathing his particular experience at the moment (9:21). Job begs for death, while Qoheleth despises life and strives mightily to sustain it. Job considers the stillborn more favored than he (3:13), a sentiment shared by Qoheleth (6:3–5). To one whose pain wracks his body day and night, death becomes an occasion for rejoicing. Qoheleth's hatred for life grows out of

---

29. W. Zimmerli, "Zur Struktur der alttestamentlichen Weisheit," *ZAW* 51 (1933), 177–204 (English translation, *Studies in Ancient Israelite Wisdom*).

his search for profit. He sees no evidence that God distinguishes between the good and the wicked, the clean and the unclean, the one who sacrifices and him who does not. In Qoheleth's view the race does not go to the swift or the battle to the strong, but time and chance play indiscriminately. The dead are more fortunate than the living, Qoheleth believes, since the latter know that the skull (death) grins at the banquet.

Death's lurking shadow tempers everything Qoheleth does. His liberating word (9:7) constitutes a desperate attempt at grasping as much of life's bounty as possible before youthful vigor fades. The fact that God has already approved his revelry offsets the awful limitations imposed upon man, who enjoys only a portion. Furthermore, that tiny portion of life's goodies remains within God's control. God dispenses his gifts arbitrarily, whether from love or hate no one knows.

Written in an age when all values had lost their power to compel confidence and sustain hope, Job utters the lone individual's agonizing cry and the collective experience of God's people. Experience had failed to confirm the belief that virtue receives its reward. Those with weak elbows and sensitive hearts found themselves ground into dust by men who disregard justice and mercy. When a malevolent deity oppresses innocent people, a matrix of tragedy or resignation forms. Such a situation calls forth Job's Promethean defiance of tyranny in high places. The wonder of his dissent constitutes a wellspring from which surges his courage to strike back with words, the only weapon available to mortals. This source, the memory of a prior relationship both profound and mutual, enables Job to wrestle with the Lord in confidence that God can be trusted despite all evidence to the contrary. The traditions to which he was heir and personal validation of their major proclamation had taught Job that the divine word should be pursued, not eluded. Astonishingly, Job takes for granted what he wishes to overthrow, the principle of retribution. This dilemma justifies describing Job as a bankruptcy of rationality. The final note struck in Job, quiet submission in divine presence, exploded for all times the magical assumption in religion. The blasphemous notion that God is slave to man's concept of justice shatters to bits. God cannot be manipulated by worship or ethics.

Like Job, Qoheleth calls into question the entire human enterprise. "Emptiness of emptinesses, the greatest profitlessness, everything passes into nothingness." These words sum up his message. Neither religion, nor sensuality, nor anything in between, can cancel the eternal decree—"You must die." Qoheleth gives no credence to the ancient belief in a loving God who guided the destiny of the fathers.[30] Such godless monotony and sheer bondage to fate do not propel Qoheleth into suicide. Rather this dissenter shrugs his shoulders, utters the resigned "Who knows?", and chases life with abandon. Did that elusive chase give birth to the refrain "striving after the wind"?

SIRACH AND 2 ESDRAS

Presumably Sirach's incorporation of traditions from Israel's sacred history gave him a means of dealing with the problem posed by Job and Qoheleth. Although affirming life's bondage and lamenting the eternal decree, "You must die," Sirach refuses to despair over his inheritance of maggots and worms. Instead he bursts into hymnic praise for the creator whose works reflect infinite wisdom and purpose. Sirach's escape into realms of metaphysics and psychology approaches bad faith. Forced into this refuge by dissidents who denied divine goodness and power, Sirach strove mightily to answer questions raised by such skeptics. His dissent made use of an ancient debate form consisting of the formula "Do not say," a direct quotation, and a reason why one should not utter such words.

---

30. Others discover a subterranean faith in Qoheleth. His message exposes reason's inadequacy and the futility of all human striving, thus summoning the sages back to genuine monistic wisdom characterized by the fear of the Lord. See especially H. Gese, "Die Krisis der Weisheit bei Koheleth," *Les sagesses du Proche-Orient ancien* (Paris: Presses Universitaires de France, 1963), pp. 150–51.

Sirach's dissent does not extend to God. Instead, he turns heavenward in prayer and song.[31]

The author of 2 Esdras struggled with the problem of divine inactivity and consequent injustice. Faced with Perdition's ravenous appetite, Ezra squeezes little comfort from the angel's assurance that he will receive a heavenly reward. From his lips rises the familiar Joban cry, also uttered in different words by Qoheleth: "It would have been better if no one had been created." Second Esdras belongs to another significant corpus of protest literature, apocalyptic.[32] This literature struggles with the problem of evil in a world devoid of divine action. No longer blessed with an inspired word, the apocalyptist searches sacred texts for clues about God's time-table. Adverse political conditions dictate pseudonymity and enigmatic language, and anticipated deliverance prompts historiography that makes use of distinct epochs. God's action moves to the end of history. Apocalyptic protests against an oppressive hegemony, on the one hand, and divine indifference, on the other. Whereas wisdom pushed God's activity to the beginning of time, apocalyptic opts for the other extreme. The sages found some comfort in the conviction that God had created the universe so as to reward virtue and punish vice. Apocalyptists drew solace from the hope that God would soon set history right. The apocalyptist faced persecution bravely, confident that God could rescue him from the fire but faithful whether deliverance came or not (Dan. 3:16–18).

THE HUMAN DILEMMA: THEOLOGICAL IMPLICATIONS

Both within wisdom and elsewhere the human dilemma gave birth to dissent so extreme that a death wish surfaced. Besides Job, others begged for an early death. Elijah found the chal-

---

31. See the author's "The Problem of Theodicy in Sirach," *JBL* 94 (1975), 47–64.
32. For recent analyses of this literature, see P. D. Hanson, *The Dawn of Apocalyptic* (Philadelphia: Fortress, 1975); J. Schreiner, *Alttestamentlich-jüdische Apokalyptik* (München: Kösel, 1969); and K. Koch, *Ratlos vor der Apokalyptik* (Gütersloh: Mohn, 1970) = *The Rediscovery of Apocalyptic*, SBT 2/22 (London: SCM, 1972).

lenge of Baalism too strenuous; Jonah could not endure loss of
reputation; Samson refused to be the object of mockery any
longer; Tobit begged for relief from his sorry lot; Joanna had
borne the yoke of false accusation long enough. (How vastly
different from the aged Simeon's prayer for death now that he
had seen the Christ child!) All of these death wishes constitute
acts of defiance. They admit defeat. Life has overwhelmed
God's noblest servants.

The resiliency of Israelite faith enabled traditionists to record
such dissent and thus to take it into account rather than to snuff
out the flaming query. Indeed the pluralistic nature of Israel's
faith and traditions, as has been shown in preceding chapters,
derives from its openness and responsiveness to life in all of its
multiplicity, and perhaps for this reason its literature has survived with impact unto this day. For dogma tends to harden,
threatening the very life that gave it birth. Burning questions
of identity, conscience, and integrity fell upon the parched surface of creedal religion like gentle rain, infusing new life. Such
bursts of vital energy occasioned ruptures in the hardened crust
of Israel's confessions; fresh shoots sprouted, reached for the
sun, and bore rich fruit.

Traditionists incorporated lively dissent into patriarchal traditions and neutralized it by subjecting skepticism to the reality
of divine compassion. Birth narratives dared to introduce
human incredulity into conversation between God and the father of the Israelites. Even the ancestor of faithful Israel insisted on keeping God honest. Similarly, the wilderness and
Sinai traditions juxtaposed divine wrath and theophanic confession of his long-suffering. By joining dissent to confessional
streams of tradition, guardians of Israel's traditions achieved a
neutralization of attacks against God.

This phenomenon occurs in wisdom literature as well. Positive and negative proverbs stand alongside one another, and
wholly negative voices lose their impact when set within
canonical collections. A striking example appears in Prov.
30:1-6, where skepticism elicits opposing confession, which in

turn evokes a warning not to tamper with finished traditions. In Job blasphemous dissent alternates with a mixture of profound faith and hardened dogma. In a sense the literary genre of disputation readily lends itself to such interweaving of dissent and confession. Prose gives way to poetry, then surfaces again. Job attacks God and friends, who utter dissent in equal measure. Even Satan enters the act, begging to differ with God, and receives a challenge to justify his cynicism. Set within a literary work that culminates in majestic theophany, radical protest boasts divine approval. Job alone has spoken truth about God! Thus an unresolved tension within the book manifests itself.

Traditionists even found ways to incorporate a work that rejects everything they stood for. Qoheleth's striving for totality, particularly his broken questions, gave the impression of vacillation on his part. Furthermore, the final *double entendre* enabled the faithful to affirm their creator, and justified the addition of an epilogue that provided a clue for understanding the book. By this means skepticism's point, though blunted, was allowed to stand in this watered-down version. Sirach reversed Qoheleth's practice of introducing *positive* traditions only to refute them; here radical dissent finds expression within a context that warns against such folly. Although Sirach voices protest against God's conduct, the prefaced "Do not say" functions to neutralize the impact of dissent. Still, the doubting thought is not altogether silenced.

In short, tradition found ways to baptize radical skepticism, either by the context within which it was set or by the addition of neutralizing observations. The effect of juxtaposing creedal affirmation and profound denial electrifies, for dissent against a loving God turned enemy cannot be termed idle banter. Thus the force of skeptical argument burns within the consciences of generation after generation. At the same time, the intensity and eloquence of protest testify to the transforming power of vital faith. Concealed within the human shriek is an awful recognition that God alone in all the universe is worthy of su-

preme devotion. Precisely here resides the power of dogma and
its opposite. In a word, truth resides in creed *and* in skepticism.

Israel had no monopoly on the problem of divine integrity.
That mass of scar tissue stretches beyond its temporal and
spatial borders, uniting past and present. The fundamental
problem of human existence, the question of God's trustworthiness, constitutes the single most significant theological issue
today. Belief in divine goodness, essential to viable faith, suffers
because of life's ambiguities. Death, "the worm at the core of
man's pretensions to happiness" (William James), cancels all
virtue in a single moment. Undeserved suffering and precipi-
tous death force one to ask, "Can God be trusted?" Both revelation and providence depend upon one's response to this crucial
question.

Dissent literature demonstrates Israel's basic honesty in dealing with theological questions. No issue was too delicate to
ponder, no matter too dangerous to explore its merits. Indeed,
its Lord openly invited expostulation, confident that his servants' devotion could endure fiery testing. Furthermore, literature of protest implies fundamental trust in God: one can
argue with his creator. Dissent rises in behalf of One who has
withdrawn or who appears in a new role as antagonist. The
bold servant appeals to God against God! In addition, dissent
literature elevates human reasoning to extraordinary heights.
In a sense, the skeptic proclaims far and wide the utter seriousness with which Israel asked about its place under the sun. Like
the Queen of Sheba, it asked difficult questions of itself and its
Lord. Unfortunately, no Solomon gave the final word about
the human dilemma! Sooner or later death will give that decisive verdict.[33]

---

33. My colleague Walter Harrelson assisted me greatly in reflecting upon the
theological implications of dissent. I wish by this means to express my gratitude
to him for perceptive reading and patient listening.

Part IV

SCRIPTURE

Chapter 11

Tradition and Canon

Robert B. Laurin

"Canon is an incident, and no more than that."[1] In this simple comment by Samuel Sandmel lies the heart of the matter. For tradition history demonstrates the fundamental point that the development of canon was a legitimate search for authority by the community, but that final canonization was an illegitimate closure of that process by the community at one moment in its history. Thus what we call "canon" is only "an incident, and no more than that" in what should be seen as a continuous process to be entered into at each period in the believing community's life. We must not finally ask "what was properly canonical?" (an historical question), but rather "what is authoritative for the believing community?" (an existential question). The canon has been and still should be only a corporate means for determining the witness to the revelatory presence of God, the real basis of authority and life for the community of believers. Canon is an ever-contemporary word. So we need to make a distinction between "canonizing" (the dynamic process of tradition growth) and "canonization" (the static event of tradition closure). Canonization has been untrue to the canonizing process of tradition history.

THE PURPOSE OF CANON

The establishment of a canon or "standard" was always at heart a demand for theological authority. On the one hand,

1. S. Sandmel, "On Canon," *CBQ* 28 (1966), 207.

the believing community needed an authoritative witness to God's encounter with them by which to organize their life and verify their hope. On the other hand, the community had the conviction that certain traditions or witnesses out of the welter of other witnesses uniquely bore that authority. They heard certain words in the Spirit, that is, "accompanied by a mode of presence of the one of whom they speak."[2]

The development of a canon, therefore, was a natural and legitimate move on the part of Judaism and Christianity, particularly given their own self-understanding. The traditions witness to a universal revelatory work by God (Amos 1–2; Isa. 45:1; John 10:35; Rom. 2:12–16), but also claim the special election of a people of God as the unique interpreter of the meaning of his presence in the world and as the body through whom he acts uniquely in the world (Exod. 19:4–6; Amos 3:1; Heb. 1:1–2; Rom. 3:2). So regardless of whether or not it made the right decision (and it certainly was only a majority decision) the believing community had the valid task of establishing an authoritative witness to God's revelatory presence.

All of this, then, has two particular values. First, it provides a means of determining revelation within the context of the believing community. For centuries the people of God lived without official limits, constantly in need of some authoritative base. With the formation of canon there came a more uniform tradition for the people as a whole to which appeal could be made. Now the judgment could be disengaged from the tradition of a local shrine or synagogue or individual church, and brought within the view of the wider people of God. But, of course, even with the corporate decision about canon this did not settle the matter of revelational witness. In spite of any claim that "we must place ourselves under Scripture," no one in fact ever does, or indeed can. Everyone distinguishes between what is authoritative and nonauthoritative for him on the basis of some personal or sectarian criterion.

2. J. Barr, *The Bible in the Modern World* (New York: Harper & Row, 1973), p. 131.

Second, the canon provides a means for achieving unity within the faith. The canon, as a corporate decision, witnesses preeminently to certain crucial events—the acts and disclosures of God—and it is around these that the people of God are formed. And thus in the proclamation of these events with their interpretation unity within the faith may be found.[3]

THE PROCESS OF CANON

The historical stages in the development of the Old Testament canon are well known, and there is widespread consensus, apart from a few details, about this process. However although the historical process is fairly clear, the functional reasons for the process are not. Put in another way, the growth of the canon was always the product of a search for theological authority, but there is not agreement as to how certain traditions functioned so as to produce the particular grouping of writings we call the canon.

One of the things that emerges clearly in traditio-historical studies is the many-layered character of a given pericope. So although it is true that canonization was an historical process rather than a theological decision by a council, it is also misleading. The historical process was rife with theological conviction. Certain traditions spoke to the heart of the community in ever-changing ways at different stages. They "functioned" differently at different times while all the while bearing witness through the Spirit to the Spirit. James Sanders is certainly correct when he states: "One needs to understand the need of the later believing communities in their rereading of a tradition in order to understand what went on in canonization."[4]

All of this has, therefore, very important implications for our understanding, not only of the historical process of canonization, but also of how the canon should function for the believing community in any age. As previously indicated, the history

---

3. These points are treated in more detail in several of the above chapters; cf. especially the discussions by W. Harrelson, Chapter 1, and D. A. Knight, Chapter 7.

4. J. Sanders, "Reopening Old Questions about Scripture," *Interp* 28 (1974), 327.

of tradition growth should speak to us about the need to distinguish between "canonization" and "canonizing," between a static and a dynamic approach to the canon, between historical and existential judgments, if the believing community is to play its proper role. For the almost universal opinion among Judaism and Christianity, apart from such as the Jewish apocalyptists or Montanus, is that there was something unique about the biblical period or part of the biblical period, and about the manner and content of God's revelation during that time. But is this correct? The history of tradition growth would seem to suggest otherwise.

The canonical tradition developed in three stages. (1) It was formed because of a conviction of authority in the face of corporate need for guidelines. (2) It was limited as scripture because of a need to contemporize and stabilize authority in the face of heresy. (3) It was closed or canonized because of a crystallizing of authority in the face of radical political and psychological threat.

(1) *The formation of tradition.* The acceptance of separate traditions as authoritative was based on the conviction that they preserved God's word and provided a norm for life. This is well known, even if the reasons for the conviction are not. The particular concern at this point, however, is to remember the important phenomenon that there was great diversity in the traditions, both in terms of text and theology, that were circulating and being accepted by divergent groups within Israel.[5] The diversity, however, was not in affirmation about Yahweh who was at the heart of reality. Amos and Amaziah, or Jeremiah and Hananiah, differed greatly over the nature of human responsibility and divine involvement, but each witnessed to the same Yahweh. When the prophet Ezekiel promised that Yahweh would not spare Tyre from the ravages of Nebuchadrez-

5. Consider the double psalms, the double narratives, Ps. 18 and 2 Sam. 22, Samuel and Jeremiah in LXX and MT, Habakkuk in Pharisaism and at Qumran; cf. P. R. Ackroyd, "The Theology of Tradition: An Approach to Old Testament Theological Problems," *BTF* 3 (1971), 56–58.

zar (Ezek. 26–28), only later to correct himself (Ezek. 29), he was a false prophet only about the application of Yahweh's power, not about the powerful presence of Yahweh in that situation. The same can be said about the strong differences between Job and Ecclesiastes.

The point is that diverse traditions were circulating in Israel and being accepted by different groups within the community.[6] The formation of tradition, therefore, was based on a conviction about Yahweh among a given group at a given moment in history. This very human process sometimes misdirected the conviction or misread the tradition or bent it to particular sectarian concerns. Yet the tradition was retained and incorporated with other traditions eventually, because of a recognition of diversity in conviction. This suggests the central point that *the function of tradition was to witness to a person (Yahweh) not to an event.* Thus its authoritative reference must always be seen as a dynamic process, not a static point.

(2) *The limitation of tradition.* Just as the formation and preservation of tradition were motivated by the need for an authoritative witness by which the people of God could direct their lives, there were periodic times when these traditions were edited and delimited to preserve the unity of the people. For as traditions multiplied, so did variant claims for authority which tended to disrupt that unity. In Josiah's day there were claims for the validity of idol worship and theology left from Manasseh and Amon. But Josiah, rediscovering the authoritative word, made official proclamation of the proper contents of revelation (2 Kgs. 22–23). In Ezra's day there were claims for eclectic worship which had developed during the days of exile and later. So Ezra reaffirmed the authoritative word regarding pure worship and practice (Neh. 8–10). In the days of Ben Sira, when the prophets are first mentioned as authoritative, the

---

6. Ibid. Ackroyd draws attention to the social diversity among orthodox groups (who produced the major historical surveys) and between orthodoxy and sectarianism (e.g., Jews and Samaritans).

evidence is not clear, and so the issue is not certain (Sir. 44–49). But at Jamnia in 90 A.D. there were claims from Jewish and Christian apocalypticism. On the one hand, the growing doctrinal attacks against Judaism by the early church brought the need to establish a list of authoritative books. The church, which used a larger grouping reflected in the Septuagint, was circulating oral and written traditions proclaiming the coming of the Messiah. But, on the other hand, the increasing growth and use of a larger, often apocalyptic, literature among groups in Judaism, such as at Qumran, also brought about the need for a canonical decision.

The point of all this is that the community at certain moments in history felt the threat of disunity, and so legitimately sought to preserve its unity by getting its traditions-house in order. This is the function of canon at the stage when it was delineated as *scripture*, that is, the body of writings in which the community uniquely heard the Spirit speak. But it is important to notice two things that were happening.

First, there was a dynamic dialogue between tradition and community. It was the body of believers interacting with the various witnesses, believing that it was legitimately involved in deciding the issue of authority, that determined scripture. As Sanders writes: "This presupposes the basic view that the believing communities are essentially pilgrim movements challenged dynamically, generation by generation, and even morning by morning, to take another step on the way to obedience and faith."[7]

Second, the development of scripture was a process of contemporizing various diverse traditions and of allowing diverse traditions to exist side by side as each bore theological, contemporary witness. The community at each stage in its scriptural history saw contemporary value in traditions from various periods, because it saw a unity in witness to Yahweh, not in the

---

7. Sanders, "Reopening Old Questions about Scripture," p. 329.

theological forms of that witness. The developing shape of the Decalogue or the composite character of the Deuteronomistic or Chronicler's histories are evidence of this. It was the conviction of one group at one moment in history that these traditions were the authoritative norm *for them.* Two histories could exist side by side at one stage in canon because, though diverse in the ways they dealt with the same events, they both witnessed to the same *Heilsgeschichte.*

The common theme of the Old Testament is that Yahweh is involved in the world of people and nature to bring about the completion of his creation. This is true not only of the final canonical form, but also of individual traditions.[8] Thus this shows that the biblical communities, in their acceptance of varying traditions, recognized that the Spirit was witnessing to diverse ways or sides to God's actions in this common purpose. This presents us, therefore, with an hermeneutic. The key to interpreting or evaluating the traditions is not to isolate a theology of form (e.g., covenant, Torah), but of movement with Yahweh toward *šālôm.* This is the normative authority that the communities saw in the traditions, and why they resisted harmonization of those traditions into a standard form. There was recognized a diversity in God's ways toward achieving his will for people, and they at that moment were diverse human beings who could hear that multifaceted witness represented by differing traditional forms.

The fact that the traditions were changed, modified, and expanded by the community at various periods shows significantly that the basic stance of the people of God toward tradition was always to be a dynamically involved one, since Yahweh was dynamic and developing his will. This is the meaning of contemporizing the traditions in the establishment of scripture. A thoughtless, mechanical preservation of tradition in its ancient form could give a unity to the people by having a common

8. Cf. Jer. 29:11: ". . . plans for fulfillment (*šālôm*), not for frustration/incompleteness (*rāʿāh*)."

authority. But it would provide a stultifying unity, since it
blocked the growth of the people, and ultimately of the purposes of Yahweh, by denying the involvement of those people
with Yahweh. Simple acceptance of the past brought *Heilsgeschichte* to a halt, or at least diverted it. Each generation was
to be at the exodus, at Sinai, in the wilderness (Deut. 5:2–3),
not just in some role-playing sense, but in the actual sense of
hearing God address them through the ancient words so that
they could understand their own function in moving toward
conquest, toward freedom, toward rest, toward *šālôm*. This
meant, therefore, contemporizing, adding elements not part of
the original event.[9] Each generation was to "test the spirits,"
to find "a mirror for [their own] identity,"[10] to add to the
tradition, since they were part of the process. They were not
attempting, in establishing scripture, to codify or standardize an
earlier generation's hearing of God or responding to God as the
norm for all generations. They themselves became participants
in the tradition process by "canonizing" the ancient witness for
their own moment in history through a flexible approach to the
traditions.

The book of Amos provides a clear example of this. The
prophet was concerned to awaken Israel to the fact that it had
become dead to its true role as the people of God. They had
become mere preservers of the tradition, and thus had lost the
meaning of the tradition. The people of Israel had preserved
the form of the tradition, but had lost the witness of the tradition in that act. So Amos' role, as that of the other prophets,
was to reaffirm the validity of the tradition by contemporizing
that tradition. He sought to reshape the tradition so that the
people would truly hear the tradition addressed to them. Amos
therefore apparently radically reshaped the "Day of Yahweh"
tradition by applying it to Israel in a negative way (Amos

9. The Song of Moses (Exod. 15:1–18) is a good example, where verses 1–10 deal
with the exodus, and verses 11–17 with the conquest. Cf. also Amos 9:8a/8b–15.
10. J. Sanders, *Torah and Canon* (Philadelphia: Fortress, 1972), p. xv.

5:18–20), but in actuality was restoring the theology of the tradition that had got lost. He was pointing the people to the fact that the tradition was not a matter of form, but of witness to Yahweh involved in the world to achieve the completion of creation. This meant, therefore, at that historical moment, destruction for Israel who had blocked Yahweh's purpose by their social and political behavior. The people had failed to be the people by being participants with Yahweh, and a major reason for this was their passive attitude toward the tradition.

Amos did a similar thing when he repeated the old "salvation history" list, but also contemporized or reshaped it by adding the words about Nazirites and prophets (Amos 2:9–12). Those two events were also part of salvation history, events that were for Israel at that moment more existential, more meaning-bearing, because they could be identified with more easily than the events of the distant past.

So all this—the diversity of traditions in one developing scripture and the contemporizing of traditions in that expanding scripture—shows that the people of God saw the norm in tradition in its witness to Yahweh, not in its theological formulation or shape. This indeed is what is represented in the use of the Old Testament by the New Testament or by the Targums and Midrash. They used the Old Testament not in terms of what the Old Testament writers always meant for their own day, but for what the Old Testament writers meant when seen in light of the events of their day.

The Old Testament process of developing scripture, therefore, is highly instructive. There is a necessity for unity in the faith—the purpose of scripture—but that unity is deceptive if it is seen as allegiance to a form of tradition formulated by a previous generation. That unity is in a dynamic, responsive attitude toward the ever-present God witnessed to in the tradition. Thus the Old Testament scriptural tradition at its various stages is useful in showing us what was contemporary norm for the people of God at those stages, but not in giving us what is exclusive contemporary norm for us. It gives us examples of how to contemporize tradition, and by its common witness to God involved in history for *šālôm* it provides a normative kind of tradition. But by this it only gives selected examples, not a closed catalogue of all examples that can witness to God.

(3) *The closing of tradition.* The establishment of a closed canon—our present collection—was based on the emergence of a particular view of revelation. Pressured by radical heretical claims at the time of Jamnia, given greater threat by the disruption caused by the destruction of the temple, Judaism moved to close its canon by reaching to the past for an authoritative base. In a sense, it was pressured by heresy in the heat of controversy to overstate its case and take an extreme position. It developed a view that prophetic inspiration had occurred only in the period between Moses and Artaxerxes,[11] or that the Holy Spirit had disappeared from Israel after Haggai, Zechariah, and Malachi had died.[12] Thus the search for authoritative tradition and the periodic delimitation of that in scripture came to an end. It is true that in Judaism the Rabbinic literature developed an authoritative position during subsequent centuries and achieved a quasi-canonical status, but there was still a distinction made from canon.

A similar situation developed in the emerging church. Although there was a controversy over the apocryphal/deutero-canonical materials, the discussion was not about an open canon but about the contents of a closed tradition. Including the apocrypha as deutero-canonical works did not open the canon, but simply expanded its size. For the church the incarnation was a revelational watershed. Because of its belief that Jesus was the fulfillment of the revelatory process witnessed to in the Old Testament, it affirmed that there were two periods of revelation—before Jesus Christ and after him. Thus it was again a

11. Cf. Josephus, *Against Apion* I, 8.
12. Tosephta Sotah 3:2.

particular view of revelation that considered the Old Testament canon closed.

The history of tradition shows us, therefore, a positive involvement of community with tradition as the people sought to contemporize the past witness to revelation, and by that to witness to the same God in their own life and day. The function of tradition was to be contemporized by each generation through adaptation, expansion, and addition. Therefore the development of scripture (canonizing) was a legitimate search for unity of faith in the face of threat, a search that embraced textual and theological variants. But canonization was an unfortunate freezing of tradition growth. Canonization was untrue to tradition history and its contemporizing process. It was an overreaction to threat that gave special status to one historical moment, and thereby crystallized one set of tradition for all groups and for all time. It thus provided a kind of harmonization of diverse traditions that had been rejected in the process of tradition growth. It is interesting to note that the church rejected the harmonization attempts by Marcion and Tatian, but accepted the principle with a closed canon. Thus it inhibited later generations from participating in the struggle to ascertain authority for themselves and deadened the tradition to the letter of the law. It opened the way for the continuing struggle in Judaism and Christianity between the recognition of authority in later traditions and the pressure of canonization to assume a special value or sanctity to a particular set of traditions.

The *canonizing* of tradition was based on a recognition of the dynamic and ever-present work of the Spirit in speaking to each generation of the people of God about what was authoritative for its life. This is presumably why the process passed over many apparently significant works, that is, works that have been felt to be significant by later people at other times (e.g., Ben Sira or 4 Maccabees). It is also why the process accepted works which many in later times have considered to be less significant (e.g., Esther, Song of Songs). What was important for canon was not content, but the community conviction of the authority for that moment of certain works, even if that significance was only partially understood. Post-canonical generations have not always felt that conviction, and have thus wrestled with justifying those works through allegory or some other means.

The canonizing process, therefore, teaches us to accept each stage in the developing canon as having authority in witnessing to how each generation heard God's will for themselves. But we do not take each stage as necessarily authoritative for our lives, including the final stage. We ask if it speaks to our own *"Sitz im Leben."* Maybe our *"Sitz"* is more akin to the Yahwist stage, for example, than the final canonical stage. Brevard Childs claims that "the final shape of the Pentateuch is canonical, that is, normative for the life of faith, because it reflects the fullest form of the church's understanding of God's revelation."[13] But the history of scriptural growth would seem to suggest otherwise. No stage, not even the New Testament, is the final or more authoritative stage. The people of God in every generation must engage in the canonizing process, that is, must hear the Spirit convincing it of God's word for itself in its own situation.

The *canonization* or closing of tradition was based on radical political and psychological threat, and the need for a safe tradition. Thus the continuing work of the Spirit was forgotten in the attempt to find theological security. The process of tradition growth recognized diversity in the nature of reality and accepted mystery in the ways of God. It resisted harmonization into a single theology or explanation of life. It witnessed to the need to accept loose ends. It was an example of each generation's doing theology not just repeating theology. Canonization, however, solidified one theology.

13. B. Childs, "The Old Testament as Scripture of the Church," *CTM* 43 (1972), 721.

James Barr comments that the closing of the canon had the practical advantage of providing a body of material of manageable size, showing "something of a reasonable balance between different genres, periods and points of view."[14] But this is hardly a convincing case for a closed canon, particularly in light of the Mishna and Talmud, or in view of the need to be responsive to the ever-new actions of God.

Barr also speaks of the Old Testament canon as a "classic model" for faith, a model "reaffirmed, restated and reinterpreted in Jesus."[15] He is therefore opposed to a continuous process of tradition growth as having a deteriorating effect on tradition.

> The effect of this, I would suggest, is to cause a deterioration in the character of tradition, which easily becomes a mechanism for the manipulation of the unchanging and objective scripture. The tradition is no longer the total and existential life of the people of God; its range and depth is limited by the existence in scripture of the objectified classic model of understanding. . . . The model was fixed by scriptural form because it was believed to be sufficient.[16]

But if safety in faith is the issue, why not then canonize only the first stage of tradition growth? This would presumably avoid any deterioration of tradition. And was not security in faith the implicit argument of those who agreed to the closing of the canon? The issue, it seems, is rather the continuing vitality of the community's involvement with the Spirit, and this is always chancy but absolutely necessary. The centrality of the exodus event was not an insurmountable problem for the Old Testament period, nor the centrality of the Christ event for the New. This is always the task of interaction with developing tradition, a task suggested by the Old Testament tradition itself (Deut. 13:1–5; 18:20).

14. Barr, *The Bible in the Modern World*, p. 156.
15. Ibid., p. 151.
16. Ibid., p. 128. But cf. the comment of E. Jacob, *Grundfragen alttestamentlicher Theologie* (Stuttgart: Kohlhammer, 1970), p. 45, n. 6.

Thus the canon may provide a "classic model" for faith and for the "re-presentation" of tradition, but should not be an "exclusive model." Developing authoritative tradition of a constitutive nature, not just of interpretative or exegetical character, should continue to be recognized, if not formally, at least functionally, if succeeding generations are to be true to the history of tradition.

Chapter 12

Torah and Tradition

Michael Fishbane

The post-biblical relationship between Torah and Tradition reveals a dynamic between fixed, authoritative texts and their subsequent reinterpretations, between canonical teachings and their subsequent reuse. In the present chapter, our purpose is to explore some of the modes, functions, and implications of this dynamic. Indeed, a consideration of post-biblical Tradition is pertinent insofar as preceding chapters have explored dimensions of tradition in the biblical period.[1] But this consideration is doubly pertinent inasmuch as the post-biblical relationship between authoritative texts and their reuse *also* exists in the biblical period—for in the earlier period we can apprehend the later phenomenon in its nascent, pre-canonical modes.[2]

Accordingly, two phases of Torah, in its relation to Tradition, will be treated. In the first phase, the term "Torah" will denote specific authoritative teachings in the *pre-canonical* Hebrew Bible. It is here that we shall consider the phenomenon of pre-canonical "canonical" texts. By contrast, in the second phase, "Torah" will denote the received, *canonical* He-

1. In the following discussion the capitalized form of "Tradition" refers to the modes of interpreting biblical scripture by post-biblical Judaism as a whole or by any of its various groups, the "Judaisms." The lower-case form, "tradition," is reserved for the pre-canonical development of the materials, as treated elsewhere in this book.

2. For two earlier, but substantially different, treatments of inner-biblical interpretation see I. L. Seeligmann, "Voraussetzungen der Midraschexegese," VTS 1 (1953), 150–81; R. Bloch, s.v. Midrash, DBS 5 (Paris: Librairie Letouzey et Ané, 1957), especially cols. 1267–76, and references to other works.

brew Bible and the entirety of its authoritative teachings. In both cases, then, Torah will stand for teachings whose authority and formulation precede their reuse by Tradition. Indeed, it is precisely in the nexus between fixed and free formulations, authoritative and innovative texts, and durative and punctual functions that the Torah-Tradition dialectic unfolds.

What follows, then, is a treatment of the relationships between Torah and Tradition in the biblical and early post-biblical periods, and their theological implications. However, given the variety of texts, it is first necessary to provide an organizing focus for analysis. To do this, as well as to use an appropriate literary form, we will present most of our discussion as a midrashic exposition of the Decalogue. To use the Decalogue in this way is to choose a specific text whose various teachings were reinterpreted by ongoing biblical and post-biblical traditions (and frequently with precise reference to the Decalogue formulation). Used heuristically, then, the Decalogue will provide a focus for our consideration of the relationship between authoritative teachings and their ongoing reinterpretations.

TORAH AND TRADITION: FORMS AND FEATURES OF THE BIBLICAL, PRE-CANONICAL PHENOMENON

I am YHWH, your God, who took you out of the land of Egypt. As the paradigmatic expression of YHWH's power for his people in servitude, the exodus gave shape to many later hopes for return from the Assyrian and Babylonian exiles (Isa. 11:11–16; Jer. 16:14–15; Mic. 7:15). But these various formulations do not reflect the language of the authoritative Pentateuchal recension in Exod. 1–15. They witness typological uses of the exodus motif rather than exegetical traditions *verbally dependent* upon the formulation found in the book of Exodus. Even the clearer echoes of the exodus scenario in Deutero-Isaiah (cf. 43:16–20; 51:9–11; 52:12; 63:11–12) lack the specific verbal tension effected, for example, by Ezek. 20:4–11, 33–36, which withstands a point-by-point comparison with the language of Exod. 6:2–9. Indeed it is just by virtue of this terminological relationship to Exod. 6:2–9 that the power and paradox of Ezekiel's midrashic reinterpretation—of a "new" exodus done in wrath against Israel—are accentuated.

The foregoing provides a concise case whereby tradition deliberately used an authoritative Torah-teaching as a didactic foil. But such midrashic reformulations could also be produced through a freer handling of an authoritative teaching. Isa. 19:19–25—which combines several eschatological oracles coming at the conclusion of the oracles against Egypt (Isa. 19:1–18)—provides a case in point. These texts show a theologically audacious transposition of the exodus motif found in Exod. 1–12. To make this transposition self-evident, Isa. 19:19–25 can be most suggestively juxtaposed with Exod. 3:7–9; 8:16–24 [8:20–28]. Thus, in the Exodus Cycle, YHWH saw the torment of "my people" (*'ammî*), heard their cry (*ṣa'ăqātām*), and saw the Egyptians oppressing (*lōḥăṣîm*) them; he sent (stem: *šālaḥ*) Moses as a deliverer to bring them out (3:7–9). In 8:16–24, for example, YHWH sent a sign (*'ōt*) that the Egyptians might know (stem: *yāda'*) his power; Pharaoh temporarily relented to let the Israelites sacrifice (stem: *zābaḥ*) to YHWH in Egypt; but Moses refused: the Israelites would only worship YHWH outside Egypt. Pharaoh also begged Moses to pray (stem: *'ātar*) for him. Punishment for Pharaoh's noncompliance with Moses' demands was that YHWH would plague them. (The stem *nāgap* is found in 7:27 [8:2]; 12:23; and Josh. 24:5.) By means of an exegetical-terminological counterpoint, Isa. 19:19–25 touches on all the aforementioned points—but in a revolutionary way. Now the Egyptians have oppressors (*lōḥăṣîm*) and cry (*yiṣ'ăqû*) to YHWH; now an altar to YHWH, in Egypt, will be a sign (*'ōt*) that he will send (stem: *šālaḥ*) them a deliverer. Through these acts of deliverance YHWH would be known (stem: *yāda'*) to the Egyptians, and they would sacrifice (stem: *zābaḥ*) to him. YHWH would plague (*nāgap*) the Egyptians, but in the end he would respond to their prayers (stem: *'ātar*). Finally, the third oracle (vss. 24–25), which calls Egypt "my people" (*'ammî*), bristles with irony. Understandably, the Septuagint and Targum renationalized it.

This midrash has thus produced the most extreme transposition of a national historical memory conceivable. Through explicit counterpoint, the private experience of Israelite redemption has become the verbal key through which universal redemption was annotated. Isaiah has bequeathed to Egypt Israel's most personal memory for the sake of peace. The metamorphosis is stunning and suggests fixed formulations in the pre-canonical phase of biblical literature. It suggests an instance of a pre-canonical "canon," or "canon within the canon."[3]

You shall have no other gods instead of me. You shall not make any sculptured image, or any form of what is in the heavens above, or on the earth below, or in the waters under the earth. This command of divine exclusiveness is supplemented by an anti-iconic proscription. But whereas no reason is given in the Decalogue itself, one is suggested in the sermon in Deut. 4:12–24. In Deut. 4:12 and 15 the reason given is that the Israelites did not see any form at Horeb. This text continues with a specification of the proscribed forms (vss. 16–18). As in the Decalogue, these commandments are associated with prohibitions neither to make (vs. 23) nor to bow down to such forms (vs. 19), and with references to both the exodus (vs. 20) and God's angry zeal (vs. 24).

But the expository power of this sermon extends beyond a free amplification of the opening section of the Decalogue. It contains, in fact, a true midrash. So as to recognize it, one need but recall that a frequent item in anti-idolatry polemics is the ironic juxtaposition of the fashioning of an idol and God the Creator (cf. Isa. 40:12–16; 44:6–20; 45:18–25; 46:1–11; Jer. 10:2–16; cf. Ps. 115). From this vantage point we return to Deut. 4:16–19 and note that it precisely reiterates the crea-

---

3. I owe this phrase to, among others, J. Sanders, *Torah and Canon* (Philadelphia: Fortress, 1972), p. xv.

tion sequence of Gen. 1–2:4a—but in reverse order! This creation account has thus been subtly used to "carry" a midrashic teaching which, reciprocally, gains power by virtue of the hermeneutical tension evoked by the superimposition of an anti-iconic polemic over the structure of a received text.

You shall not bow down to them or worship them. For I, YHWH your God, am a zealous God, visiting the guilt of fathers on their children, to the third and fourth generation of them that reject me. This Torah-teaching determines a certain theological position. The adaptation of a text to a later theological viewpoint or different moral sensibility is also a hallmark of later midrash. The above-cited text provides a case in point. The stated issue of intergenerational punishment is probably not one of judicial redress, for that was customarily handled by the ordinances of jurisprudence. In such cases, the specific offender was always punished (cf. Deut. 24:16 and Exod. 21:31). The issue seems, rather, to be infractions made directly against God, for example, acts of idolatry. In such cases, punishment is divine and transgenerational.[4] Reference to punishment to the third and fourth generation is found both in the Decalogue (Exod. 20:2–17; Deut. 5:6–18 [5:6–21]) and in the list of divine attributes (Exod. 34:6–7; Num. 14:18–19).

But later generations were uncomfortable with the implications of this theological teaching. Reinterpreting a related proverb which describes the visitation of fathers' guilt on their children, Ezek. 18 attempted to teach hope to those in exile and delimit the scope of their guilt (note vss. 2–4, 19–20).[5] Similarly, in his oracles of consolation Jeremiah also reinterpreted this proverb as a teaching for the new age (31:29–30). However, it is the sermon in Deut. 7:9–10 which shows a closer

4. On the possibility of a dual standard of justice as regards civil and divine punishment, see M. Greenberg, "Some Postulates of Biblical Criminal Law," in *Yehezkel Kaufmann Jubilee Volume*, ed. M. Haran (Jerusalem: Magnes Press, The Hebrew University, 1960), 20–27 (English section).

5. As his examples and argument suggest, Ezekiel attempted to overcome the dual standard of punishment by treating divine infractions as civil ones, viz., to argue against vicarious punishment for the children of those sent into exile.

relation to the wording of the Decalogue and its transformation. Whereas vs. 9 strikes the chord of long-term grace to the faithful, vs. 10 sharply continues: "And He will requite those who reject Him, directly to destroy him; He will not delay to hate him but will repay him in his presence." The received formulation has thus been controverted by later tradition.

As we have seen in previous sections, another aspect of inner-biblical midrash is the free adaptation of a fixed text. Of the two versions of divine attributes in Exod. 34:6–7 and Num. 14:18–19, the former is clearly the more expansive. It will be, therefore, instructive to juxtapose it to Mic. 7:18–20—as it appears that just such a text has been restyled in the praise of vs. 18 and reappropriated in the appeal of vss. 19–20.

Exod. 34:6–7	*Mic. 7:18–20*
O YHWH, YHWH!—a *God compassionate* and gracious; [who] assuages [his] *anger*, is great in *steadfast kindness*, and maintaining *kindness* to the thousands; *forgiving iniquity*, *rebellion* and *sin* . . .	Who is a *God* like you, [who] *forgives iniquity*, passes over the *rebellion* of the remnant of his inheritance; [who] has not kept his *anger* forever, as he delights in *kindness*?! May he again be *compassionate* to us, cleanse our *iniquities*, and cast into the depths of the sea all our [!] *sins*. O be *steadfast* with Jacob and *compassionate* with Abraham, as you swore to our ancestors in days gone by.

Once aware of this reuse of the formula in Micah, we can recognize a further transformation. Just as the redactor of the minor prophets utilized word repetitions to link the separate books (e.g., Hos. 14:2 [14:1] and Joel 2:12; Joel 4:16 and Amos 1:2; Amos 9:12 and Obad. 19; Hab. 2:20 and Zeph. 1:7; Hag. 2:23 and Zech. 1:3), so is Mic. 7:18–20 linked to Nah. 1:2–3. In this reuse of the "attribute-formula" (Exod. 34:6–7) in Nah. 1:2–3 terms of compassion are transformed into terms of war: "who maintains (*nōṣēr*) *kindness*" becomes "who *rages* (*nôṭēr*) against his *enemies*" (cf. Lev. 19:18); "*assuages* anger" (taking *'erek* to be like the stem used in, e.g., Jer. 30:17) becomes "*long* of anger"; and "great in . . . *kindness*" becomes "mighty in *power.*"

The various reuses of the formula concerning divine attributes considered in this section thus demonstrate diverse modes of inner-biblical midrash—whereby an authoritative pronouncement-text was either re-formed or reformulated by later tradition in the light of their ideologies and concerns.

Observe the Sabbath day, to keep it holy . . . do not do any manner of work because. . . . The ritual prescription of the Sabbath in the Decalogue is given two motivations. It serves both as a social celebration of the completed fact of creation (Exod. 20:11) and as a recollection of the Egyptian slavery and the redemption from Egypt (Deut. 5:15). In both cases, the explanation serves an adaptative-integrative function for the changing motivations of the faith-community centered in an authoritative Torah-teaching.

But what is the content of "to keep it holy" and "do not do any manner of work"? All the earliest teachings on this commandment, through which the life of the observing community unfolded, are not preserved. Yet there are passages, such as Exod. 16:25–26, 29; 34:21; 35:1–3; Jer. 17:21–22; and Neh. 10:32 [10:31]; 13:14–21, which contain references to this commandment together with legal clarifications and/or amplifications of it. These latter texts point to another inner-biblical aspect of Torah and tradition whereby various ritual-legal teachings clarify, amplify, and protect the authoritative Torah-teaching.

With the close of the canon, this type of elaboration-exegesis became increasingly significant; the diverse collations of biblical laws and their amplifications had to be harmonized, on the one hand, and integrated with the new post-biblical customs or clarifications, on the other. The result of this midrashic process was the collections of legal tradition known collectively as *midrash halakhah*. But such processes of harmonization and text-blending can be detected much earlier, both between books of the Pentateuch and between the Pentateuch and later materials. As regards the former, let us note a case showing the relationship between the Book of the Covenant (Exod. 21–23) and Deuteronomy.

The law in Exod. 22:30 [22:31] occurs independently of a related context. It proscribes the eating of unslaughtered carcasses—prescribing their use as fit for dogs—and adjures the Israelite to be holy. Exod. 23:19 concerns the pilgrimage-offering of first-fruits and, in this cultic connection, prohibits the practice of boiling a kid in its mother's milk. Strikingly, Deut. 14:21 *combines* these two teachings and incorporates them at the conclusion to the code of laws on forbidden/permitted foods. Again there is a reference to Israelite holiness—although here it is unconditional—and allows the carcasses to be given to the sojourner. A comparison of the texts points up the new Torah-teaching:

Exod. 22:30; 23:19	*Deut. 14:21*
And be a *holy* people to me, and *do not eat* ripped field carrion; throw it to the dog. . . . Bring the first of your produce to the shrine of YHWH; *do not boil a kid in its mother's milk.*	*Do not eat* any carcass; [either] give it to the sojourner . . . or sell it to the stranger: for you are a *holy* nation to YHWH your God; *do not boil a kid in its mother's milk.*

Not only is the Deuteronomic ideology concerning the sojourner and Israelite given expression in Deut. 14:21, but so is the ongoing process of reuse of authoritative texts. Coming at the conclusion of the code of food legislation, Deut. 14:21 not only incorporates the prohibition of eating carrion in a collection of food laws, but also *transforms* the prohibition of boiling a kid in its mother's milk from a cultic prohibition to one concerned with food regulations in the widest sense. This new literary context for the latter undoubtedly aided later rabbinic elaborations which considered this law within the parameters of dietary regulations—as we shall see below.

As regards the process of *midrash halakhah* between Pentateuchal and non-Pentateuchal sources, let us turn to the Passover rite. In Exod. 12:8–11 the Paschal offering is to be roasted (*ṣlî 'ēš*), *not* boiled; but Deut. 16:7 expressly commands that "you shall boil (*ûbiššaltā*) [it]." Whether these differences (including the type of designated animal, cf. Exod. 12:5 and Deut. 16:2) reflect geographical or historical variations is unclear. What is clear is that the later reflex of the Paschal rite, recorded in 2 Chr. 35:10–18, was bothered by these two differing authoritative teachings. The solution was one of harmonization, despite the apparent awkwardness of the result.[6] Thus after vs. 12 states that the sacrifice was done "as is written in the Book of Moses" we read (vs. 13): "And they *boiled* (*wayĕbaššĕlû*) the paschal-offering *in the fire* (*bā'ēš*), as per the statute." Through this exegetical process of harmonization later tradition preserved the variously received Torah-teachings and bridged any apparent discrepancy between them. This example is already at that historical frontier wherein Tradition looked back to the diverse Torah-teachings of many periods and saw one uniform Torah. With this dehistoricizing and monolithicizing process, textual superfluities and contradictions were exegetically transformed. This matter, as stated, became particularly prominent *after* the canonization of scripture; but already here we again see an incipient "canonical consciousness."

Thou shalt not commit adultery/desire your neighbor's wife. The Decalogue not only contains theological and cultic teachings, it also includes social-moral matter. The commandments mentioned above will serve as the basis of two different innerbiblical examples of the relationship between Torah and tradition.

6. Cf. M. Z. Segal, *Parshanuth Ha-Miqra'*, 2d ed. (Jerusalem: Qiryat-Sefer, 1971), p. 6.

The first involves a situation in which the theme of adultery and seduction provides the root metaphor for a wisdom tradition admonition to beware of the temptations of falsehood. In the process, Prov. 6:20–35 actually reshapes the teachings-admonitions in Deut. 6:4–9 and the Decalogue (5:6–18 [5:6–21]) in a creative way. The skill of this reformulation can be observed by a juxtaposition of the relevant passages:

Deut. 5:6–18 [5:6–21]; 6:4–9	*Prov. 6:20–35*
Hear, Israel, what I command (6:4, 6)	Heed, my son, the commands (vs. 20)
When you dwell and journey, when you lie down and rise up (6:6)	When you go about, when you lie down and awaken (vs. 22)
Bind them on your hand (6:8)	Bind them on your heart (vs. 21)
I am a jealous/zealous God; for YHWH will not clear the guilty (5:9–11)	For the jealous/zealous fury of a man [betrayed] (vs. 34); . . . whosoever has intercourse with his fellow's wife will not be cleared of guilt (vs. 29)
Honor your father and your mother (5:16)	Heed . . . your father . . . your mother (vs. 20)
Do not commit adultery (5:17 [5:18])	Whosoever had adultery with a woman (vs. 32)
Do not steal (5:17 [5:19])	Theft *topos* (vss. 30–31)
Do not desire your fellow's wife (5:18 [5:21])	Do not desire . . . your fellow's wife (vss. 25, 29)

The second example involving the issue of adultery derives from prophecy, where it often serves as a motif: Israel's infidelity to YHWH was imaged through the *topos* of whoring after other gods/husbands-ba‘alim (e.g., Hos. 2; Ezek. 16; 23). But it is Jer. 3:1 that makes specific use of a Torah-text on this theme. A juxtaposition of his sermon with its Deuteronomic source will facilitate analysis.

Deut. 24:1–4	*Jer. 3:1*
If a man marry . . . if he has found against her *'erwat dābār* . . . he will divorce her from house . . . he will not be able . . . to return (*lāšûb*) to [re]marry her . . . And do not profane the earth. . . .	If a man divorce . . . can he return (*yāšûb*) to her? Will not this earth be defiled? Yet you have whored after many suitors . . . *wĕšôb 'ēlay.*

The Deuteronomic law is prescriptive and precise; the formulation is set within a prodosis-apodosis form. The subject is "a man." Jeremiah has reused this law in a radically new way in Jer. 3:1. Through his prophet, God asks a question about the Deuteronomic law. God is the subject; Israel is the wife who has been adulterous. This allegorization of the Torah-teaching is already a reinterpretation by later tradition. And while the term *'erwat dābār* of Deut. 24:1 was variously interpreted in later Tradition,[7] Jeremiah is hereby giving it a sexual sense ("unchaste matter"). But his reuse of the terminology of the Deuteronomic law goes yet further and centers on the clause: *wĕšôb 'ēlay*, "therefore *return* to me." The text is ambiguous with two principle difficulties: (1) If this clause is to be understood as a question with God as subject (viz., "will you, therefore, return to me?"), then it is rhetorical with the implication that Israel's infidelity has now prevented her restoration; whereas (2) if the clause is affirmative ("therefore, return"), it either suggests that Israel repent *before* God divorces her or argues that God will break his own law and take her back ("therefore, you *will* return to me"; and cf. b. *Yoma* 86b). However the ambiguity be resolved, the power of the reinterpretation is that, through the allegory, Jeremiah has transposed the legal term "return" into a theological key so that it denotes the question of Israel's religious return or repentance; moreover, in doing so, he has broken the original symmetry of the

---

7. Cf. LXX to Deut. 24:1; *Antiq.* IV, viii.23; M. *Giṭṭ.* IX–X; Matt. 19:3, 9.

law in which the husband is the active agent. A series of re-interpretations unfolds, then, in Jeremiah's use of Deut. 24:1–4. The hermeneutical tension effected is allegorical and didactic. It suggests yet another inner-biblical mode of the relationship of ongoing tradition to Torah, for with the reinterpretation the plain-sense of scripture has been undercut.

Let us pause here to reflect. The inner-biblical dynamic of Torah and tradition, as thus far analyzed, reveals the reuse (controlled or creative), transformation, readaptation or blending of transmitted teachings having an authoritative aspect. Tradition emerges as a relationship to past authority—be that an historical memory, a theological proclamation, or a commanded behavior. Tradition, in its relationship to Torah, has thus far been seen to be both conservative and innovative. As an innovative process, tradition is a mode of hermeneutics, a process of interpretation, which *actualizes* a received, authoritative text in a new context. Through tradition, a sacred teaching remains effective in new life situations. As a conservative force, tradition provides for cultural continuity and cohesion by *preserving* the authoritative memories of the past. From an analytical perspective, an hermeneutical tension is created between the primary Torah-teaching and its new use in tradition. Where this tension is explicit it provokes didactic irony or establishes validity for the new teaching; where this tension is implicit—as in text-blending or harmonization—tradition has deliberately obscured its own exegetical processes so as to create a *new Torah* authority. This points to an aspect of the dialectic between Torah and Tradition which we shall later examine: it involves that process in which new traditions succeed primary Torah-teachings and, in so doing, threaten to supercede them.

Before concluding this presentation of pre-canonical modes of the relationship between Torah and tradition, we must note two final aspects which, equally, become significant in the post-canonical phase. These two aspects deal with an historicization of received teachings: in the first instance, we shall note examples of the historicization of nonhistorical materials; in the second instance we shall note examples of the re-historicization (or revitalization) of prophetic materials.

The historicization of the nonhistorical. The phenomenon of adding superscriptions to the psalms should certainly be regarded as a type of inner-biblical exegesis. Some superscriptions, notably those which indicate musical accompaniment or mode, are undoubtedly original—but others are suggestive for our purposes. Thus the ascription of Ps. 51 to David, when he repented to God after Nathan censured him for taking Bathsheba, can be understood as a later interpretation in the light of 1 Sam. 12. By the ascription of this event to a late liturgy of repentance, the liturgy is historicized—in the sense that it is relocated within a specific national-historical context. A reciprocal dynamic is thus effected. From the standpoint of the psalm the superscription provides a national-historical setting; and from the standpoint of the historical event, the psalm provides its spiritual exfoliation (cf. Pss. 57; 59; 60). Such an interpretational transformation of a received liturgy affects Ps. 30 as well. It has been intriguingly suggested that the superscription in vs. 1, "for the dedication of the Temple," nationalizes and historicizes the psalm—thereby transforming it from one of personal lament and hope into one that reflects on the sorrow and hope of the nation in exile without a temple at the joyous time of its rededication.[8] The nexus between ongoing tradition and received "Torah" has, here too, created a new and independent Torah-teaching.

The re-historicization of the historical. This example deals with prophecies and their revitalizations. Such reuses of authoritative prophecies have both a negative and positive aspect: negative, insofar as they point to a failed prophecy needing reascription; and positive, insofar as these prophecies remained vital and significant to the people.

---

8. H. Ludin Jansen, *Die spätjüdische Psalmendichtung, ihr Entstehungskreis und ihr "Sitz im Leben"* (Oslo: Dybwad, 1937), p. 99.

The prophecy in Jer. 25:11–12; 29:10 is such a case of a reused and vital prophecy. An oracle of seventy years of doom is also attested in Isa. 23:15–17 and the neo-Assyrian annals.[9] In the book of Jeremiah it is applied to the period of subjugation to Babylon. Recited in 605 B.C.E., according to Jer. 25:11–12, the seventy-year oracle would have been fulfilled in 535. Judeans in the exile, and those just returned after Cyrus' decree in 538, must undoubtedly have considered this oracle to have applied to their time. The Chronicler certainly did and so cited Jeremiah (2 Chr. 36:21) to the effect that Cyrus' decree came "to fulfill the oracle of YHWH by the mouth of Jeremiah" (vs. 22). He therefore took over the Jeremian oracle and implicitly construed it as spoken in 609/8 (the year of the death of Josiah and beginning of the Egyptian hegemony over Judea). The Chronicler, moreover, reinterpreted the meaning of seventy years and took them to refer to the necessary period of atonement for the transgressed sabbatical years.

Zechariah (1:12) also reused this oracle. Speaking in 522/1 and urging the returnees to rebuild the temple, he announced God's will that the seventy years were almost up—as they would have been in 517 if he interpreted the oracle as having been recited at the Judean exile in 587/6. In this light, one wonders whether the rebuilding of the altar in 517/6 (cf. Ezra 6:15) was not also motivated by such an interpretation of this oracle. Strikingly, Daniel 9 also refers to this oracle, but for him it is not yet complete; however, he reinterpreted the seventy years as referring to seven heptads. Other reapplications of the authoritative term "seventy" occur in Dan. 10–12, where they are interpreted in terms of seventy weeks.

These ongoing applications or interpretations of the Jeremian oracle are very striking. There is a continuous chain of reinterpretation down to the Seleucid period. But the late book of Daniel also preserves other reinterpretations of earlier oracles. It has been pointed out that Dan. 11 reuses prophecies

---

9. R. Borger, *Die Inschriften Asarhaddons, Königs von Assyrien*, AfOB 9 (Graz: Weidner, 1956), 15, Epis. 10, Fass. a:2b–9, b:19–20.

from the books of Numbers and Isaiah.[10]   It seems further likely that Dan. 11 also reapplies a prophecy from the book of Habakkuk. The oracle in Dan. 11:27: "and the . . . kings . . . will speak deceit; but it will not succeed, for the end remains for the appointed time," refers to the period of Seleucid domination over Palestine. It appears to be a reuse of Hab. 2:3a: "There is still a vision for the appointed time . . . and it will not deceive"—where the historical horizon is different.[11]   The historical enemy for Habakkuk is the neo-Babylonian Chaldeans.

The upshot of these two types of "historicization" confirms our earlier discussions on authoritative Torah-teachings and ongoing interpretations. We have again seen that tradition takes the shape of interpretative adaptations, additions, and revitalizations of received teachings. Israelite culture did not, then, scaffold in a vacuum but on the firm bedrock of forms of authority. Indeed, in the foregoing, we saw that even originally non- or ahistorical texts were a potential seedbed for historical reuse. We are, therewith, already alerted to the appropriation and reinterpretation by later Tradition of *all* the received texts of authority. Finally, let us observe that the preceding examples reinforce an earlier impression: what might be termed a "canonical consciousness" unfolded from the beginning in ancient Israel.

It is to the blossoming of such a consciousness, together with an accompanying analysis of its theological implications, that we now turn.

TORAH AND TRADITION: FORMS AND FEATURES OF THE POST-BIBLICAL, CANONICAL PHENOMENON

We now turn to a consideration of the received MT as "Torah." The latter, in its canonical entirety, now forms the

10. See H. L. Ginsberg, "The Oldest Interpretation of the Suffering Servant," *VT* 3 (1953), 400–404.

11. I have treated this in a study on the continuity of midrashic forms and terms from cuneiform to Rabbinic literatures; see "The Qumran Pesher and Traits of Ancient Hermeneutics," in *Proceedings of the VIth World Congress of Jewish Studies* (Jerusalem: World Union of Jewish Studies, 1976), vol. 1.

basis of religious authority in relation to subsequent tradition and reinterpretation. For the post-biblical Judaisms, the MT not only contained divine revelations but constituted *the* Divine Revelation. As a closed, inscribed revelation it contained —implicitly or explicitly—God's will for Israel. Its multiple torahs and traditions came to constitute *the* Torah. The unfolding of new Traditions would now be set over against this authoritative totality. With this shift to a full "canonical consciousness" both a recognized textual authority and authoritative interpreters emerge. Interpretation and exegesis of the Torah became the mode through which new Traditions were articulated. The canonical MT became the bedrock and point of reference for Tradition and "traditional life," that is, a life lived "out of" interpretations of Torah. "What is Scripture? Interpretation (Midrash) of Torah" (b. *Qid.* 49a).

The formation of a canonical Torah set the tasks of the exegesis to follow: a closed authority which contained God's one revelation would, if restricted, be static at best and of mere antiquarian interest at worst. But for that teaching to be pertinent it had to remain vital to the life of later generations. A serious theological issue had to be overcome: the memories, teachings, and variations of the original revelation had to be related to continuing needs. Thus the need for a continuity of revelations would, with a canon, unfold through post-canonical exegeses. And, as regards the "laws and statutes of the Torah" which constituted the revelation, each of the post-biblical Judaisms claimed to continue the pre-exilic covenantal community and possess the correct interpretation of "Torah." A dialectical process was therewith engaged: the authority of the one revelation was set against the many emergent interpretative Traditions which claimed to continue its validity for the new community. Hence a vital concern of Tradition was to constitute itself as an authoritative teaching, indeed as *the* authoritative teaching-interpretation of Torah. How this was done, as well as a more detailed articulation of the foregoing matters, must await our exploration of exegetical Traditions of the post-biblical Judaisms. Both to facilitate analysis and to integrate the two phases of our study, we shall return to some of the cases of legal exegesis, or *midrash halakhah*, noted in the first section, and see how later Traditions reinterpreted them. In contradistinction to *midrash halakhah*, speculative and homiletical exegesis came to be known as *midrash aggadah*. We shall thus also return to a motif and a prophecy considered above. The theological implications of post-biblical midrash of Torah shall accompany and follow our examples.

The exodus: In the Hebrew Bible the exodus served as the typological paradigm of redemption for ongoing generations, as we saw. This continued to be the case in the post-biblical period (cf. 1QM XI,9–10). The expansive Targumic paraphrases to Exod. 12:42 (especially T. Neofiti) further fixed the night of the Passover (Nisan 15) as the expected time of future redemption.[12] The same conclusion appears in *Mekhilta de R. Ishmael, Bo'* XIV (to Exod. 12:42) in the name of R. Joshua; R. Eliezer only stressed the general period (cf. also b. *R.H.* 11a).

Idolatry: As we have noted, a feature of tradition is that it arises in a new and different time period from that of the original authoritative teachings. To the extent that a Torah-teaching remained valid but that later generations had also either compromised or modified its observance, an exegesis might develop to justify the new practice. Such an interpretative exigency was necessary in connection with the second commandment, which forbids the making or worshiping of images (Exod. 20:4–5; Deut. 5:8–9). Thus while Josephus stressed the uncompromisability of this law in conjunction with an attempt by Petronius to set up an image of Gaius Caligula (*Antiq.* XVIII,viii,2), R. Simeon bar Yohai already found it necessary to forbid the use of sculpted images for decorations (cf. *Mekhilta de R. Simeon, Kî Tisa'* [to Exod. 34:17]). Indeed, figurative images appeared in synagogues both within

---

12. See R. Le Déaut, *La nuit Pascale* (Rome: Institut Biblique Pontifical, 1963), especially pp. 263–338 (includes New Testament typology).

and without Palestine. Scriptural justification for this practice was needed and was accordingly found through a midrashic expansion of Lev. 26:1. Building on the command not to "bow down" to such images, the (1J) Targum permitted one to lay a figured mosaic floor ". . . but not to worship it." The Torah provided authoritative teachings; any divergence or modification of its expressed commands required justification through midrashic exposition of scripture. But let necessity not obscure the audacity of the result: *Tradition teaches a new Torah;* exposition of scripture threatens to succeed scripture. We shall expand on this below.[13]

Observe the Sabbath. In the first section we referred to ways that various biblical texts clarified or amplified the unnuanced apodictic commands, "observe the Sabbath day" and "do not do any manner of work" on the Sabbath, in accordance with ongoing needs and customs. By the post-canonical stage, such halakhic constructions of the law were collated and/or further systematized. Thus, for example, Qumran literature preserves an early attempt to classify and systematize the range of laws for Sabbath "observance" (cf. CD X,14). A legal collection of such laws appears in CD X,14—XI,18. Many of these deal with issues either not fully dealt with in scripture (e.g., Exod. 16:25–26, 29 says that one may neither go out to the field nor leave one's home on the Sabbath; CD X,20–21 gives an expanding exegesis to this law and both defines and protects the spatial character of Sabbath rest) or not at all clarified by scripture (e.g., the phrase *"observe* the Sabbath day" in Deut. 5:12 is interpreted in CD X,14–17 as watching the setting sun so that the temporal character of the Sabbath would be safeguarded).

Both of the above parenthesized examples show a double dynamic common to post-canonical exegetical Tradition: on the one hand, there was *dynamic* exegesis; on the other, *protective*

---

13. Cf. the Targumin (Onq., 1&2J) to the previously considered passage on retribution in Exod. 34:7. The biblical text is radically transformed by the addition of the possibility of repentance (cf. Ezekiel. 18)!

exegesis. The former refers to the radical character of exegesis which often extends or interprets scripture against its plain-sense, but for the sake of ongoing contemporaneity; the latter refers to the human exegetical process which safeguards the divine law from human encroachment and/or transgression. The principle that "Tradition [i.e., authoritative human exegesis] is a [protective] hedge to the [divine] Torah" is cited in M. *Avot* III,13 (cf. I,1; VI,6 and *Mekhilta de R. Ishmael, Bo'* VI [to Exod. 12:8]).[14] A significant dialectic which arises between Torah and Tradition is hereby disclosed: on the one hand, there is the awareness that exegesis renders the text flexible, malleable, and relevant; on the other hand, there is the danger that the divine word will be reinterpreted beyond recognition. Accordingly, from the first, we witness a reciprocity which tries to put the one, the dynamic exegesis, in the service of protective exegesis. In this manner the Torah is protected, the observer is safeguarded from transgression, and scripture remains alive for new generations. With this in mind we can understand the principle taught in M.*Sanh.* XI,3: "Greater stringency accords to [the observation of] the words of the Scribes than to [the observation of] the words of the [written] Torah." But, as we noted about the Targum to Lev. 26:1, the danger that Tradition will encroach upon scripture and, with its new authoritative clarification, supplement it, is a real one. The following example makes this abundantly clear.

We earlier dealt with the law forbidding boiling a kid in its mother's milk. The blended text in Deut. 14:21 gave the earlier formulations in Exod. 22:30 [22:31]; 23:19 a new dietary context. And yet later Tradition was bothered by the threefold repetition of the injunction. Since the assumption of a meaningless superfluity of texts was not acceptable, the variations served as pretexts for further teachings into the dietary regulations. Thus in M.*Ḥull.* VIII,1 these repetitions allow the new

14. Note the interpretation of Eccles. 10:8 in b. *Shab,* 11a, and cf. already CD I,16 for the overall notion.

inference that no meat whatsoever may be cooked in milk, and in M.*Ḥull.* VIII,4 there is the further prohibition of eating the two together. Thus the formation of a canon, as exemplified here, produced a curious historical dialectic. The diverse historical strata of earlier traditions were de-historicized with the result that variations and/or multiple accounts of a teaching had to be re-apprehended. But while Midrash intends to elicit new meanings for Torah—which is its primary authority—it does not arise to obliterate it. And yet, such is the dialectical process of Torah and Tradition that this danger can and did happen—as when Targum Onqelos replaced the Torah text of Deut. 14:21 with the new legal exegesis: "You shall not eat meat with milk!" Hereby the danger inherent in the dialectical process between a divine Torah-revelation and a human exegetical Tradition has been disclosed. Tradition has superceded the Torah-teaching and has become an independent authority. Indeed, in this case, Tradition has replaced Torah itself!

As in our discussion of the first phase, so here we shall conclude our series of examples with two instances of "historicizing" exegesis. Both instances—the historicization of the nonhistorical and the re-historicization of prophecies—show the dynamic appropriation of the entire MT by later Tradition. As regards the first instance, Tannaitic midrash provides numerous examples wherein Pentateuchal themes and events were applied to nonhistorical texts in such books as Psalms and Canticles.[15] By such exegesis, later Tradition averred that no literary sphere of scripture was neutral or without witness to the significant events of Israelite history.

The second sphere of historicizing exegesis involves the re-historicization of the historical, whereby earlier prophecies were infused with new content. As is known, in the Qumran *pesher*-commentaries various MT prophecies become codes to be atomistically deciphered. Prophecies were related to the sec-

---

15. This subject has been treated by N. N. Glatzer, *Untersuchungen zur Geschichtslehre der Tannaiten* (Berlin: Schocken, 1933), pp. 45–61.

tarian community, which claimed to continue the covenantal teachings of biblical Israel. The previously cited Hab. 2:3 was thus reinterpreted in 1QpHab VII,5–8 to refer to the particular life and expectation of the Qumran covenanters. But such a reapplication of biblical texts was not limited to prophecies; it could take the form of *florilegia*. Thus in 4QFlor I,18–19, which deals with the rebellions of the enemies of God, Ps. 2:2 was interpreted for the life of the Qumran historical community, whereas the Sibylline Oracles (3,669–70) interpreted the passage as referring to Gog—possibly depending upon a similar rabbinic Tradition (b. *Ber.* 7b; b. *Av. Zarah* 3b; *Tanḥ., Noaḥ* 24 [Buber]).

Taken altogether, these preceding instances of post-biblical exegesis provide the complement to the earlier examples of inner-biblical interpretation. As we have seen, all areas of the MT were potentially available to ongoing Tradition—each according to its mode and genre: motifs were typologized, laws were extended or clarified, nonhistorical texts were historicized, and prophecies were revitalized. No sphere of Torah was excluded from post-biblical exegetical Tradition. The Hebrew Bible in its variety and in its totality was a living organism for the theocentric life of later generations.

The new Torah-teachings were "radical" in a double sense: they were grounded in *biblical roots* and produced *extremely innovative* results. Granted, the processes of interpretation produced tensions and dialectics between past and present, between dynamic and protective exegesis, and between human exegetical words and the divine words of revelation. But it must be stressed that the very notion that scripture can be perpetually renewed and readapted by human words is itself a radical idea. And no less radical is the complementary observation that without human words of interpretation the divine word of scripture would be static and closed. Let us now supplement these implications with another series of reflections on the post-biblical relationship between Torah and Tradition.

TORAH AND TRADITION: THEOLOGICAL IMPLICATIONS

The restoration to Zion, after the proclamation of Cyrus, was built around the "Torah of Moses" (Neh. 8:1–5). In the pre-exilic period, one was dependent on the priests for Torah-instruction (Lev. 14:57) and on the prophets for the unrequested word of God. Yet one might also "consult (*lidrōš*) YHWH" (1 Kgs. 22:8), that is, through divination. In the post-biblical period, the functions of requesting ritual knowledge from priests continued (Hag. 2:10–19), as did the unrequested word of God. But there now arose the *sōpēr*-scribe who would "consult (*lidrōš*) the *Torah* of YHWH" (Ezra 7:10), that is, interpret and teach Torah (Neh. 8:7–8). Torah and its interpretation became the bulwark of the restored covenantal community.[16] Thus the Torah was the subject of panegyrics (Pss. 19; 119) and exhortations (Ps. 1). The admonition at the end of the book of Malachai ("Remember the Torah of Moses my servant, the laws and ordinances which I commanded him at Horeb for all Israel," 3:22 [44]) underscores the emphasis on the pre-exilic Torah for the remnant that returned. Indeed, groups formed and separated (stem: *bādal*) themselves from the very beginning on the basis of knowledge and study (*mēbîn*) of Torah (Neh. 10:29–40 [10:28–39], especially vss. 29–30 [28–29]; cf. these terms in Isa. 56:3; Ezra 10:8; Neh. 9:2; 13:3; CD VI,14; 1QS V,2,10; VIII,13; and in Ps. 119:34; Neh. 8:3, 7–8; CD, II,14; VI,2; VIII,12, respectively).

The authoritative, canonical place of Torah in the post-biblical Judaisms sponsored a decisive theological implication: all new covenantal life would be read "out of" Torah. Life was a practical application of Torah; Torah was the one source of divine teachings for theological, ritual, and socio-ethical matters ("All is in it," M. *Avot* V,22). Authentic religious life was life with Torah and in relationship to it. Accordingly, the diverse

16. Cf. b. *Sukkah* 20a; b. *Sanh.* 21b.

streams of Tradition in the post-biblical Judaisms unfolded through exegeses on Torah (cf. Sir. 38:1–39:8; Jub. 23:26; 1QS VIII,12–16; M. *Avot* V; Matt. 13:51–52). Correct interpretation was vital. There was one written Torah; but many oral Torahs of interpretation laid claim to continue the covenant community of ancient Israel.

Canonical consciousness thus fostered an exegetical consciousness which, in turn, evoked rivalries over the authenticity of interpretation. The Qumran sectarians both saw their uniqueness precisely in their interpretations of Torah (cf. CD VI,2–VII,6; 1QS V,8–9; VIII,1–2, 12–16), and mocked their rivals' exegesis (cf. 1QH II,32; 4QpNah I,2,7; CD I,18). Among the Pharisees, the legal constructions of Hillel—who had officially introduced hermeneutical rules for exegesis (Tos. *Sanh.*, VII,11)—were often different from those of Shammai (e.g., M. *'Eduy.* I,1–3) and even led to extreme divisiveness (b. *Shab.* 17a; 88b). It is said that they "complained" about each other's interpretations (M. *Yad.* IV,6–8). Similarly, Josephus reports that the Sadducees rejected the interpretations of the Pharisees as they were not in the written Torah (*Antiq.* XVIII,x,6); another source states that they broke with the Pharisees who "afflict themselves" (with the burden of the oral law).[17] And finally, Paul's remarks in 1 Tim. 6:3–4 show an opposition that took the form of mocking the interpretations of another group, of refuting them, and of denying the method itself (cf. Matt. 15:1–3; Mark 7:1–3; Col. 2:8).

Given the decisive significance of interpretation for the early post-biblical Judaisms, the pivotal position of the teacher can well be appreciated. Interpretation was the basis of Tradition. The theological significance of this cannot be minimized; for whereas the written Torah preserved God's revealed will to ancient Israel in the past, God's present will was a human, *interpreted* will. Revelation was dependent upon proper exegesis. At Qumran, the teacher was known as the "interpreter of

---

17. *Avot de Rabbi Nathan*, Schechter edition, A, chap. V, p. 26.

Torah" (CD VI,7); he had appropriate knowledge of the laws and mysteries (1QpHab II,2; 1QS VIII,15). It was he who interpreted the law for the community during the "epoch of wickedness" (CD XV,9–10; 1QS VIII,12; IX,20); they were dependent upon his interpretations for their salvation: "he leads them in the ways of his [God's] heart" (CD I,11). Given this dependence upon a teacher for right interpretation and observance, it is significant that Mishnah *Avot* opens with a recitation of a chain of tradition that links the Tannaitic sages to the revelation at Sinai and, therewith, invokes *post facto* authority for their modes of interpretation. The aforesaid dependence of revelation upon exegetical tradition was pointedly stated thus: "A matter whose source is in the words of Torah has its application in the teachings of the scribes" (b. *Sanh.* 88b).

Two points follow directly. First, the preceding emphasis on a true interpreter and his authority suggests that it was by virtue of their exegetical traditions that the post-biblical Judaisms could justify themselves—for each felt that its interpretation led to right belief and right observance. And indeed, the covenanters of Qumran believed that they would be justified and saved at the hour of apocalyptic judgment because of their trust in the Teacher of Righteousness and his interpretations (e.g., 1QpHab VII,1–VIII,3). The fundamental relationship between right interpretation and right observance is thus underscored and discloses a significant theological implication of Tradition during this period. Nor was it a marginal matter, for it finds various expressions in Tannaitic sources as well. Thus, for example, the *Avot de Rabbi Nathan* preserves an episode in which an individual who did not know the exegesis of a biblical law of purity, as practiced by R. Yohanan ben Zakkai's circle, was chided: "If this is how you have practiced, you have never eaten clean heave-offerings in your life!"[18]

This point leads to another: the emphasis on Tradition as an

18. Ibid., A chap. XII end, p. 56.

interpretative unfolding of Torah meant a new emphasis on study. Among the covenanters at Qumran, all had to study one-third of the nights of the year (1QS VI,6–8); and indeed people were ranked by accomplishment in Torah and interpretation (1QS V,20–23; VI,4,9,14). Among the Pharisees, Torah was a pillar of the world (M. *Avot* I,2) and its study particularly emphasized (e.g., M. *Avot* II,14,16; III,7–8). Indeed Hillel taught: "The common man cannot be righteous" (M. *Avot* II,5). This remark does not so much denigrate simple piety as aver that significant religious merit lay in the true interpretative understanding of the divine will (cf. b. *Ber.* 47b). Herein lies a religious deepening of the Greek educational ideal of *paideia*: to do God's will one must first know it. Early Tannaitic sources often stressed the twin matters of study and practice (religious duty) and debated their relative merits. One discussion, between R. Tarfon and R. Aqiba, was resolved by R. Aqiba who decided in favor of Torah—since it leads to practice (b. *Qid.* 40b). The task of extending and interpreting the divine will produced, then, a new form of piety: a piety of study and interpretation, a piety of Tradition and its ongoing legitimation. A further theological implication is thus disclosed: through pious study and interpretation God's ongoing will could be known; through human exegesis of Torah the covenant of ancient Israel could be preserved and made present for succeeding generations.

Taken altogether, both Torah and Tradition are reciprocally necessary and interdependent. Torah needs Tradition for its continued life and authority; Tradition needs Torah for its roots and frame of reference. Of the two, Torah is the more fundamental; for only through Torah, or over against it, could any claim of continuity be made regarding the ancient covenant. But Torah did not stand alone: the post-biblical Judaisms variously affirmed both Torah *and* Tradition—in their complementarities and in their dialectical tensions.[19] The

19. This includes the Sadducees. As shown by J. Z. Lauterbach ("The Sadducees and the Pharisees: A Study of Their Respective Attitudes towards the Law," in

theological implication of this is clear: a post-biblical religious life which claimed to continue the covenant of ancient Israel was a life—howsoever modified—lived in relationship to the written Torah. Torah was thus constantly reactualized—be it through observance, interpretation, or expectation—by all the groups of the period. On this view, moreover, Torah, given in the past, was always being given through each new teaching of Tradition (cf. T. Onq. Deut. 5:19 [5:22]).

The preceding further underscores a vital theological implication. When Tradition became the very means through which Torah was rendered understandable for the ongoing theocentric community, the original revelation was considered incomprehensive without its mediation and expanding power (and cf. 1QS V,8–12). The theological audacity of this is counterbalanced only by its life-giving power. In an early Tannaitic sermon interpreting: "And God spoke all these words" (Exod. 20:1)—words spoken immediately before the Decalogue—R. Eleazar ben Azariah understood *"all"* these words" as both the words of divine revelation *and* the various— even contradictory—words of human exegesis (b. *Ḥag.* 3a–b). Herewith, the past Torah remains part of the present Tradition; and the living Tradition becomes part of the original Torah. Revelation was not once but, through Tradition, con- tinuous: "The Holy One, blessed be he, speaks Torah out of the mouths of all rabbis" (b. *Ḥag.* 15b). This temporal-spiritual tension between Torah and Tradition is, finally, reflected in the classical Jewish blessing, still recited at the communal reading of the Torah: "Blessed are you, Lord our God, King of the universe, who has chosen us from all the nations and has *given* us the Torah. Blessed are you, Lord, who *gives* the Torah."

Studies in Jewish Literature, Festschrift Kaufmann Kohler [Berlin: Reimer, 1913], 176–98), they did not reject Tradition per se. In contrast to the Pharisees, they did not attempt to attach Tradition to the written Torah. But this fact also excludes them from some of the implications which follow.

Chapter 13

Tradition and Biblical Theology[*]

Hartmut Gese

The appropriate form for presenting biblical theology or
even Old Testament theology alone is a controversial subject.
In fact, it is even problematic to determine exactly how its subject matter should be distinguished from a systematic-theological
(dogmatic) presentation of biblical *doctrine.* Nevertheless,
we can proceed from the justification given biblical theology in Johann Philipp Gabler's Altdorfer inaugural address
in 1787, *"De iusto discrimine theologiae biblicae et dogmaticae
regundisque recte utriusque finibus"* ("On the correct distinction between biblical and dogmatic theology and the proper
determination of the goals of each"). According to Gabler,
biblical theology has a basically historical orientation and
should clarify the different theological positions of the writings
and (as we would say today) of the traditions combined in the
biblical corpus: *"Est theologia biblica e genere historico,
tradens quid scriptores sacri de rebus divinis senserint"* ("Biblical theology is of an historical nature, transmitting what the
holy writers thought about divine matters"). Systematic theology can present dogmatics supported by biblical texts, but in
contrast to this, biblical theology emerges from historical analysis of individual texts and should therefore present the historical differences. With the impressive discovery and expansion of
historical knowledge in the nineteenth century, this biblical
theology progressively took on the form of a history of religion.
Not only an historical but increasingly also a dogmatic dis-

[*] Translated by R. Philip O'Hara and Douglas A. Knight.

tinction fundamentally between the Old and New Testaments accompanied these discoveries. As a result, the comprehensive biblical-theological perspective gave way to separate Old and New Testament theologies. The New Testament discipline maintained a conscious tie to the canon, thus setting limits to the disintegration of New Testament theology into a history of primitive Christian religion. In part this was due to the proximity of the discipline to dogmatics, but also because the New Testament materials had gone through a much shorter historical expansion than had those of the Old Testament. In comparison, the Old Testament field often lost sight of its connection with the canon. As a "collection of the national literature of Israel," the Old Testament became the main source for reconstructing a history of Israelite religion, and this took the place of a biblical theology.

Since the 1920s this development, which had been particularly evident within Protestant circles, has been replaced by a general effort to reflect upon the distinctive tasks involved if one is to make a description that is both historical and also theological. The various contributions and suggested solutions cannot be reviewed here, but it would be well to mention the essential viewpoints and their consequences:

(1) In contrast to a history of Israelite religion, Old Testament theology must relate to Old Testament literature as *canon*. However, it is not enough for this theology to adopt—simply for practical reasons—the canon and its historical affirmation. Instead, this canon must be theologically grounded in the heart of the Old Testament itself.

(2) Only the *testimony* of the Old Testament—and not Israel's piety—can constitute material for Old Testament theology. Depending on one's proximity to Kerygmatic Theology, this basic premise was underscored and the testimonial character determined. However, such a premise derives from the very relation of Old Testament theology to the canon—regardless of one's own theological position. This is true to the extent that

the canon as such is characterized as a binding witness and consequently a religious "foundation"—and thus is more than a document of religious piety or religious "praxis."

(3) In contrast to a dogmatic presentation of theological doctrine, a theology of the Old Testament must be *historically* derived from the Old Testament itself. However, that cannot mean merely describing the historical character of a *theologoumenon* but must also involve determining its historical conditionedness, indeed its very essence which resides in its origins and in its historical crystallization and development. This historical character must be preserved regardless of whether Old Testament theology takes the form of a more or less systematically structured design, or describes the content in the form transmitted in the Old Testament, or presents its historical development, or is conceived as some combination of these approaches.

(4) It is not simply that in an Old Testament theology the relation of the materials to *history* must not become lost; indeed, this relation must determine its very structure. The historical path (*"Heilsgeschichte"*) witnessed to in the Old Testament is not merely one among several features of the Old Testament, but is of fundamental significance for every element of Old Testament theology. However, with respect to its content it does not suffice simply to understand Old Testament theology as a theology of *"Heilsgeschichte,"* especially since some important Old Testament materials cannot be subsumed under the rubric of history. Rather, theology must be understood essentially as an historical process of development. Only in this way does such a theology achieve unity, and only then can the question of its relationship to the New Testament be raised. Thus when individual *theologoumena* can be located in history, they acquire thereby a significance extending beyond historical precision and delimitation; they become classified functionally in this developmental process.

Contributions to Old Testament theology since the 1950s

illustrate progress in two directions. On the one hand, G. von Rad, drawing on the previous work of several predecessors, utilized the results of form criticism for the method of Old Testament theology. Since the Old Testament as a literary work develops from kerygmatic intentions, form criticism can to a considerable extent expose this kerygmatic structure, and a presentation of the traditions recovered by modern form criticism leads automatically to a presentation of the Old Testament kerygma. Thus, "retelling" (*"Nacherzählung"*) can be the "most legitimate form of speaking theologically about the Old Testament." The lively discussion following von Rad's work questioned whether form criticism was not being taxed too greatly in its significance for theology since the content behind the form should be more important than the form itself. Furthermore, the question was raised whether simply accepting the Old Testament view of history, instead of assessing the Old Testament traditions critically, would do justice to the task of Old Testament theology. Nevertheless, this whole discussion was not able to eliminate the impression that theological relevance resides not only in the "content" of Old Testament materials but also in its form-critical assessment and formation —and indeed that distinguishing between these two aspects is itself no mean problem.

On the other hand, the question of the unity or center of the Old Testament became acute as a result of the awareness, emerging from form criticism and tradition history, that the Old Testament displays a variety of elements and lines of tradition. Careful attention had been paid the Old Testament witness in its individual parts, and this raised the question about some overriding content. It was thought that a systematic presentation transcending historical description would become possible if one could somehow determine the center of the Old Testament. Yet there is still a problem of how this complies with the basic character of the Old Testament as a witness to a specific history and not simply to human historical-

ity (*"Geschichtlichkeit"*).   Moreover—and this question is felt
to be especially urgent—how can both Testaments be related to
each other if New Testament theology is presented in an
analogous manner?

This aspect of biblical theology has been expressed increasingly clearly in recent years, although the means for accomplish-
ing it are more contested now than ever before. As much as it
is emphasized that the Old Testament is open to the New Testament, viewing the Old Testament as an entity *sui generis*,
fundamentally different from the New Testament in many
ways, nonetheless has just as great a countereffect. It is often
felt that the Testaments are separated by a sizable historical
gulf, occupied by the so-called apocryphal literature. This gulf
is made even wider by the usual habit of devaluating the post-
exilic Old Testament texts. With all of this, little is to be
gained by referring to the subsequent history of Old Testament
texts in the New Testament or by pointing out the complementary function of the New Testament with respect to the Old
Testament. For if the New Testament is not simply to become an appendage to the Old Testament, then the Old
Testament, if fundamentally different, must remain behind at
the threshold of the New Testament. The demand for an
historically, not dogmatically, oriented biblical theology, however, arises from the feeling that our present historical and
theological knowledge and methods could disclose the internal
and external coherence between the Old and New Testaments.
This would transcend the fundamental distinction between Old
and New Testament theology, which is affected essentially by
systematic points of view, and it would transcend also the non-
binding character of a mere history of Israelite religion.

If we are to do justice to the above-mentioned demands on an
Old Testament theological method, then out of necessity we
must look to tradition history, which has gained special importance in modern research of the Old Testament. For, if (1)
Old Testament theology needs to proceed from the canon and

yet also to understand this canon as something which is theologically grounded and not just historically given, then it must appeal to the theological development which led to the formation of the canon, and this is the history of tradition. (2) This makes it evident that not only the individual text but also the whole Old Testament has a testimonial character. Tradition does not grow as a document of piety but in its function for the life of faith—namely, as a witness to revelation and to its history. Tradition with no compelling character is unthinkable. (3) Tradition history resulted from a refinement of historical work on the tradition corpus in the Old Testament. And (4) precisely this structure of the Old Testament articulates the relation of the Old Testament to the history of Israel: what is handed down does not deal only with its experience of history; rather, stretching throughout history, tradition reflects Israel's experience of God in its history, and this historical character of revelation assumes tangible form as a process of tradition formation. The most recent development in the discipline of Old Testament theology confirms this significance of tradition history. Von Rad is particularly concerned not to bring foreign criteria to bear on an Old Testament theology but to let the Old Testament, in light of its formal structure, speak for itself in a "retelling" manner. This approach is essentially founded on traditio-historical research of the Old Testament. And with a possible traditio-historical connection between the two Testaments, the question about the relation of the Old Testament to the New could finally be liberated from the fruitless conflict over references and antitheses between their respective contents. As a result, one could instead turn to the question of how the Old Testament may provide a traditio-historical foundation for the New Testament.

Consequently, it is absolutely necessary for the method of biblical theology to become aware of the significance, indeed the essential function that tradition history can have for it. We can attempt to determine the importance of tradition history for biblical theology in three directions: (1) with respect to the text as a whole; (2) with respect to the total subject matter of biblical theology, the canon, and the relationship between the Old and New Testaments; and (3) with respect to the theological consequences of laying a traditio-historical foundation for biblical theology—revelation history.

THE TEXT AS A WHOLE

The basic task of biblical theology consists in facing the multiform complex of texts, which differ sharply in their history and subject matter, and attempting to describe the theology of this complex. Simply setting out what all the texts might have in common would mean losing essentials which appear in the individuality of a text. But even for practical reasons such a process of reduction is quite impossible since a text's theological whole is more than the sum of its individual theological parts. On the other hand, we also cannot get at this plurality of theologies through merely juxtaposing them all in a biblical theology, for example, in historical order. For there is undoubtedly an internal connection among the texts (or their theologies) which gives this plurality a character extending far beyond their simple compilation.

This fundamental problem of biblical theology, that of comprehending unity in plurality, does not exist only with respect to the extensive complex of texts, but as a rule is present even in a single original text. For a biblical text is not the product of an author in the literary sense, even if we ignore all redactional arranging and reworking. For instance, a psalm is affected by a certain range of form, language, and ideas—existing antecedent to the psalm and having its own theological import—even though the author expresses his own, occasionally even his very personal "position" in this psalm. These antecedent theological elements are by no means mere externalities, as if they were only the media used for the author's real message. Rather, in his selection of precisely this form and formulation we can perceive how the author classifies his own message. There is such a variety of formal and linguistic structures that the author is not compelled to follow a simple schema, but appropriates selectively and affirmatively. In fact, the structures of form and language are so much alive that with their inherent power they can actively convey the author's message. The author stands within a particular tradition both unconsciously and consciously.

We are advocating that biblical theology has the task of determining the theology of the whole tradition and that it can accomplish this neither by isolating a dogmatic doctrine as the unifying factor of the whole, nor by descriptively rendering historical diversity as the assemblage of the whole, but only by attempting to grasp the totality as a cohesion. Consequently, this task confronts (a) the individual text with its preliterary antecedents, (b) the development of the text as literature with its own literary classification, and (c) the growth of the text tradition into a corpus embracing the whole.

The Individual Text

The genesis of Old Testament texts usually includes an early stage of oral tradition. And even when the text appears in writing from the very outset, it is possible to speak of a prior stage, viz., its basis in the antecedent traditions. Tradition history in the narrower sense describes the preliterary, oral transmission of the text or its contents; in its broader sense, tradition history describes a text's formal and substantial presuppositions, taken from tradition. So ascertained, this formation of the text is of decisive theological importance—by no means simply a *quantité négligeable* or just a factor of very limited or circumscribed significance. The reason for this great importance is that the biblical texts grow out of *life processes* and exist in *life contexts*.

In the first place, this is true in the immediate sense in which form criticism and genre criticism speak of the *"Sitz im*

Leben." Certain life processes in Israel lead to certain texts.
The fact that the older historical traditions are totally under the
influence of the legend-form (*"Sage"*) can be traced back to the
life situation in which historical events were narrated (and
heard). The background for the collections of priestly instructions, the *tôrôt*, is the process of educating and instructing; for
the laws it is that of adjudication. The prophetic reproaches
and warnings derive from the process of prophetic proclamation
of judgment. Cultic songs, whether lament, hymn, or song of
thanksgiving, grow out of the vital process of cultic celebration.
Even artistic wisdom sayings are unimaginable without the
didactic discourse of the sages or without the ancient schools.
This list of examples can be expanded as desired. In this regard, even late, purely literary appropriation of a genre should
not be automatically excluded on principle from such basis in
life processes. For even if at this point there is no longer an
actual life process behind the text, this artificial connection to a
suitable form shows that the writer is endeavoring to associate
consciously, in a sublimated manner, with this life process. It is
therefore not surprising when such texts, cut off from their direct processes in life, later find their way back to these life processes (e.g., when songs expressing individual piety become
cultic songs again).

Thus we see that biblical texts relate to life processes in that
these texts in their early stages grow out of such processes, or at
least can be understood form-critically in terms of such processes. This is true in a deeper sense as well: what takes place
in these life processes is what makes Israel into the biblical
Israel. In these situations Israel's faith takes on form; revelation becomes apparent as lived life (*"gelebtes Leben"*) and can
be articulated and proclaimed. As the great historical events
are narrated and heard, Israel's memory is formed, and it becomes conscious of divine guidance in its history. Objective re-
porting of history can never manage to express history as it is
lived or experienced, yet this is possible for the legend, which

grows out of the living process of narrating and listening. The life process of prophetic preaching is an immediate effluence of divine inspiration. Israel's piety survives in the processes of cultic life, giving birth to the cultic song. And the regulations of Israel represent its life lived, or at least perceived, under the aspect of revelation.

The Bible does not teach us revealed truth in doctrinal form. Revelation comes in the form of truth experienced in Israel's life processes—and even at that, this lived life is almost immeasurably diverse and even seemingly contradictory. This fact, of course, is connected with the very nature of this revelation. It is not revelation of the deity as such. It is the revelation of God as Self, in a self-disclosure to his personal counterpart, Israel. It is the revelation of the divine "I" in association with the "Thou." It is revelation in an exclusive relation, in an ultimate union between God and humanity: "I am YHWH, your God." Revelation in this exclusive personal relationship therefore enters into the very life of this Israel and is rooted in Israel's life processes. And the secret of Israel and of its historical path all the way to the point of identifying with all humanity—this is the essence of biblical revelation as truly human revelation, of divine self-disclosure projected into human life.

The biblical text thus begins in the life process of Israel. And only the traditio-historical approach can constitute the method for tracing this dimension of a text back into the lived life of Israel. Only tradition history opens up, as it were, the basis of the text in Israel's life processes. Yet this is not limited to the point of origin. Just as the individual legend develops into a literary form, into the form of a text, and just as the corpora of Torah and law are crystallized from the life context, and just as the process of prophetic preaching assumes a form amenable for transmission, and just as the various possible and actually spoken proverbs converge into the form of a text which stands the test of practical instruction, and just as apostolic parenesis leads to the church epistle, and just as apostolic tradition yields the peculiar form of gospel—so also it is essential to describe the traditio-historical path all the way until the text is formed, and not only to penetrate back to some original situation. For the life context of the text unfolds fully on this very path to the textual whole. This is true first of all because only those life processes which the future also finds important can leave transmitted texts; only that which has proved itself can become stable tradition. Secondly, it is true because certain bodies of material develop which alone present the form appropriate for the subject.

This can be clarified with the help of an example. We can certainly assume that there were very many prophetic incidents in Israel about which no text reports because these incidents did not lead to the formation of some text. As decisive as these events may have been in the particular situation, their importance was too ephemeral for a long-lasting tradition or for transmission in the form of a text. On the other hand, inclusion of incidents in the continuing tradition must be differentiated from the determination of their form. Quite similar life processes can lead to completely different forms of tradition. The prophetic proclamation of Elijah and Elisha unfolded in historical processes, were "fulfilled" in them, in such a way that the legitimate form for tradition was the prophetic legend, presenting the living experience of these processes. However, prophetic proclamation in the eighth century was not "fulfilled" solely in the events of Assyrian domination. These historical processes constitute only the beginning, and the fullness of what was proclaimed would not be actualized until the future. Accordingly, in this case tradition usually had to retain the prophetic word in its direct form. It is especially interesting how the forms of tradition overlap in Isaiah. We can see clearly that the legend-form in Isaiah can single out only one element of the Isaianic proclamation, the positive reference to the Zion tradition. Thus while tradition is being formed into a text, significant processes of selection and interpretation are occurring, and the life of Israel is as much behind these processes as it is behind the initial formation of tradition.

The Literature

With literary fixation of a text, tradition relates to it differently in several respects. In contrast to the rather fluid preliterary form, it is possible to change the fixed form only through a conscious act of intervention. The transmitted text carries its own authority, and a traditionist who engages this text must reckon with this, especially since he will in most cases be related to the circle preserving the tradition of this text. However, this does not mean that the tradition is confined to only editorial corrections and compositions and that otherwise the formation of tradition is terminated. On the contrary: since only those items are transmitted which meet the demands of life, literature does not exist for itself but has vital functions in life; therefore by being true to these functions it assumes a new form in the context of life. Deuteronomy does not attain significance only for the Deuteronomic reform; it represents a theological movement which affects and forms life in Israel long after the time of Josiah. Complexes of historical texts cannot be characterized simply as biblical archives; they give an account of Israel's past in order to provide a point of orientation for present self-understanding. Prophetic traditions describe future expectations as events which already begin to be fulfilled now in the real present.

The continued authenticity of a text is reflected in its redaction, composition, reinterpretation, and above all its selection and incorporation into new text complexes that are being formed. Only tradition history, which includes this viewpoint and thus embraces also redactional and compositional history, is in a position to describe and assess properly the theological developments occurring here. This continuing history of tradition can show how, for example, additions to a text—beyond simply replenishing it as may be necessary—can result in an actualization of the text which opens it up to a totally new theological perception. Through apocalyptic additions a complex of prophetic texts can acquire an altogether new character, representing old truth on a new ontological level. This is more than merely requisite modernizations or adjustments to modern ways of thinking; preservation of the truth of the old text is at stake. Thus if apocalyptic thought significantly broadens the perspective in which revelation is perceived, then prophetic tradition, which of course had led to this expansion, can be viewed in this new light. If in a new ontology the Davidic king becomes the messiah, then the ancient Davidic traditions can be understood anew—indeed have to be understood in a new way if one wants to comprehend the truth retained in them. Ps. 110 does not maintain old truths out of necessity, but directs them toward a new plateau. We find ourselves today in the wake of an historical research which is interested primarily in the origin of an historical phenomenon and which exists in order to reconstruct "historically" this origin, in contrast to the later tradition; in this approach we are governed by our own modern perception of reality. Consequently, we are accustomed to evaluating this continuing history of tradition as something which is of secondary importance in comparison with the actual origin of the text. Yet as valuable as this historical viewpoint is, it will not do justice to the character of biblical literature as tradition. The import of additions and supplements, of redaction and composition, is not that "genuine" and "nongenuine" materials are mixed together or that a "counterfeit" impression according to the interests and taste of the successors is created— as if we should be grateful that all of this can be annulled by critical analysis. Rather, the texts incorporated into the tradition were living phenomena, and the point is for us to preserve them in their life context and not allow them to be reduced to merely historical documents.   This conservative character in tradition formation becomes understandable when we consider how tradition grows toward a whole.

The Totality

Tradition does not represent a series of individual stages in the material and formal evolution of truth.   In such a case each stage would have to eliminate antiquated, no longer adequate elements, or at least "modernize" them rigorously.   On the other hand, tradition is also not a compilation of materials perceived as truth at some point in time.   In such a case it would have to confine itself to a rigid, non-innovative preservation of ancient texts.   In contrast, tradition is like a living process of growth in which the old is preserved while being understood as the new.   For example, a new understanding of the creation event is recorded in the Priestly text of Gen. 1:1–2:4a, but this does not require that an older notion, such as that in Gen. 2:4bff., be regarded as untenable and be eliminated.   The edition retains the older tradition because it is still truth; indeed the story of the so-called Fall could not be understood at all without it.   Yet through a definite form of complementary co-ordination the older tradition is not without relation to the younger.   In this way tradition becomes a polyphonic choir of voices without relativistically surpressing any part.   Intelligible co-ordination and subordination yield a totality and not merely coexistence.   Tradition does not attempt simply to compile but also to mold a whole.

This formation of a totality is a necessary consequence of the fact that tradition grows along a continuum of meaning.   New truth exists in revelatory identity with old truth: the same Israel experiences the same God, even when this experience becomes more advanced.   This later experience, also immersed and amplified in being, does not suppress and replace the earlier experience, and this is in accord with the growing structure of history in which the past affects the present and the future is

embryonically existent in the present.   Just as revelation is tied
to Israel's history and is fulfilled in it, so also Israel's formation
of tradition is connected with its history, and the path is re-
traceable only through traditio-historical means.   As little as
history is a mere succession of incidents, so little is tradition a
mere juxtaposition of materials.   A totality must necessarily
emerge.

This growth toward a whole comes into view most clearly in
the material ties between tradition strata.   At this point we can
perceive a developmental continuum of notions, motifs, elements, and structures, and this can describe content-related
tradition history in its wider sense, embracing the history of a
concept, the history of a motif, and similar entities.   A line
leads from the Davidic king to the messianic ideal-king of Isa. 9
and of Isa. 11, to the messiah of peace in Zech. 9, to the heroic
messiah of Zech. 13; this is not a development in which one
stage replaces another, but in which the former is retained so
that a whole is formed.   The notion of Moses as· the *'ebed
YHWH* ("servant of YHWH"), which in turn corresponds to
the prophetic conception of Elijah, constitutes a representation
of revelation in man; this becomes understood as the personifi-
cation of Israel and thus leads to the Deutero-Isaianic *'ebed*-
notion and, on the other hand, paves the way for the conception
of the Son of Man.   Wisdom theology can conceive of wisdom as
a preexistent, personal, mediating figure, as the "co-enthroner
of God," which is transformed into *logos*-Christology.   These
developments are often described today along merely religio-
historical lines, whereby one considers the diverse possibilities
of foreign, external influences as a basic impetus for development.   But this manner of viewing the situation does little
justice to the essence of tradition formation.   Only that which
promotes the growth process, that which is already implicit in
the present, that which accords with the entirety of tradition
can be appropriated or can have influence.   And referring to
external, political-historical conditions as the decisive basis for

the theological "superstructure" ("*Überbau*") of tradition fails to recognize that precisely the theological tradition determines how external history will be experienced; only this subjective experience and not an objective historical event itself could be relevant for the "superstructure." For example, the Assyrian domination can be "processed" according to the view of an Isaiah or that of an Ahaz. Only traditio-historical description related to the contents can understand tradition formation as such. It does not get lost in the quest for individual historical factors, for these cannot be properly evaluated by themselves but only in the total structure.

Against this viewpoint of the growing whole it cannot be objected that formation of tradition, like any historical occurrence, is subject to an untold number of contingencies which prohibit us from viewing the result as a developed whole. For by regarding the persistence of traditions as a result of chance one overlooks the life process which is active in the formation of tradition and which creates a totality. To be sure, the history of tradition is replete with contingencies; how much has been destroyed through external influence, how significantly have expansions and developments been hindered from without! Yet we do not disturb the contingent character of history if we pay attention instead to the lively thrust of tradition, replacing omitted elements, compensating for discontinued developments, eliminating meaningless and disruptive elements and wrong directions. If tradition formation is the living answer to the challenges of history in this external sense as well, then we have no gounds for speaking of accidental results. On the contrary, historical catastrophes appear to have benefited the formation of tradition considerably.

One could ask whether irreplaceable elements did not become lost in the course of history, as filled with misfortune as it is. What would it mean if, through an improbable occurrence, archaeology would supply us with an original testimony from a familiar Old Testament prophet? Should this document properly belong to the prophet's canonical tradition? As important as such a discovery would be for historical research, it cannot correct the formation of tradition. For this prophetic utterance—not "heard," not esteemed, not transmitted—did not enter the life process of tradition formation. Only preaching which was heard, understood, and received constitutes the truth which sustained the life of Israel. This utterance found subsequently may be as "correct" as it can be, yet it is not truth in the sense of revelation to the Israel that lived. Revelation obtains its *organon* only in the formation of tradition.

This example makes it evident how different the historical viewpoint can be from the traditio-historical perspective, and we must recognize that only tradition history (to be sure, in its double sense) can describe biblical theology. It is only by these means that the historical as well as the kerygmatic character of revelation becomes manifest; it is only by these means that revelation can be understood as something which entered Israel's history and yet which forms a totality. Tradition history can become the method of biblical theology because it goes beyond historical facts and religious phenomena and describes the living process forming tradition.

THE CANON AND THE RELATIONSHIP
BETWEEN OLD AND NEW TESTAMENT

Canonization is the final result in the formation of tradition. The path from the text's origin in life situations, via complexes of tradition in the form of literature, and on to a comprehensive corpus of tradition leads to the final collection and compilation, the canon. Of course, this progressive consolidation of tradition is not possible without a substantive process behind it which directs the development of tradition toward a goal. But at this point we need to restrict our attention to the more formal side of the phenomenon.

Just as a long process is needed in order to accomplish the pre-canonical consolidation of tradition, so also canonization itself is to be understood as a process. At the outset, the canonized text is neither a plumb-line of orthodoxy nor a sacred, inviolable text. Rather, the textual corpus in the pre-canonical period passes almost imperceptibly over into the canonical period. There is less change in the character of the text than there is in the Jewish community which is maintaining it. What is the nature of this process?

In the context of a comprehensive theocratic reorganization of the post-exilic Jewish political structure, Nehemiah's administration achieved relative independence through direct subordination to the Persian province of Transeuphrates, but under Bagoas internal difficulties resulted from conflicts between civil and religious powers (fratricide by the high priest within the temple, defilement of the temple, sacrificial tax, and more). Against this background, Ezra in 398 B.C. leads the Jewish community into a binding relationship to the codified Jewish "law," and this obligation is given external and legal form. This new obligatory character of the corpus of tradition represents the transition to the stage of canonization. At first little change occurs in the manner of relating to the more or less fixed textual tradition of the Pentateuch; even after Ezra the Pentateuchal text can be submitted to limited additions and redactions. We can observe the new relation to the text most clearly in the liturgical phenomenon of word-oriented worship ("*Wortgottesdienst*"), introduced by Ezra. The community, that is, "all who were able to hear with understanding," gathers not in the temple but in the square before the Water Gate. Following specific liturgical forms of giving reverence to God, the reading and interpreting of the text begin; indeed the present text in Neh. 8 speaks of Levitical instruction on the text, that is, preaching. This marks the beginning of sermons in synagogal and Christian worship, and this new liturgical relation to the text is the actual sign of canonization. The binding character of the text is expressed, and so is its authoritative and closed totality. In the face of this, any actualizing now is understood as interpretive preaching. Alongside worship in the temple, a new form of obligatory and conscious appropriation of the revelation retained in tradition comes to the fore. The process of tradition formation had prepared the way for this long in advance, especially in the Deuteronomic demand for consciously internalizing tradition, but now it finally became possible by the virtual end of the development of the Torah.

One might think that the canonization effected at this point is tied to the preceptive character of the Torah, that is, that the form of the binding text derives from the character of the precepts themselves. However, we are dealing here with more than just commandments, which are of course a priori compulsory and which had for a long time been practiced as such in the form of the Decalogue and other legal collections. In addition to the law in its strict sense there is a plentitude of other materials in the Pentateuch which can by no means be regarded as accessories. Through the establishment of the Priestly document as the foundation and through the addition of older materials in the Tetrateuch, the *heilsgeschichtliche* structure acquired essential significance from the outset. And on the other hand, the legal material, even in Deuteronomy, often has a didactic character (for teaching "order") and thus extends beyond the normal practice of law. The understanding of Torah current in Ezra's age could have affected Pentateuchal canonization, but it is so complex (consider the influences from sapiential theology) that more was at stake in this canonization than simply elevating a certain legal tradition to the position of binding law. Instead, we must consider that the essence of revelation, the bestowal of being in community before God and with God, includes law at a decisive point, and we must comprehend the obligation being expressed in canonization in terms of this essence of revelation.

For this reason we can also understand that the canonization of the Pentateuch was only the beginning of a canonization process and that this process did not apply to the Torah tradition alone but to the entirety of tradition: the historical tradition about the prophets succeeding Moses in the period following the Mosaic *Urzeit*, the prophetic tradition itself, the sapiential tradition, the "cult-lyrical" tradition, and the rest. With the conclusion of the prophetic age—the first signs of the end of this tradition formation can be sensed in Zechariah—the second part of the canon takes its place beside the Torah, before the close of the third century B.C.: the completed prophetic tradition, including both the historical tradition of the post-Mosaic age (which is understood as a prophetic period) as well as the tradition of the prophetic utterances. But it was never doubted that canonization did not end here. The Psalter was practically closed already, yet it could not be fitted into this prophetic section. The formation of apocalyptic tradition, which had previously occurred in direct contact to the prophetic traditions for the purpose of adding to and editing them, was continued in independent form. Sapiential tradition, as old as it might have been, now came to full bloom for the first time. These were joined by the historical tradition of the post-exilic period and many other elements. The extent and form of a third part of the canon remained open for a long time, even though the fact of such an additional section was recognized and recorded, for example, in the prologue to Sirach where mention is made of "the other books coming down from the fathers," "the remaining books" besides the law and the prophets.

When was this third part completed, and what was its extent? This question is controversial primarily for dogmatic reasons. According to the late Jewish (after 70 A.D.) theory of the canon, the third part is also delimited by the traditio-historical boundary-line of Ezra, or the time of Artaxerxes; in fact, determination of all three canonical sections is attributed to Ezra (4 Ezra 14:45). Here the third part of the canon has the small scope of the Masoretic tradition, and this is attested to by Josephus (*Against Apion* I,40) who in all probability stands chiefly in Pharisaic tradition. We are informed that in Jamnia ca. 100 A.D. an affirmative decision was made that these controversial writings belong to this third canonical section. This indicates that this delimitation of the canon per se is not early, but at most the principle may be early insofar as only those writings were accepted which appeared old and enjoyed a certain respect. Synagogal worship does not usually have the third part of the canon in its scriptural readings, and this fact shows that for this stage of liturgical development the third section cannot in its entirety be presupposed as canonical.

The New Testament is familiar only with the law and the prophets (e.g., Matt. 5:17; 7:12) as completed parts of the canon, and possibly also the psalms (Luke 24:44) as the beginning of a third section. However, the number of writings that are cited or that are implicitly presupposed extends far beyond the later Masoretic limit, and it can indeed even surpass the normal Septuagint circle, which is more comprehensive than the Masoretic (cf., e.g., the citation from 1 Enoch 1:9 in Jude 14–15). This corresponds entirely to the archaeologically ascertainable evidence of tradition formation prior to the upheavals of 70 A.D.: a flowering formation of tradition with a plentitude of writings, especially apocalyptic and sapiential but also historical and other types, with a variety of mixed forms. Disregarding perhaps the psalms, one cannot draw a line between writings which have acquired definitive canonical status and those which have not or have not yet achieved canonical maturity. At the most, inferences can be made about common recognition on the basis of circulation.

These circumstances can permit only one judgment—that a third part of the canon was in the process of being formed in the period prior to the New Testament. Certain individual writings had already attained greater or quasi-canonical recognition; others were only beginning to win recognition and distribution or were even still in the developing stage, and still others clearly in a traditio-historical marginal position were not able to move beyond a narrowly limited circle of tradition and therefore had to withdraw from the common formation of tradition. In this traditio-historical stage of the development of the Old Testament, the events of the New Testament take place and are then followed by the formation of the New Testament tradition. In other words, there existed no closed Old Testament prior to the New Testament, and—provided that we do not reject the formation of the New Testament tradition in principle—we can speak really of only one single tradition process at the end and goal of which the New Testament appears.

A unity of the Bible is not to be established artificially through exegetical cross-references between the Old and New Testaments. A unity exists already because of tradition history. The gulf supposedly between the Old and New Testaments does not exist traditio-historically at all, and no dubious bridges are needed to span it. There is a difference between the Old and New Testaments insofar as the New Testament represents the goal and end, the *telos* of the path of biblical tradition. With the death and resurrection of Jesus, that event takes place toward which the earthly *Heilsgeschichte* of biblical revelation is moving. The apostolic principle, tied to those who witnessed Jesus' resurrection (for Paul, the Damascus incident), defines the end of forming the New Testament and thus the biblical tradition. In the process, of course, the apostolic tradition can be shaped by the circle forming around the apostle, as is only to be expected when considered traditio-historically; as a rule it is only in this way that the total amplitude of apostolic testimony can assume the form of tradition. There is no opposition in content or in tradition history between the Old Testament and the New Testament. The Old Testament prepares for the New in every respect: the doctrine of the new covenant, the structure of Christology, etc.

Objections to this view could be raised on formal and fundamental grounds. Formally, the New Testament seems to separate itself from the Old Testament through the Greek language and through new literary forms. In answer to this, we can point out that even during the forming of Old Testament tradition a transition could be made to "ecumenical" languages, Official Aramaic and then Greek. Certainly, deeper reasons, not just superficial ones, lead to this transition, which we find, for example, in Dan. 7 and in Wisdom of Solomon. Yet we must note that the intellectual world of Hebrew does not simply disappear with this but helps to determine thinking in these trans-cultural languages. Regarding the other point, the new literary forms of gospel and apostolic epistle result traditio-historically of necessity from the subject matter itself; they are developed for the first time in the formation of New Testament tradition. But aside from these, the individual parts of the New Testament are to be understood form-critically entirely in terms of the Old Testament.

On fundamental grounds, the post-Christian Jewish viewpoint must result in rejecting the unity of biblical tradition because the legitimacy of the New Testament tradition is repudiated. Remarkably, though, Judaism does not continue developing Old Testament tradition parallel to the Christian forming of tradition (the latter would then appear to be a digressive, premature conclusion to the biblical tradition; cf. the Samaritan tradition). On the contrary, it leads to as extensive a reduction as possible and to a canonization of the third part of the canon, thereby terminating the whole tradition process. Through this reduction to the indispensable texts, which moreover as *kĕtûbîm* ("Writings") were not even made cultically equal to the first two parts of the canon, they rejected developments which appeared to be faulty from their perspective after 70 A.D. They appealed entirely to Ezra as the starting-point of the canon. Thus the Old Testament was closed through a reform in the spirit of Pharisaism, which rejected the Hellenistic Old Testament. Alongside the Old Testament, halakhic and aggadic explication of the Torah emerged as a new formation of tradition.

This later Jewish view of the Old Testament has, strangely enough, also become a widespread Christian view in modern times. To a certain extent, one has carried out the same canonical reduction, has ceased regarding the later Old Testament traditions as genuinely biblical, and has thereby made it impossible to preserve the continuity from the Old to the New Testament. In turn, even the pre-Hellenistic Old Testament was thought to be more strongly affected by "Jewish legality," which one was unable to understand at all. Actually, the preaching of the literary prophets was the only point where one dared to draw close connections to the New Testament. Consequently, the New Testament's whole understanding of the Old Testament was brought under suspicion, even though the method with which the New Testament interprets the Old Testament is in principle no different from that of later strata of the Old Testament, and is fully consistent traditio-historically. A biblical theology had become impossible through this view; two entities were set in juxtaposition: the Old Testament leading to Jewish religion and the New Testament leading to Christian religion. Access to a biblical theology can be opened only by revising, through the traditio-historical perspective, this fundamental evaluation of the relationship between the Old and New Testaments. This would also affect the way we perceive the relationship between Judaism and Christianity. We would have to recognize that the relation is not a juxtaposition ("*Nebeneinander*") but an interpenetration ("*Ineinander*"). Christianity would have to perceive itself as old-new Israel and would have to identify with the Old Testament history of experience. Judaism would have to recognize that it has not moved past Christianity, but that it has consciously taken a holding position prior to the messianic encounter.

REVELATION HISTORY

Biblical theology can be described traditio-historically; it can be comprehended as a continuous, holistic process. In this totality, no single level or element can be torn out of its context and absolutized. For example, as useful and important as it is to determine the theology of the historical Isaiah, biblical theology cannot be content with this historical viewpoint nor with translating this historical view into a systematically developed theology. It must perceive Isaiah's traditio-historical roots not simply as an historical condition but as an essential classification and connection: without the truth of the theology of Zion we cannot understand the truth of Isaiah, who transcends the old theology of Zion. Biblical theology must also see that the biblical Isaiah is not the historical Isaiah but the dynamic force, the Isaiah tradition, which stems from Isaiah and achieves its effect traditio-historically, stretching from the first redaction all the way to the New Testament view of "fulfillment."

Just as we cannot, in view of the holistic character of biblical theology, absolutize preliterary tradition, or the formation of the text, or certain redactional stages, or the canonical composition—so also we cannot understand the *telos* of the New Testament as the "final" form which has surpassed and thus done away with all prior forms. The New Testament has absolute character with regard to the *telos* which appears in it—but not absolute over against the Old Testament traditions leading up to it. Precisely because the Old Testament is "contained" in the New, we cannot divorce it from the latter. Practically speaking, the New Testament is not understandable without the Old because the New Testament lays its foundation in the Old. We often fail to realize this because we are no longer conscious of the Hellenistic Old Testament and because we regard "Hellenistic" and "Old Testament/Jewish" actually as strict alternatives. Without Sir. 24 *logos*-Christology is cut off from older wisdom theology, and theological evaluation of such development within revelation history has become impossible. Also, setting different theologies within the New Testament in sharp and mutually exclusive contrast to each other, which then leads to a desperate search for a "canon within the canon," stems from this disengagement of the New Testament way of thinking from that of the Old Testament. On the one hand, one does not see the multiplicity of traditio-historical starting-points or the linguistic and interpretational fields which must be appropriated from the late Old Testament. And on the other hand, one often presupposes a much too simple and exaggerated theology within late Old Testament texts; this could be shown especially for the concept of the law. A New Testament theology is not feasible until it becomes a part of biblical theology.

Tradition history renders a biblical theology possible because it can describe revelation as history—not as a history of stages which relieve each other and are annulled in succession, but as a total process in which being is made known in the self-disclosure of God. As revelation is truly human-oriented disclosure of God, it does not appeal to a specific human situation but seizes the human entirely, that is, in one's historical dimension. This full revelation can only be revelation *history*. God's self-disclosure in union with the "Thou" can unfold only as a *process*, as a proceeding toward the goal—that God himself appears in the deepest depth of the human, in his uttermost distance from God.

Biblical theology is the comprehending presentation of this revelation history, which leads through all stages of human existence in the historical process. It is the secret of Israel to have been shown this path all the way to the inclusion of the whole world, to have perceived it, and to have handed down this truth. Biblical theology has the task of teaching us to comprehend this tradition, this path.

INDEXES

Index of Passages

Index of Authors